NEW REVISED CAMBRIDGE GED PROGRAM

Writing Skills

Cathy Fillmore Hoyt

CAMBRIDGE Adult Education
Prentice Hall Career & Technology
Englewood Cliffs, New Jersey 07632

Pre-press Production: **Topdesk Pre-Press, Inc.**
Acquisitions Editor: **Mark Moscowitz**
Production Editor: **Shirley Hinkamp**
Interior Design: **LCI Designs**
Cover Photo: **The Stock Market/Craig Tuttle**
Prepress Buyer: **Ray Keating**
Manufacturing Buyer: **Lori Bulwin**
Scheduler: **Leslie Coward**

© 1993 Prentice-Hall, Inc.
A Simon & Schuster Company
Englewood Cliffs, New Jersey 07632

Printed in the United States of America

10 9 8 7 6 5 4 3 2

ISBN   0-13-116963-7

Prentice-Hall International (UK) Limited, *London*
Prentice-Hall of Australia Pty. Limited, *Sydney*
Prentice-Hall Canada, Inc., *Toronto*
Prentice-Hall Hispanoamericana, S.A., *Mexico*
Prentice-Hall of India Private Limited, *New Delhi*
Prentice-Hall of Japan, Inc., *Tokyo*
Simon & Schuster Asia Pte. Ltd., *Singapore*
Editora Prentice-Hall do Brasil, Ltda., *Rio de Janeiro*

New Revised Cambridge GED Program

Executive Editor	Senior Editor	Editor
James W. Brown	Robert McIlwaine	Doreen Stern

Writers	Consultants/Reviewers	Photo Researchers
Beverly Ann Chin	Marjorie Jacobs	Page Poore
Gloria Levine	Cecily Bodner	Ellen Diamond
Karen Wunderman	Diane Hardison	
Stella Sands	Dr. Margaret Tinzman	**Electronic Design**
Michael Ross	Nora Chomitz	
Alan Hines	Bert C. Honigman	Molly Pike Riccardi
Donald Gerstein	Sylvester Pues	

Contents

To the Student

The following pages will introduce you to the Writing Skills Test and to the organization of this book. You will read about ways you can use this book to your best advantage.

What Is the Writing Skills Test?

The Writing Skills Test of the GED Tests examines your knowledge of the conventions of written English and your ability to write.

What Kind of Questions Are on the Test?

The Writing Skills Test is composed of two parts. Part I tests your knowledge of the conventions of written English: usage, sentence structure, and mechanics (punctuation, capitalization, and spelling). Part II tests your ability to write an expository essay.

In Part I, you will read paragraphs made up of ten to twelve sentences. Each sentence in each paragraph is numbered. You will be given 75 minutes to complete the 55 multiple-choice items. The majority of the questions ask you to locate and correct errors in the sentences. The errors may be in spelling, punctuation, capitalization, usage or sentence structure. Other items ask you to rewrite or combine sentences.

The paragraphs you will read on Part I of the Writing Skills Test contain errors that beginning writers are most likely to make; thus, as you use this book to study writing skills, you should learn to avoid those types of errors.

About 35 percent of the items on this part of the test will check your knowledge of correct sentence structure. Another 35 percent will test your knowledge of usage. The remaining 30 percent concern the mechanics of writing: spelling, punctuation and capitalization.

In Part II, you will be asked to write a 200-word essay in 45 minutes in which you state your opinion about a certain topic or explain something. You will support your opinion or defend your explanation with specific details, reasons, and/or examples. There are no correct answers for this portion of the test. Your essay will be judged for its overall effectiveness. Readers will not be critical of the opinion you present; they will be interested in how effectively you present it. The score given to your essay will be based on how clear, well-organized, and generally free of errors it is.

What You Will Find in This Book

This book gives you a four-step preparation for taking the Writing Skills Test. The four steps are as follows:

Step One: Prediction

In this first step, you will find the Predictor Test. This test is very much like the actual Writing Skills Test, but Part I—the part that tests your knowledge of the conventions of English—is half as long as the actual Writing Skills Test, Part I. Part II, the part in which you write a composition, is the same length as the actual GED.

By evaluating your performance on the Predictor Test, you will get a sense of your strengths and weaknesses. This information will help you to plan your studies accordingly.

Step Two: Instruction

The instruction section has two parts. The first part, "Writing Skills, Part I: Grammar," covers the conventions of English usage, sentence structure, and mechanics (punctuation, capitalization, and spelling). It also shows you how to edit writing, that is, how to locate and correct errors in usage, sentence structure and mechanics.

The second part, "Writing Skills, Part II: Essay Writing" provides a variety of writing activities to prepare you to practice the writing process. Instruction in the writing process itself takes you through the steps by which you plan, organize, write, revise, and edit a successful essay.

Both parts of the Instruction section are divided into units. Each of the three units in Part I covers one of the aspects of writing skills that will be tested in Part I of the Writing Skills Test: usage, sentence structure, and mechanics. The units, in turn, are divided into chapters, such as subject-verb agreement, complete sentences and spelling. Each chapter begins with a Preview and ends with a Review. The Previews and Reviews are made up of questions that cover the material taught in that chapter. There are very few multiple-choice questions in Part I, in order to give you the maximum amount of practice in writing sentences correctly.

Part II is made up of three chapters. The first chapter provides a variety of writing activities to prepare you to learn the writing process. The second chapter explains and provides practice with the writing process. The third chapter reviews the writing process. Each chapter is divided into lessons that include writing activities.

Step Three: Practice

This section gives you valuable practice in answering questions like those you will find in Part I of the actual Writing Skills Test, and in writing the type of essay required in Part II of the test. There are two parts to this section: *Practice Items* and a *Practice Test*. Both are structured very much like the actual Writing Skills Test. Both types of practice activities have 55 items in Part I, the same number of questions as are in Part I of the GED Test, and one essay question in Part II, as in the real GED Test. You can use your results to track your progress and to give you an idea of how prepared you are to take the real test.

Step Four: Simulation

Finally, this book offers a simulated version of the Writing Skills Test. It is as similar to the real test as possible. The number of questions, their level of difficulty, and the way they are organized are the same as you will find on the actual test. Taking the Simulated Test will be useful preparation for taking the GED Test. It will help you find out how ready you are to take the real exam.

The Answer Key

At the back of this book, you will find an answers and explanations section. The Answer Key contains the answers to the items in all the Previews, Exercises, Reviews, and the Test in Part I, as well as the answers to the items in Practice Items, the Practice Test, and the Simulated Test. It not only tells you the right answers for grammar items, but it also explains why the answers are right. It names the topic in grammar you need to know to answer a question successfully. The Answer Key contains model essays and guidelines to help you score essays you write. You can benefit a great deal by carefully consulting the Answer Key.

Using This Book

The book has been designed to give you several choices. Whether you are working with an instructor or alone, you can use this book to prepare for the Writing Skills Test in the way that works best for you.

Take a Glance at the Table of Contents

Before doing anything else, look over the Table of Contents and get a feel for this book. You can compare the headings in the Table of Contents with the descriptions found in the preceding pages. You might also want to leaf through the book to see what each section looks like.

Take the Predictor Test

Next, you will probably want to take the Predictor Test. As the introduction before the test explains, there is more than one way to take this test. Decide which is best for you. It might be best for you to take the test in two separate sittings; take Part I one day and Part II on another day.

Your performance and score on the Predictor Test will be very useful to you as you work with the rest of this book. It will help you identify your particular strengths and weaknesses, which can help you plan your course of study.

Beginning Your Instruction

After you have an idea about what your strengths and weaknesses are, you are ready to begin instruction. You may begin with either Part I or Part II, or you may wish to work on both of them at the same time. It is best to work through the first three chapters in Part I in order.

Each of the three units of Part I is divided into chapters. Each chapter begins with a Preview and ends with a Review. To find out whether you need to study the lessons that make up a chapter, take the Preview. If you score 100 percent on the Preview, skip ahead to the Review. If you score 80 percent or better on the Review, you can be satisfied that you understand the material in the chapter. Go on to the Preview at the beginning of the next chapter. You can continue skipping ahead in this fashion until you score below 80 percent on a Review. At that point, go to the first lesson in the chapter and begin work.

You should work on the chapters in Part II in order. The first chapter will get you started on daily writing activities that will help you improve your writing skills. The second chapter introduces the writing process, and the third chapter reviews that process.

Using the Practice Section

Because there are two parts in the instruction section, corresponding to the two parts of the Writing Skills Test, you have several choices about how to use this book. You may complete the instruction section for Part I and proceed directly to the related Practice Items and Practice Test. You may do the same for Part II and the related parts of the Practice section. Or, you may wish to complete the Instruction section for both Parts I and II before going on to the Practice Section. The choice is up to you.

Taking the Simulated Test

Finally, once you have completed the Instruction and Practice sections, you can take the Simulated Writing Skills Test. This will give you the most accurate assessment of how ready you are to take the actual test.

Try Your Best!

As you study the lessons and complete the activities and tests in this book, you should give it your best effort. In those sections that can be scored, try to maintain at least 80 percent correct as you work through this book. If you maintain 80 percent scores, you are probably working at a level that will allow you to do well on the GED Test.

What Is the GED?

You are preparing for the GED Tests. The initials GED stand for General Educational Development. You may also have heard the tests referred to as the High School Equivalency Tests. The GED diploma is widely regarded as the equivalent of a high school diploma.

The GED Test is a way for millions of adults in the United States and Canada to get diplomas or certificates without returning to high school. Each year about half a million people take advantage of the opportunity to take the GED Tests.

Who Recognizes the GED?

The GED is recognized by employers, unions, and state and federal civil services. Vocational institutes, colleges, and universities accept students who have obtained a GED. All fifty states and parts of Canada use the GED Test results to issue high school equivalency credentials. However, each state has its own standards for what constitutes a passing grade. For information on the requirements in your state, contact the High School Equivalency Program of the State Department of Education in your state's capital.

What Is Tested on the GED Test?

The material found on the GED Tests is based on the subjects covered in most high schools around the country. Thus you will be learning about the subject areas that you would be most likely to study if you attended four years of high school. However, the focus of the GED Tests is not on content, but on skills. You will not have to memorize specific dates, names, and places. For example, whether you recall the date of a battle or the title of a novel is less important than whether you can read and understand a passage on history or literature.

You have already been using many of the thinking skills that will be tested on the GED. For example, many people must do some writing in their lives, and the GED includes a test of writing skills. A lot of people read in their jobs or for pleasure, and reading skills are tested, too. Many people use basic mathematics for such things as figuring out a budget or doubling a recipe, and the GED includes a test of basic math skills.

Instead of testing your memory, the GED tests your ability to get information and apply your thinking to that information.

How Is the GED Structured?

The GED is actually five separate tests. With one exception, the test is composed entirely of multiple choice questions. The one exception is the 200-word essay that you will be required to write as part of the Writing Skills Test.

The chart below describes the structure of the five tests:

Test #	Test Subject	Number of Items	Minutes Allowed
1	Writing Skills Part 1—Multiple Choice Part 2—Essay	55 1	75 45
2	Social Studies	64	85
3	Science	66	95
4	Interpreting Literature and the Arts	45	65
5	Mathematics	56	90

Introduction

Imagine that you were going to take the GED Test today. How do you think you would do? In which areas would you perform best, and in which areas would you have the most trouble? The Predictor Test that follows can help you answer these questions. It is called a Predictor Test because your results can be used to predict where your strengths and your weaknesses lie in relation to the actual Writing Skills Test of the GED.

The Predictor Test is like the actual GED Test in many ways. It will check your skills as you apply them to the kinds of items you will find on the real test. The items are like those on the actual test.

How to Take the Predictor Test

Because there are two parts to the actual Writing Skills Test, there are two parts to the Predictor Test. Here are two ways you can take the test:

(1) It may be best to take the Predictor Test in two sittings. You can complete either part first. After you finish one part of the test, put the test aside and complete the other part at another time.

(2) If you want, you can take the Predictor Test in one sitting. Start with Part I. As soon as you finish Part I, begin Part II.

You should time yourself to see how long you take to complete each part of the test. If you finish Part I of the Predictor Test within 38 minutes, you are right on target. You should complete Part II of the Predictor Test in about 45 minutes, the same amount of time allowed for Part II on the actual test. Do not worry, however, if it takes you longer to complete Part II at this stage of your work.

When you are done, check your answers by using the answer key that begins on page 10. Put a check by each item in Part I that you answered correctly. Score your essay according to the instructions in the answer key. You might like to have a teacher or someone else score your essay as well.

How to Use Your Score

At the end of the test, you will find a Performance Analysis Chart. Fill in the chart; it will help you get a general idea about which areas you are more comfortable with, and which give you the most trouble. As you work through Part I in this book, you will complete several short exercises—Previews and Reviews—that will help you pinpoint your strengths and weaknesses in grammar. Part II of this book will help you with writing essays.

TIME: 38 minutes

Directions: The items in Part I of this test are based on paragraphs that contain numbered sentences. Some of the sentences may contain errors in sentence structure, usage, or mechanics. *A few sentences, however, may be correct as written.* Read each paragraph and then answer the items that follow it. For each item, choose the answer that would result in the most effective writing of the sentence or sentences. The best answer must be consistent with the meaning and tone of the rest of the paragraph.

FOR EXAMPLE:

Sentence 1: **Although it may take only two hours to watch the average motion picture takes almost a year to make.**

What correction should be made to this sentence?

(1) replace <u>it</u> with <u>they</u>
(2) change <u>take</u> to <u>have taken</u>
(3) insert a comma after <u>watch</u>
(4) change <u>almost</u> to <u>all most</u>
(5) no change is necessary

The correct answer is **(3)**. In this example, a comma is needed after the introductory words <u>Although it may take only two hours to watch</u>.

Items 1 to 9 are based on the following paragraph.

(1) People spends a lot of money each year on cold remedies. (2) Many of these products dont really help to prevent or cure colds. (3) In fact, some may even be harmful. (4) Several types of cough medicine contains alcohol and can be habit-forming. (5) The Food and drug Administration reports that mouthwashes can't really fight colds. (6) Gargling with mouthwash may make your sore throat feel better. (7) But salt water probably works just as well. (8) One scientist is named Linus Pauling he believes taking a lot of vitamin C can help prevent the common cold. (9) Other scientists, however, disagree, they say careful research does not support Pauling's claim. (10) In any case, large doses of vitamin C can be harmful to some people. (11) These people include pregnant women the elderly, and people with certain health problems. (12) Maybe the cheapest cold remedies—home remedies, such as tea with lemon and honey—are really the best.

1. Sentence 1: **People spends a lot of money each year on cold remedies.**

   What correction should be made to this sentence?

   (1) change spends to spend
   (2) change the spelling of a lot to alot
   (3) insert annually after money
   (4) insert a comma after year
   (5) change cold to Cold

2. Sentence 2: **Many of these products dont really help to prevent or cure colds.**

   What correction should be made to this sentence?

   (1) replace these with which
   (2) change the spelling of dont to don't
   (3) change the spelling of to to too
   (4) insert a comma after prevent
   (5) replace cure with in curing

3. Sentence 4: **Several types of cough medicine contains alcohol and can be habit-forming.**

   Which of the following is the best way to write the underlined portion of this sentence? If you think the original is the best way, choose option (1).

   (1) contains alcohol and can be
   (2) contains alcohol. And can be
   (3) contain alcohol and can be
   (4) contain alcohol and were
   (5) contained alcohol and can be

4. Sentence 5: **The Food and drug Administration reports that mouthwashes can't really fight colds.**

   What correction should be made to this sentence?

   (1) change Food to food
   (2) change drug to Drug
   (3) change reports to report
   (4) change the spelling of can't to cant
   (5) no correction is necessary

5. Sentences 6 & 7: **Gargling with mouthwash may make your sore throat feel better. But salt water probably works just as well.**

   Which of the following is the best way to write the underlined portions of these sentences? If you think the original is the best way, choose option (1).

   (1) better. But salt water probably works
   (2) better. But salt water probably worked
   (3) better, but salt water probably works
   (4) better but salt water probably works
   (5) better but, salt water probably works

6. Sentence 8: **One scientist <u>is named Linus Pauling he believes</u> taking a lot of vitamin C can help prevent the common cold.**

Which of the following is the best way to write the underlined portion of this sentence? If you think the original is the best way, choose option (1).

(1) is named Linus Pauling he believes
(2) named Linus Pauling he believes
(3) named Linus Pauling believes
(4) named Linus Pauling, he believes
(5) named Linus Pauling, he believe

7. Sentence 9: **Other scientists, however, disagree, they say careful research does not support Pauling's claim.**

What correction should be made to this sentence?

(1) remove the comma after <u>scientists</u>
(2) replace <u>disagree, they</u> with <u>disagree. They</u>
(3) change the spelling of <u>careful</u> to <u>carefull</u>
(4) change <u>Pauling's</u> to <u>pauling's</u>
(5) no correction is necessary

8. Sentence 11: **These people include pregnant <u>women the elderly, and</u> people with certain health problems.**

Which of the following is the best way to write the underlined portion of this sentence? If you think the original is the best way, choose option (1).

(1) women the elderly, and
(2) women the elderly and
(3) women. The elderly and
(4) women, the elderly, and
(5) women; the elderly, and

9. Sentence 12: **Maybe the cheapest cold remedies—home remedies, such as tea with lemon and honey— are really the best.**

If you rewrote sentence 12 beginning with

<u>Even though home remedies, such as tea with lemon and honey, are cheap,</u>

the next word should be

(1) it
(2) they
(3) also
(4) and
(5) best

Items 10 to 19 are based on the following paragraph.

(1) Many jobs is being created in the fast-food industry. (2) We are beginning to see a change in who fills these openings. (3) The birthrate went down in the 1970s, and there are fewer teenagers to fill counter positions than in the past. (4) We probably found more retired people working at fast-food places in the future. (5) Already, there are more college graduates than there used to be among managers at many fast-food restaurants. (6) The fast-food business has grown, and it has, at the same time, become more complicated to run. (7) Fast-food companies are looking for people which are able to think, speak, read, and write clearly. (8) Today's fast-food managers have many responsibilities, several of these require the use of a computer. (9) Managers have to set sales goals other tasks include figuring how much food has been used and how much wasted. (10) A manager needs good communication skills if when he or she is training new workers. (11) More than ever before, fast-food jobs at all levels went to those with the best thinking and language skills.

10. Sentence 1: **Many jobs is being created in the fast-food industry.**

    What correction should be made to this sentence?

    (1) change <u>is</u> to <u>was</u>
    (2) change <u>is</u> to <u>are</u>
    (3) change <u>created</u> to <u>create</u>
    (4) insert a comma after <u>created</u>
    (5) no correction is necessary

11. Sentence 3: **The birthrate went down in the 1970s, and there are fewer teenagers to fill counter positions than in the past.**

    If you rewrote sentence 3 beginning with

    <u>Because the</u>

    the next word should be

    (1) birthrate
    (2) 1970s
    (3) teenagers
    (4) counter
    (5) past

12. Sentence 4: **We <u>probably found more retired people working</u> at fast-food places in the future.**

    Which of the following is the best way to write the underlined portion of this sentence? If you think the original is the best way, choose option (1).

    (1) probably found more retired people working
    (2) will probably find more retired people working
    (3) found more retired people probably working
    (4) probably found more retired people, working
    (5) probably found more retired people. Working

13. Sentence 5: **Already, there are more college graduates than there used to be among managers at many fast-food restaurants.**

    What correction should be made to this sentence?

    (1) remove the comma after <u>Already</u>
    (2) change the spelling of <u>college</u> to <u>collage</u>
    (3) insert a comma after <u>be</u>
    (4) change <u>managers</u> to <u>Managers</u>
    (5) no correction is necessary

14. Sentence 6: **The fast-food business has grown, and it has, at the same time, become more complicated to run.**

If you rewrote sentence 6 beginning with

As the fast-food business has grown,

the next word should be

(1) and
(2) it
(3) at
(4) the
(5) more

15. Sentence 7: **Fast-food companies are looking for people which are able to think, speak, read, and write clearly.**

Which of the following is the best way to write the underlined portion of this sentence? If you think the original is the best way, choose option (1).

(1) are looking for people which are
(2) were looking for people which are
(3) are looking for people which is
(4) are looking for people who are
(5) are looking for people, which are

16. Sentence 8: **Today's fast-food managers have many responsibilities, several of these require the use of a computer.**

What correction should be made to this sentence?

(1) change have to has
(2) replace many with a variety of different
(3) change the spelling of responsibilities to responsabilities
(4) remove the comma after responsibilities
(5) replace the comma after responsibilities with a semicolon

17. Sentence 9: **Managers have to set sales goals other tasks include figuring how much food has been used and how much wasted.**

Which of the following is the best way to write the underlined portion of this sentence? If you think the original is the best way, choose option (1).

(1) goals other tasks include
(2) goals, other tasks include
(3) goals and other tasks include
(4) goals. Other tasks include
(5) goals other tasks includes

18. Sentence 10: **A manager needs good communication skills if when he or she is training new workers.**

What correction should be made to this sentence?

(1) change needs to need
(2) insert a semicolon after skills
(3) replace skills if with skills, and if
(4) remove if
(5) replace he or she with they

19. Sentence 11: **More than ever before, fast-food jobs at all levels went to those with the best thinking and language skills.**

What correction should be made to this sentence?

(1) remove the comma after before
(2) insert a comma after levels
(3) change went to go
(4) remove those with
(5) change the spelling of language to langauge

Items 20 to 28 are based on the following paragraph.

(1) People are sending more and more mail, but the U.S. Postal service is hiring fewer and fewer workers. (2) Computers are responsible for the reduced hiring. (3) Fewer people are payed to sort the mail now that zip codes are used. (4) A computer operator types the first three numbers of the zip code. (5) The computer immediately tells the person into which tray he or she should toss the letter. (6) Even computer operators are being replaced, some computers read addresses directly. (7) Computers make delivery more efficient. (8) Computers can also check postal workers' efficiency. (9) It can figure how much mail a carrier or clerk is sorting each minute. (10) Computers even store information about when each carrier leaves the post office and plans to return. (11) Doing more work at less cost, postal clerks are being replaced by computers. (12) However, when it comes to reading messy writing humans still do as well as or better than computers.

20. Sentence 1: **People are sending more and more mail, but the U.S. Postal service is hiring fewer and fewer workers.**

What correction should be made to this sentence?

(1) remove the comma after <u>mail</u>
(2) replace <u>mail, but</u> with <u>mail. But</u>
(3) change <u>Postal</u> to <u>postal</u>
(4) change <u>service</u> to <u>Service</u>
(5) change <u>is</u> to <u>was</u>

21. Sentence 3: **Fewer people are payed to sort the mail now that zip codes are used.**

What correction should be made to this sentence?

(1) change <u>are</u> to <u>is</u>
(2) change the spelling of <u>payed</u> to <u>paid</u>
(3) replace <u>the mail</u> with <u>it</u>
(4) replace <u>now</u> with <u>because</u>
(5) change <u>are used</u> to <u>will be used</u>

22. Sentence 5: **The computer immediately tells the person into which tray he or she should toss the letter.**

What correction should be made to this sentence?

(1) change the spelling of <u>immediately</u> to <u>imediately</u>
(2) change <u>tells</u> to <u>told</u>
(3) insert a comma after <u>person</u>
(4) replace <u>he or she</u> with <u>they</u>
(5) no correction is necessary

23. Sentence 6: **Even computer operators are being replaced, some computers read addresses directly.**

What correction should be made to this sentence?

(1) change <u>are being</u> to <u>were</u>
(2) change <u>replaced, some</u> with <u>replaced. Some</u>
(3) remove the comma after <u>replaced</u>
(4) insert <u>who</u> after <u>computers</u>
(5) change the spelling of <u>addresses</u> to <u>adresses</u>

24. Sentences 7 & 8: **Computers make delivery more efficient. Computers can also check postal workers' efficiency.**

The most effective combination of sentences 7 and 8 would include which of the following groups of words?

(1) They can make delivery
(2) Computers can make it
(3) Not only computers make
(4) and can also check
(5) but also postal workers

25. Sentence 9: **It can figure how much mail a carrier or clerk is sorting each minute.**

Which of the following is the best way to write the underlined portion of this sentence? If you think the original is the best way, choose option (1).

(1) It can figure how much
(2) They can figure how much
(3) It can figure, how much
(4) They can figure, how much
(5) It could figure how much

26. Sentence 10: **Computers even store information about when each carrier leaves the post office and plans to return.**

Which of the following is the best way to write the underlined portion of this sentence? If you think the original is the best way, choose option (1).

(1) leaves the post office and plans
(2) leaves the post office and is planning
(3) leaves the post office and when plans
(4) leaves the post office and to plan
(5) left the post office and were planning

27. Sentence 11: **Doing more work at less cost, postal clerks are being replaced by computers.**

If you rewrote sentence 11 beginning with

Because they do more work at less cost,

the next word(s) should be

(1) postal clerks
(2) it
(3) workers
(4) post office
(5) computers

28. Sentence 12: **However, when it comes to reading messy writing humans still do as well as or better than computers.**

What correction should be made to this sentence?

(1) insert a comma after writing
(2) change do to done
(3) replace as well as with as well
(4) change the spelling of than to then
(5) no correction is necessary

Answers are on pages 10–11.

PREDICTOR TEST – PART II

TIME: *45 minutes*

Directions: This is a test to see how well you can write. In this test, you are asked to write an essay in which you present your opinions about an issue. In preparing your essay, you should take the following steps.

Step 1. Read all of the information about the topic. Be sure that you understand the topic and that you write about only the assigned topic.

Step 2. Plan your essay before you write.

Step 3. Use scrap paper to make any notes.

Step 4. Write your essay on a separate sheet of paper.

Step 5. Read what you have written. Make sure that your writing is legible.

Step 6. Check your paragraphing, sentence structure, spelling, punctuation, capitalization, and usage; make any changes that will improve your essay.

TOPIC

Credit cards are responsible for changes in the ways many Americans spend their money. Some of these changes have been for the good, while others have caused problems for consumers.

Write an essay, approximately 200 words long, explaining some of the effects of the credit card. You may describe positive effects, negative effects, or both. Be specific, and use facts, reasons, and examples to support your view.

When you take the GED Test, you will have 45 minutes to write about the topic you are assigned. Try to write the essay for this test within 45 minutes. Write legibly and use a ballpoint pen so that your writing will be easy to read. Any notes that you make on scrap paper will not be counted as part of your score.

After you complete this essay, you can judge its effectiveness by using the Essay Scoring Guide and Model Essays in the answer key to score your essay. Your GED essay will be judged on how clearly you make the main point of your essay, how thoroughly you support your ideas, and how clear and correct your writing is throughout the composition. You will receive no credit for writing about a topic other than the one assigned.

Answers are on pages 12-18.

ANSWERS AND EXPLANATIONS FOR THE PREDICTOR TEST – Part I

1. **(1)** *Usage/Subject-Verb Agreement—Noun-Verb Pairs/Sentence Correction.* A plural subject, People, requires a plural verb, spend.

2. **(2)** *Mechanics/Contractions/Sentence Correction.* The contraction, don't, is the short form for do not. The apostrophe replaces the o in not.

3. **(3)** *Usage/Subject-Verb Agreement/Sentence Revision.* The plural subject, types, requires a plural verb, contain and can be, despite the interrupting phrase, of cough medicine.

4. **(2)** *Mechanics/Capitalization/Sentence Correction.* Capitalize all main words in the proper name of an organization such as the Food and Drug Administration.

5. **(3)** *Sentence Structure/Sentence Fragment/Sentence Revision.* Connecting words, such as but, and, and or, are not used to begin a sentence.

6. **(3)** *Sentence Structure/Run-On Sentence/Sentence Revision.* Two complete ideas are incorrectly fused into a run-on sentence. The construction in choice (3) eliminates the run-on by making scientist the subject of believes.

7. **(2)** *Sentence Structure/Comma Splice/Sentence Correction.* Do not join two complete ideas with a comma.

8. **(4)** *Mechanics/Punctuation/Sentence Revision.* Separate items in a series with commas.

9. **(2)** *Usage/Pronoun-Antecedent Agreement/Construction Shift.* <u>Even though home remedies, such as tea with lemon and honey, are cheap, they are really the best.</u> The subject of the next idea refers to the home remedies. The pronoun <u>they</u> agrees with the antecedent <u>remedies</u>.

10. **(2)** *Usage/Subject-Verb Agreement—Noun-Verb Pairs/Sentence Correction.* The plural subject, jobs, requires a plural verb, are.

11. **(1)** *Sentence Structure/Subordination/Construction Shift.* Because the birthrate went down in the 1970s, there are fewer teenagers to fill counter positions than in the past.

12. **(2)** *Usage/Verb Tense/Sentence Revision.* Look for clues to tense within the sentence. The word future indicates the need for future tense, will find.

13. **(5)** *Mechanics/Spelling/Sentence Correction.* College, a frequently misspelled word, is correctly spelled. It is easy to confuse the endings ege, age, edge, idge.

14. **(2)** *Sentence Structure/Subordination/Construction Shift.* As the fast-food business has grown, it has become more complicated to run.

15. **(4)** *Usage/Pronoun Reference—Relative Pronoun/Sentence Revision.* The pronoun which refers to things; who refers to people.

16. **(5)** *Sentence Structure/Comma Splice/Sentence Correction.* Two complete ideas are incorrectly joined by a comma. The error is corrected here by using a semicolon to separate the two ideas.

17. **(4)** *Sentence Structure/Run-On Sentence/Sentence Revision.* Two complete ideas are incorrectly fused into a run-on sentence. The error is corrected by forming two separate sentences.

18. **(4)** *Sentence Structure/Subordination/Sentence Correction.* When joining ideas of unequal rank in a sentence, use only one subordinator at a time.

19. **(3)** *Usage/Verb Tense/Sentence Correction.* Make sure the verb tense is consistent with that used throughout the paragraph. Here, present tense is required.

20. **(4)** *Mechanics/Capitalization/Sentence Correction.* Capitalize all important words in a proper noun, such as the U.S. Postal Service.

21. **(2)** *Mechanics/Spelling/Sentence Correction.* The past tense of pay is spelled paid.

22. **(5)** *Usage/Pronoun Reference—Agreement with Antecedent/Sentence Correction.* A pronoun should agree in number with the noun it replaces. The noun person requires he or she.

23. **(2)** *Sentence Structure/Comma Splice/Sentence Correction.* Two complete subject-verb structures should not simply be joined by commas. Here, each is made into a complete sentence.

24. **(4)** *Sentence Structure/Coordination— Combining Sentences/Construction Shift.* Computers make delivery more efficient and can also check postal workers' efficiency.

25. **(2)** *Usage/Pronoun Reference—Agreement with Antecedent/Sentence Revision.* A pronoun should agree in number with the word it replaces. Here, Computers should be replaced by They.

26. **(1)** *Sentence Structure/Parallel Construction/Sentence Revision.* The sentence is correct as written. The verbs <u>leaves</u> and <u>plans</u> are parallel.

27. **(5)** *Sentence Structure/Modification— Dangling Modifier/Construction Shift.* <u>Because they do more work at less cost, computers are replacing postal clerks.</u> Postal workers are not the ones doing the work at less cost. It is because the computers do more work at less cost that the computers are replacing the postal workers.

28. **(1)** *Mechanics/Punctuation/Sentence Correction.* Use a comma after the subordinate idea when it comes first in the sentence.

Scoring Your Essay- Part II

Introduction to Holistic Scoring

The following GED Essay Scoring Guide provides a general description of the characteristics found in GED essays that are scored by the Holistic Method.

GED ESSAY SCORING GUIDE

Papers will show *some* or *all* of the following characteristics.

Upper-half papers make clear a definite purpose, pursued with varying degrees of effectiveness. They also have a structure that shows evidence of some deliberate planning. The writer's control of English usage ranges from fairly reliable at 4 to confident and accomplished at 6.

6 Papers scored as a 6 tend to offer sophisticated ideas within an organizational framework that is clear and appropriate for the topic. The supporting statements are particularly effective because of their substance, specificity, or illustrative quality. The writing is vivid and precise, though it may contain an occasional flaw.

5 Papers scored as a 5 are clearly organized with effective support for each of the writer's major points. The writing offers substantive ideas, though the paper may lack the flair or grace of a 6 paper. The surface features are consistently under control, despite an occasional lapse in usage.

4 Papers scored as a 4 show evidence of the writer's organizational plan. Support, though sufficient, tends to be less extensive or convincing than that found in papers scored as a 5 or 6. The writer generally observes the conventions of accepted English usage. Some errors are usually present, but they are not severe enough to interfere significantly with the writer's main purpose.

Lower-half papers either fail to convey a purpose sufficiently or lack one entirely. Consequently, their structure ranges from rudimentary at 3, to random at 2, to absent at 1. Control of the conventions of English usage tends to follow this same gradient.

3 Papers scored as a 3 usually show some evidence of planning or development. However, the organization is often limited to a simple listing or haphazard recitation of ideas about the topic, leaving an impression of insufficiency. The 3 papers often demonstrate repeated weaknesses in accepted English usage and are generally ineffective in accomplishing the writer's purpose.

2 Papers scored as a 2 are characterized by a marked lack of development or inadequate support for ideas. The level of thought apparent in the writing is frequently unsophisticated or superficial, often marked by a listing of unsupported generalizations. Instead of suggesting a clear purpose, these papers often present conflicting purposes. Errors in accepted English usage may seriously interfere with the overall effectiveness of these papers.

1 Papers scored as a 1 leave the impression that the writer has not only not accomplished a purpose, but has not made any purpose apparent. The dominant feature of these papers is the lack of control. The writer stumbles both in conveying a clear plan for the paper and in expressing ideas according to the conventions of accepted English usage.

0 The zero score is reserved for papers which are blank, illegible, or written on a topic other than the one assigned.

Copyright 1985, GED Testing Service, September, 1985

Source: The 1988 Tests of General Educational Development: A Preview, American Council on Education, 1985. Used with permission.

HOW TO SCORE YOUR ESSAY

The following six essays are designed to be used as models for the scoring of your essay. The essays are presented in order from the essay that deserves the lowest score (1) to the essay that deserves the highest score (6).

To score your essay, first compare your essay with the model essay that received a score of 1. If your essay is better than the 1 essay, compare it with the 2 essay and so on until you are able to decide where your essay fits when compared with the six model essays.

As you score your essay, read the character trait analysis that follows each model essay. This analysis can help you to see how you might have improved your essay in order to have received a higher score.

Model Essay—Holistic Score 1

States the point of view.

Listing of unsupported opinions, needs better examples that support the writer's point of view.

Credit cards is not good for people to use. Being in debt is not good. Credit cards mean debt debt and more debt. That is not a good thing. You use credit cards and you are spending more money than you have. You are buying things you dont really need. You are wasting money. You are not keeping to your budget. Your heading for trouble. Maybe your even fighting more with your wife or your husband. Not having money hurts the family. Credit cards makes it worse. Because you never know how much you really have. And you think you are getting something for nothing. Its not good for people to think that. You appresiate things more when you work hard for them.

Character Trait Analysis

1. The organization is poor. Paragraphing would help this essay. The reader would be able to follow the ideas more clearly—and the writer might have been able to focus on groups of ideas as well.

2. The point of view is awkwardly stated.

3. The essay is primarily a list of unsupported opinions. Each opinion could have been developed with more supporting explanation. For example, instead of just saying, "You use credit cards and you are spending more money than you have," the writer could have given more detail: *Credit cards are very easy to use. This makes it easy to lose track of how much you are spending. Before you know it, you have spent more than you planned to without realizing it. This cannot happen when you are spending out of a checking account, where you must account for every dollar you spend. Therefore, credit cards make it easy to spend amounts you really can't afford.*

4. The essay should be longer to allow more room to develop ideas.

5. The essay ends without a summary or restatement of the writer's point of view.

6. The errors in punctuation, spelling, and accepted English usage interfere with the writer's purpose.

Model Essay—Holistic Score 2

Point of view is
stated.

Undeveloped
examples do
not adequately
support
the writer's
point of
view.

Restates the
point of
view.

Undeveloped
examples do
not adequately
support
the point of
view.

Conclusion is
weak.

Credit cards can be a good thing. Also a bad thing. Someone might spend more than they have. Easy to do with a credit card. But if you don't have the money, its nice to buy things. Especially if you really need them. Like something for your children. What if a person needed to buy shoes for their daughter and they didn't have any money but they could do it with a credit card. That would be good. But if the bill came and they couldn't pay? That would be bad. Hard to say. Except you can usually pay a little bit at a time. Probably that work out alright.

I think credit cards can be a good thing if you use them right. Like only for things you really need that don't cost too much money. So's you can pay the bill when it come. People could use credit cards for like children's shoes. But not stereos. Because they might not be able to pay. What I think is that people should be careful with their credit cards. Because if they don't, then there are just more problems with money.

Character Trait Analysis

1. The organization is better than the 1 essay.
2. The point of view is stated immediately.
3. The examples do not support the point of view strongly enough, because they are vague and unspecific. The writer has not explained *why* children's shoes would be an acceptable purchase with a credit card, while a stereo would not. The writer has simply mentioned items that might be bought with a credit card.
4. The conclusion is not clear. The writer has not explained what is meant by "being careful" with credit cards, or what type of "problems with money" might arise.
5. If the essay were longer, there would be more opportunity to develop the examples and to give more detail to support the writer's point of view.
6. There are many serious errors in accepted English usage.

Model Essay—Holistic Score 3

States the
point of
view.

Haphazard
listing of
ideas about
the topic.

Credit cards have make a big difference in how people spend money. People can buy things without having the money to pay for them right there. This can be a very good thing. But it can also be a very bad thing. It's a good thing if the person is careful about what he spend. Then credit card mean that the person does not have to wait so long to enjoy his money. He can buy something write away, like television set or radio. Or he can buy present for his children. If he need present for birthday or Christmas, he can buy it. That's a good thing. Credit cards give a person more choices about how to spend his money.

Restates the point of view.

Credit cards can be a bad thing if you are not very very careful about using them too often. If you don't stop and think, you start buying more than you really need. It's so easy to use a credit card, you don't stop and ask yourself, Do I need this? You just go ahead and buy. Then afterwards you are sorry, because you have spent too much. But this does not have to happen if a person is careful. If a person is careful, he can use credit cards to buy thing he would buy anyway, but he would not have to wait so long. Credit cards have change how people spend money, for the good and for the bad.

Character Trait Analysis

1. The level of organization is similar to that of the 2 essay. Better paragraphing might have helped the writer focus the ideas more sharply. The writer would have been more aware of how different ideas were grouped in the essay. For example, the first paragraph contains not one, but two ideas: that credit cards have affected how people spend money, and that credit cards can be a good thing if they are used the right way. Making two paragraphs out of the opening paragraph would have helped the writer to identify each of these two ideas, so that each could have been developed more fully in its own paragraph.

2. The examples do not adequately explain the writer's point of view. *Or he can buy present for his children* does not explain how credit cards have "made a big difference in how people spend money." It merely gives an example of something a person can use a credit card for. The example should be more closely tied to the main point of view, with a fuller explanation; for example, *Because credit cards allow more flexibility in spending, they can be used to make purchases that have to be made by a certain date, such as a child's birthday or Christmas present.*

3. The essay contains many errors in subject-verb agreement, such as *he spend.* There are other problems with accepted English usage that interfere with the essay's effectiveness.

4. The essay states its point of view very clearly at the beginning, and restates it clearly at the end.

Model Essay—Holistic Score 4

States the point of view and several reasons why the writer holds it.

I think credit cards have changed American consumers' buying habits for the better. Basically, they have given us more flexibility, which means more control over our money. I do temporary work and don't always know how much money I am going to make. Having credit cards means I can pay for some things later, when I have the money. That way I can always pay my rent and my bills on time.

Elaborates on the first reason for the point of view with an abstract example.

Elaborates on the second reason for the point of view with specific examples.

Suggests and overcomes counter-evidence; restates point of view; summarizes reasons.

More flexibility means that you can make better plans for how to use your money. If something is on sale, you can buy it and save the money, if you have a credit card. You can take advantage of the opportunity, even if you don't have the money right then.

Doing temporary work means that my income changes from week to week. But my bills don't change from week to week! I always have to pay my rent, my gas, and my electricity. Of course, I can't use my credit card to pay for those. But I can put other kinds of spending on my credit card. That way, if I have the money at the end of the month, I can pay the bill. If not, I still have at least enough to pay rent and utilities.

There are some bad points to credit cards. If people are not careful, they wind up spending way too much. But if you make a budget, decide what will go on the credit card, and what will be paid in cash, you have control over your spending. If they are used right, credit cards give American consumers more control and flexibility over spending, which is a good thing.

Character Trait Analysis

1. The level of organization in this essay is very good.

2. The essay addresses the topic immediately and explains the writer's reasons for choosing the point of view. The point of view is very clearly stated.

3. The supporting examples are better than those in the 3 essay. They are more clear and convincing, and they are more closely tied in to the writer's argument. Notice the use of specific examples in the third paragraph of this essay. The writer ties the examples very clearly to the argument. However, the examples are not as convincing as those used in the 5 and 6 essays. Check those essays for the use of specific examples that better illustrate the writer's point of view.

4. The ideas and the vocabulary in this essay are more sophisticated than those in the 1 through the 3 essays, and the grammar generally conforms to accepted English usage. However, this essay lacks the depth of the 5 and the 6 essays.

Model Essay—Holistic Score 5

Introduces subject and states point of view.

States one reason for point of view, giving supporting details.

Credit cards have had a profound impact on the way people spend money. Using credit cards can have both benefits and disadvantages. Ultimately, it is the judgment of the consumer that tips the scale.

Using a credit card means maximum flexibility in buying necessities and luxury items. For example, if an item is on sale, the consumer can take advantage of the savings by using a credit card. Using credit cards can also mean that a consumer can make purchases that would otherwise be out of reach. Many people would find it extremely difficult to save up the amounts needed to buy a major appliance or a piece of electronic equipment. With a credit card's monthly payment plan, these purchases become possible to far more people than ever before.

States another reason for point of view, giving supporting details.

On the other hand, credit card buyers can accumulate large debts in a very short time. With the increasing number of cards being offered now, it is especially easy to overspend. Many people end up buying items they don't really want or need. The high interest payments on many cards can fool people, too. They end up not only overspending, but stuck with big monthly bills.

Summarizes what has been written, restating the point of view.

As you can see, credit cards have revolutionized people's buying habits. Consumers can buy more goods and services more quickly than ever, using credit cards. Unfortunately, they can also get into debt more deeply and rapidly than they could before the days of credit cards. Only the consumer's good judgment can insure that the positive side of using credit cards outweighs the negative one.

Character Trait Analysis

1. Both the 4 and the 5 essays have a very good level of organization. This essay's style indicates that the writer has had more practice writing this type of essay. See below.

2. This essay is more interesting to read than the 4 because of the writer's greater command of the language and larger vocabulary. The writer is able to give clear and specific examples and explanations for the opinions stated, and the argument is always clear and easy to follow.

3. The essay flows smoothly and has few problems with usage.

4. Although the examples used in this essay are good, they are not as specific and vivid as those in the 6 essay. Therefore, this essay lacks the impact of the 6 essay.

Model Essay—Holistic Score 6

States the point of view and elaborates on the two sides of the argument.

Credit cards have brought the American consumer greater freedom than ever before. But they have also brought greater dangers. Because credit cards have enlarged the choices available to us, they demand that we take greater responsibility for our spending.

First reason for the point of view is given with very specific examples, including convincing details closely tied into argument.

Second reason for the point of view is given; contrasting argument shows author is aware of opposing views; again, specific, convincing details used to support argument.

Point of view restated clearly and expanded upon.

One way in which credit cards allow us to spend more responsibly is through the greater flexibility that they offer us. A wise consumer can plan to take advantage of seasonal sales, using credit cards to stock up on linens during the January white sales, or to buy a winter coat during the spring end-of-season sales. Considerable savings can result from this type of planning ahead which might not be possible to someone without the option of credit.

Yet credit cards also allow us to spend more irresponsibly. When using their credit cards consumers may tend to forget about the monthly interest payments, which are a big addition to the cost of an item. Using a credit card to pay for a restaurant meal for example, might mean that you are spending several additional dollars, just for the "privilege" of not using cash.

Freedom always brings with it responsibility. Credit cards have brought both to the American consumer. If we learn to use them wisely, we can enjoy the freedom they bring us. If not, we may find ourselves paying even more heavily than before for irresponsible spending.

Character Trait Analysis

1. The essay shows a high level of organizational ability and a solid command of the English language.

2. The writer has a smooth and confident writing style. This comes from practicing the writing process.

3. The examples that support the writer's point of view are very specific and easy to grasp. The writer ties them in very closely with the argument. Because the examples so clearly show why the argument is right, the writer pulls the reader along. Instead of just saying that "credit cards let you take advantage of sales," the writer mentions the January white sales and the spring end-of-season sales, and thereby shows the reader clearly how certain purchases have to be made at certain times to take advantage of sales and their savings.

4. This essay is not perfect. There are some awkward phrases and some errors in punctuation. However, these mistakes are not enough to detract from the overall effectiveness of this essay.

PREDICTOR TEST

Performance Analysis Chart

Part I

Directions: Circle the number of each item that you got correct on the Predictor Test. Count how many items you got correct in each row; count how many items you got correct in each column. Write the amount correct per row and column as the numerator in the fraction in the appropriate "Total Correct" box. (The denominators represent the total number of items in the row or column.) Write the grand total correct over the denominator, 28, at the lower right corner of the chart. (For example, if you got 24 items correct, write 24 so that the fraction reads 24/28.)

Item Type	Usage (page 24)	Sentence Structure (page 95)	Mechanics (page 140)	TOTAL CORRECT
Construction Shift	9	11, 14, 24, 27		/5
Sentence Correction	1, 10, 19, 22	7, 16, 18, 23	2, 4, 13, 20, 21, 28	/14
Sentence Revision	3, 12, 15, 25	5, 6, 17, 26	8	/9
TOTAL CORRECT	/9	/12	/7	/28

The page numbers in parentheses indicate where in this book you can find the beginning of specific instruction about the areas of grammar and about the types of questions you encountered in the Predictor Test.

Part II

Write your essay's score in the box at the right.

What were some of the strong points of your essay?

What were some of the weak points of your essay?

What improvements do you plan to make when you work on your next essay?

INTRODUCTION

This section of the book contains lessons with exercises and activities that can help you learn the things you need to know to pass the Writing Skills Test.

The Instruction section is divided into two parts. *Writing Skills, Part I: Grammar,* will help you to improve your skills at detecting and correcting errors in written English. *Writing Skills, Part II: Essay Writing,* can help you to become more comfortable with writing and will show you a process for writing essays.

The two parts are divided into units which are in turn further divided. There are many exercises, activities and quizzes, so you will have several opportunities to apply and to test your understanding of the material you study.

You may work through these instruction units in a number of ways. Two suggestions follow:

(1) Because Parts I and II cover different aspects of writing skills, you can work on both parts at the same time. By working on both parts at once, you can make advances in your understanding of grammar and editing while, at the same time, learning procedures for writing a composition.

(2) You can complete all of Part I before proceeding to Part II. This method will give you the opportunity to refresh and learn the conventions of English before you begin applying them to your writing.

You do not need to decide which method to follow before you start. Try one and then the other—follow the one (or another method you develop) that is most comfortable for you. You may want to discuss which method would be best with your teacher.

WRITING SKILLS

Part I-Grammar

PART 1 UNIT 1

The lessons in this part cover the conventions of written English and their application in editing. Units 1 to 3 are divided into chapters, which are in turn divided into lessons. Each of the chapters is a topic in usage, sentence structure, or mechanics. The lessons within each skill explore various facets of the topic.

It is best to work through Part I in order: begin with the first unit and continue to the test that ends the unit.

Each of the chapters in Units 1 to 3 begins with a Preview and ends with a Review. Previews and Reviews are made up of items that test how well you can apply your knowledge of the topic covered in the chapter. Previews allow you to test your present ability. If you get 100 percent of the examples in a Preview correct, you may not need to study the lessons in the chapter. To be sure, do the examples in the Review at the end of the chapter. If you get 80 percent correct, you may feel comfortable skipping the lessons in the chapter. If you get fewer than 80 percent of the examples in the Review correct, study all the lessons in the chapter.

At the end of Units 1 to 3 are sections called Test-Taking Strategies. These sections prepare you to analyze the multiple-choice items that appear on the GED Test. They will help you apply the knowledge you gain in Units 1 to 3 to editing in the format the GED uses.

You may want to work on Part II of this book at the same time you are working on Part 1. Or, you may prefer to complete this unit before you go on to Part II. Either way, you should start your work in Part I at the beginning of Unit 1.

Unit 1 Progress Chart

Usage

Use the following chart to keep track of your work. When you complete a lesson, circle the number of questions you answered correctly in the Lesson Exercise, the numbers in color represent scores at a level of 80% or better.

Lesson	Page		
		CHAPTER 1: Subject-Verb Agreement	
1	26	The Parts of a Sentence	1 2 3 4 5
2	28	Understanding Singular and Plural	1 2 3 4 5 6 7 8 9 10
			1 2 3 4 5
3	31	The Basics of Subject-Verb Agreement	1 2 3 4 5 6 7 8 9 10
4	35	Interrupting Phrases	1 2 3 4 5
5	37	Inverted Sentence Structure	1 2 3 4 5
6	39	Expletives	1 2 3 4 5
7	40	Compound Subjects	1 2 3 4 5
	42	**Chapter 1 Review**	1 2 3 4 5 6 7 8 9 10 11 12 13 14 15
		CHAPTER 2: Verb Tense	
1	47	The Principal Parts of a Verb	1 2 3 4 5 6 7 8 9 10
2	51	Verb Tenses	1 2 3 4 5
3	56	The Perfect Tenses	1 2 3 4 5
4	58	Word Clues to Tense in Sentences	1 2 3 4 5
5	60	Using Tense Consistently	1 2 3 4 5
6	62	Word Clues to Tense in Paragraphs	1 2 3 4 5 6 7 8
	64	**Chapter 2 Review**	1 2 3 4 5 6 7 8 9 10 11 12 13 14 15
		CHAPTER 3: Pronoun Reference	
1	69	Personal Pronouns	1 2 3 4 5
2	72	Pronoun-Antecedent Agreement	1 2 3 4 5
3	74	Avoiding Pronoun Shifts	1 2 3 4 5
4	76	Relative Pronouns	1 2 3 4 5
5	78	Avoiding Vague Pronoun References	1 2 3 4 5
6	80	Avoiding Ambiguous Pronoun References	1 2 3 4 5
	82	**Chapter 3 Review**	1 2 3 4 5 6 7 8 9 10 11 12 13 14 15

UNIT 1 – USAGE

Credit: Jay Seeley

Objectives

In this unit, you will learn to

• recognize the singular and plural forms of subjects and verbs

• make subjects and verbs of sentences agree

• use the correct tenses of verbs

• check sentences and paragraphs for consistent use of verb tenses

• use pronouns that agree with the words to which they refer

• select pronouns that express ideas clearly

CHAPTER 1
SUBJECT-VERB AGREEMENT

Preview

Directions: Edit the following sentences to correct all errors in subject-verb agreement. Not all of the sentences have errors.

1. There is two national anthems played at every All-Star baseball game.
2. The most popular street name in the United States are Park Street.
3. Into the crowded parking garage drives the employees.
4. Neither Frank nor Elaine works at the central office.
5. Ms. Wilson spend about two hours each day answering her mail.

Check your answers. Correct answers are on page 324. If you have all five answers correct, do the Chapter 1 Review on page 42. If you have fewer than five answers correct, study Chapter 1 beginning with Lesson 1.

The Parts of a Sentence

Every complete sentence has a subject. The **subject** tells who or what the sentence is about.

> <u>Ellen</u> repaired the typewriter this morning.

This sentence is about Ellen. The name *Ellen* is the subject of the sentence. The sentence mentions a typewriter, but the sentence isn't about the typewriter. The sentence is about Ellen, the person who fixed the typewriter.

> <u>She</u> takes a word processing class after work.

The subject of this sentence is *she.* The sentence tells about a person who is taking a class, not about word processing or about the class.

> The <u>class</u> starts at 6:30 P.M.

The subject of this sentence is *class*. In this sentence, we learn about the class.

A subject can be either a noun or a pronoun. A **noun** is the name of a person, place, or thing. It may be a general name—such as *athlete, camera,* or *city* —- or it may be a specific name — such as *José Canseco, Kodak,* or *Denver.*

The names of ideas and activities are also nouns.

> Ideas: *honesty, courage, liberty, friendship*

> Activities: *swimming, thinking, cooking*

However, a word ending in <u>-ing</u> is a verb, not a noun, when it tells what someone or something is doing.

> Noun: <u>Running</u> is Donna's favorite hobby.

> Verb: She is <u>running</u> in the Los Angeles Marathon next year.

A **pronoun** is a word that can be used in place of a noun. Some examples of pronouns that are subject pronouns: *I, you, he, she, it, we, they, anybody,* and *everyone.*

In addition to a subject, a complete sentence must have a verb. A **verb** expresses an action or a state of being. The verb in each of these examples tells what the subject does. Each is an action verb.

Ellen <u>repaired</u> the typewriter this morning.

She <u>takes</u> a word processing class after work.

The class <u>starts</u> at 6:30 P.M.

A verb that expresses a state of being can also be called a **linking verb**. A linking verb connects the subject of a sentence with a word or phrase that renames or describes the subject.

The capital of Norway <u>is</u> Oslo.

The pioneers <u>were</u> adventurous and brave.

Forms of the verb *to be* (*am, is, are, was,* and *were,* for example) are often used as linking verbs. Other verbs that can be used as linking verbs include:

appear	feel	remain	smell	stay
become	look	seem	sound	taste

Lesson 1 Exercise

Directions: Draw one line under each subject and two lines under each verb in the following sentences.

1. Henry bought a newspaper at the drugstore this morning.
2. He always reads the newspaper on the bus.
3. The newspaper on weekdays has five sections.
4. The section with the national news is the longest one.
5. Advertisements for movies start on page 6 of the last section.

Answers are on page 324.

Understanding Singular and Plural

Nouns and pronouns can be either **singular** (meaning one) or **plural** (meaning more than one). In these sentences, the subjects are singular.

The <u>customer</u> complained to the manager for over an hour.

<u>She</u> wanted a cash refund.

The sentences below have plural subjects. In each case, the subjects refer to more than one person.

The <u>customers</u> waited on the sidewalk for the start of the sale.

<u>They</u> heard about the sale on the radio.

Noun Plurals

To make nouns plural, follow these rules:

Rule 1. Most nouns are made plural by adding *s*.

house	houses	job	jobs
book	books	chair	chairs

Rule 2. If a singular noun ends in *s, x, z, ch,* or *sh,* add *es* to make the plural form.

boss	bosses	watch	watches
tax	taxes	brush	brushes

Rule 3. When a singular noun ends in *y* preceded by a consonant (any letter except *a, e, i, o,* or *u*), change the *y* to *i* and add *es*.

copy	copies	company	companies
factory	factories	city	cities

When a noun ends in *y* preceded by a vowel (*a, e, i, o,* or *u*), just add *s.*

alley	alleys	day	days
boy	boys	delay	delays

Rule 4. When a singular noun ends in *f* or *fe,* change *f* to *v* and add *es.*

leaf	leaves	knife	knives
shelf	shelves	life	lives

Nouns that do not follow one of the four rules listed above are considered irregular. All irregular plural forms are shown in the dictionary.

These nouns have irregular plural forms. In each case, the spelling of the noun changes when it is made plural.

goose	geese	tooth	teeth
woman	women	foot	feet
child	children	mouse	mice

Remember, if you are not sure how to form the plural of a noun, use a dictionary to check the spelling.

Singular and Plural Pronouns

The pronouns on the following chart can be used as subjects. Notice which pronouns are singular and which are plural. You will learn more about pronouns in Chapter 3.

Singular Pronouns	Plural Pronouns	
I, you, he, she, it	we, you, they	
this, that	these, those	
anyone, anybody, everybody, no one nobody, each, one, someone, somebody, either, neither	others, few, both several, many	

Part 1.

Directions: Underline the subject in each sentence and decide whether it is singular or plural. Then write <u>S</u> for singular or <u>P</u> for plural in the space provided.

1. ___ Someone holds the winning ticket
2. ___ Five boxes on the last truck were empty.
3. ___ That is not a good idea.
4. ___ A salesperson will help you immediately.
5. ___ We are leaving for Miami in the afternoon.
6. ___ The supervisors left the office at 4 P.M.
7. ___ She wants to hire an employee with good typing skills.
8. ___ The students asked the teacher for extra practice.
9. ___ It is not in the glove compartment.
10. ___ My brother works at the university.

Part 2.

Directions: Each of the following sentences contains at least one incorrect noun plural. Cross out each error and write the correct plural form above.

1. Because of budget problems, many citys are raising taxes.
2. Neither of his wishs came true.
3. The secretarys work at difference branchs of the same company.
4. Each of the frames is 3 feet by 2 foot, 6 inchs.
5. Our lifes changed dramatically after we won the lottery.

Answers are on page 324.

The Basics of Subject-Verb Agreement

The basic rule for subject-verb agreement is:

A singular subject must use a singular verb.

Jane *admires* the paintings of Van Gogh.

Jane is a singular subject and uses a singular verb.

A plural subject must use a plural verb.

Van Gogh's paintings *include* landscapes and portraits.

Paintings is a plural subject and uses a plural verb.

Use the basic form of a verb if the subject of a sentence is *I, you, we, they,* or any plural noun. A verb is in its most basic form when it is paired with the word *to*: to dance, to watch, to work, to win, to run, to change.

I dance	we work	athletes run
you watch	they win	cities change

When the subject of a sentence is *he, she, it,* or any singular noun, use the singular form of the verb. The singular form of most verbs is formed by adding *s* or *es.*

he dances	it works	an athlete runs
she watches	a team wins	a city changes

Some verbs have irregular verb forms. The most common irregular verb is the verb *to be*. The following sentences illustrate subject-verb agreement for this verb.

I <u>am</u> glad to meet you.

You <u>are</u> the new captain.

He <u>is</u> a computer programmer.

She <u>is</u> the new supervisor.

It <u>is</u> the largest house.

We <u>are</u> on the same team.

You <u>are</u> members of the PTA.

They <u>are</u> from the same town.

Sometimes singular subjects may appear to be plural. Other words may look plural even though they are singular. These additional rules will help you handle difficult situations in subject-verb agreement.

Rule 1: The following *indefinite pronouns* are singular and take a singular verb.

anyone	**everyone**	**someone**	**either**	**one**
anybody	**everybody**	**somebody**	**neither**	**no one**
anything	**everything**	**something**	**another**	**each**

Everyone <u>is</u> anxious to meet the new boss.

Anybody <u>is</u> eligible to apply for the loan.

Rule 2: The following pronouns are plural and take a plural verb.

both	**few**	**many**	**several**

Several <u>were encouraged</u> to continue the discussion.

Many <u>were asked</u> to join the new club.

Rule 3: The following pronouns may be either singular or plural, depending on how they are used in a sentence. Look at the phrase following the pronoun to figure out its meaning.

> **some**   **most**   **part**   **any**   **all**   **none**
>
> Some of the money <u>was spent</u> already.
>
> Some of the windows <u>were</u> open.

In the first sentence, *some* is singular and takes a singular verb. In the second, *some* refers to more than one thing. It takes a plural verb.

Rule 4: The following nouns are singular, although they end in *s*. As the subject of a sentence, they take a singular verb.

> **civics**   **athletics**   **genetics**   **news**
> **mumps**   **physics**   **politics**   **series**
> **measles**   **Unites States**   **economics**   **mathematics**

> Mathematics <u>has been</u> an important field of study since ancient times.

> Mumps <u>is</u> a disease of the salivary glands.

Rule 5: The following nouns do not have singular forms. They are plural in meaning and always take a plural verb.

> **trousers**   **pants**   **jeans**
> **shears**   **scissors**   **pliers**

> The pliers <u>are</u> in the toolbox.

> My pants <u>are</u> ripped.

NOTE: If the word *pair* precedes the noun, use the singular verb.

> The trousers <u>are</u> too long.

> The pair of trousers <u>is</u> too long.

When you edit sentences for subject-verb agreement, use this five-step test. After reading a sentence:

1. Find the subject by asking whom or what the sentence is about.
2. Determine whether the subject is singular or plural.
3. Locate the verb.
4. Determine whether the verb is singular or plural.
5. If the subject and the verb are both singular or both plural, they agree. If they do not agree, change the verb to agree with the subject.

Use the five-step method to determine the agreement of this sentence.

Microwave ovens cooks with radiation.

Step 1. By asking what the sentence is about, you determine that the subject of the sentence is *ovens.*

Step 2. *Ovens,* which ends in *s,* is plural.

Step 3. *Cooks* is the verb of the sentence.

Step 4. Because *cooks* ends in *s,* it is singular.

Step 5. The plural subject and singular verb do not agree. The verb should be changed so that it agrees with the subject.

Microwave ovens cook with radiation.

Lesson 3 Exercise

Directions: Use the five-step method to determine the agreement of the following sentences. Edit the sentences to correct all errors in subject-verb agreement. Not all of the sentences have errors.

1. The team have lost the last four games.
2. German measles frequently begins with swollen glands.
3. The pair of jeans were in the dryer.
4. No one remembers the original name of the street.
5. Tea leaves needs to be stored in a tight container.
6. A correctly written resume list your most recent job first.
7. Many experts disagrees with that answer.
8. Both shows the same talent in music.
9. Several senators was touring the flood-damaged area.
10. They realizes the importance of a healthy diet.

Answers are on pages 324-325.

Lesson 4 Interrupting Phrases

The verbs in the sentences below do not agree with their subjects. The edited versions, with the changes shown in handwriting, are correct.

The concert, sold out for three months, ~~were~~ *was* a big hit.

The president, accompanied by several staff members, ~~attend~~ *attends* many public ceremonies.

The subjects and verbs of these sentences are separated by groups of words that give more information about the subject. Because these groups of words break the normal pattern of a subject followed by a verb, they are called **interrupting phrases.**

Notice that in these two sentences, the subjects — *concert* and *president* — are singular. The corrected verb form in each sentence is also singular. An interrupting phrase that separates the subject and the verb of a sentence does not change the number of the subject.

In the two examples above, the interrupting phrases are set off by commas from the rest of the sentence. Many interrupting phrases are not set off by commas.

The increase in costs makes it difficult to keep prices down.

The debate between the candidates reveals sharp differences in opinions.

Words that immediately follow the subject, whether or not they are set off by commas, do not change the number of the subject. The subjects of both the sentences above — *increase* and *debate* — are singular. Notice that the verbs — *makes* and *reveals* — are also singular.

Before you use the five-step method given in Lesson 3 for determining sub-ject-verb agreement, cross out all the interrupting phrases in a sentence.

One of the ~~most common eye~~ problems are nearsightedness.

When the interrupting phrase is crossed out, it is easier to locate the subject and the verb. The subject of the sentence is *one.* The verb, therefore, must be changed to *is* to agree in number with the subject.

Directions: Edit the following sentences to correct all errors in subject-verb agreement. First cross out the interrupting phrases. Then use the five-step agreement test described in Lesson 3. Not all of the sentences have errors.

1. Broiling, as well as poaching, is a healthy alternative to frying foods.
2. Requirements for a driver's license varies from state to state.
3. Successful dieting, according to nutritionists, demand patience and determination.
4. One of the best salt substitutes are lemon juice.
5. Foods with a high moisture content, such as lettuce, does not freeze well.

Answers are on page 325.

Lesson 5

Inverted Sentence Structure

In most sentences, the subject comes before the verb. In some sentences, however, the subject comes after the verb. These sentences have **inverted sentence structure.**

A sentence with inverted sentence structure may begin with a phrase.

> Over there on the counter are the forms that you need to fill out.

This example has inverted structure and begins with the phrase *over there on the counter.* The plural subject *forms* agrees with the plural verb *are.*

To find the subject of an inverted sentence that begins with a phrase, cross out the phrase. That will make it easier to identify whom or what the sentence is about.

> ~~Over there on the counter~~ are the forms that you need to fill out.

Another technique is to rephrase the sentence so that the statement follows a more natural word order. The sentence above could be written:

> The forms that you need to fill out are over there on the counter.

Questions often have inverted structures. The edited version of the question below shows correct subject-verb agreement.

> Is
> ~~Are~~ the delivery date of the computers acceptable?

If a question has inverted sentence structure, change the question into a statement. Rephrased as a statement, the edited question above reads:

> The delivery date of the computers is acceptable.

Then cross out any phrases that separate the subject from the verb.

> The delivery date ~~of the computers~~ is acceptable.

Note that the verb, *is,* agrees with the subject, *date.*

Directions: Edit the following sentences to correct all errors in subject-verb agreement. Where necessary, put sentences in subject-verb order and cross out interrupting phrases. Not all of the sentences have errors.

1. At the bottom of the contract were the space for their signatures.
2. During the winter, most heating bills increase dramatically.
3. Is the doctors at the hospital this afternoon?
4. In the shuttle sits the astronauts.
5. Do the customer in Line 5 have a receipt?

Answers are on page 325.

Expletives

Read the following sentences. Notice how the sentences have been edited to correct errors in subject-verb agreement.

>   *are*
> There ~~is~~ desert regions in the northern and western parts of China.

>   *is*
> There ~~are~~ a national marble tournament held each year in the United States.

>   *is*
> Here ~~are~~ the set of blueprints for the new office building.

Each of these sentences begins with the word *here* or *there*. These words are called **expletives** when they begin a sentence. Because expletives come directly before the verb, they may appear to be the subjects of the sentences. An expletive, however, is never the subject of a sentence.

When a sentence begins with an expletive, the subject is found after the verb. The subject of the first sentence above is *regions*. Because *regions* is a plural noun, a plural verb, *are*, is needed. The subject of the second sentence, *tournament*, is singular and needs the singular verb *is*. In the third sentence, the subject is *set*, a singular noun that therefore requires the singular verb *is*.

To determine subject-verb agreement in a sentence that begins with an expletive, use the five-step agreement test given in Lesson 3.

Lesson 6 Exercise

Directions: Edit the following sentences to correct all errors in subject-verb agreement. Not all of the sentences have errors.

1. There are at least 300 people in the audience.
2. Here are the map of the Hawaiian Islands.
3. There is many ancient myths that explain forces in nature.
4. Here come the winner of the Boston Marathon.
5. There is 11 players on each team in field hockey.

Answers are on page 325.

Compound Subjects

Read the sentences below. Notice how they have been edited to correct sub-ject-verb agreement.

Swimming and jogging *are* ~~is~~ forms of aerobic exercise.

Neither Bolivia nor Paraguay *is* ~~are~~ north of the equator.

Either direct pressure or cold compresses *are* ~~is~~ used to stop a nosebleed.

Many sentences have more than one subject. In such cases, the sentence has a **compound subject.** The separate subjects in a compound subject may be connected by single connective words, such as *and, or,* or *nor,* or by paired con-nective words, such as *either...or, neither...nor, both...and,* or *not only...but also.*

When a sentence has a compound subject, these rules must be followed to determine whether the verb used should be singular or plural.

Rule 1: When two subjects are joined by *or, nor, neither...nor, either...or,* or *not only...but also,* the verb agrees in number with the subject that is closer to the verb.

Neither the coach nor the players <u>have</u> discussed the next game.

Neither the players nor the coach <u>has</u> discussed the next game.

The two subjects in both of these sentences are *coach* and *players.* In the first sentence, the subject, *players,* is closer to the verb. Because *players* is plural, the verb used, *have,* is also plural. In the second sentence, the singular subject, *coach,* is closer to the verb, requiring the use of the singular verb, *has.*

Rule 2: When two subjects are joined by *and* or *both...and*, they usually take plural verbs. It does not matter if one subject is plural and one is singular. The connective *and* combines them to make a plural subject.

Both the teacher and the students <u>were</u> ready for summer vacation.

Both the students and the teacher <u>were</u> ready for summer vacation.

Note: In a few cases, a compound subject joined by *and* is singular because the two words refer to one person, place, or thing. In this sentence, a singular verb is needed because the subject *macaroni and cheese* is thought of as one dish.

Macaroni and cheese <u>is</u> David's favorite dinner.

Lesson 7 Exercise

Directions: Edit the following sentences to correct all errors in subject-verb agreement. Not all of the sentences have errors.

1. Not only carbon but also diamonds are used in industry.
2. Either gravel or crushed rock combine with cement to form concrete.
3. The Rocky Mountains and the Andes is part of the same mountain chain.
4. Both a blanket and warm clothing is recommended when traveling in the winter.
5. Neither creams nor lotions is effective in the prevention of wrinkles.

Answers are on page 325.

CHAPTER 1 REVIEW

Directions: Edit the following sentences to correct all errors in subject-verb agreement. Not all of the sentences have errors.

1. Everyone need a passport to travel in a foreign country.
2. Neither Jesse nor Barbara are able to attend the class.
3. There is 14 offices on the West Coast.
4. One of the most common diseases in the world are malaria.
5. Both Robert De Niro and Dustin Hoffman has won Academy Awards.
6. Is Donna and Gordon planning to take a vacation this summer?
7. On 6th Street and Broadway are a new camera repair shop.
8. That typewriter, the larger of the two, cost less than $500.
9. Risa seems interested in many different kinds of music.
10. Ms. Novoa, a member of the PTA for three years, have strong opinions on the subject.
11. In large cities, the schools is often overcrowded.
12. Here are the list of phone numbers.
13. Everyone want job security and adequate benefits.
14. Are the members of the team interested in buying uniforms?
15. Either Jim or Claudia plan to drive Mr. Phillips to the airport.

Check your answers. Correct answers are on pages 325-326. If you have all 15 answers correct, go on to Chapter 2. If you have any answers incorrect, find the item number on the chart below and review that lesson before you go on.

Review	If you missed Item Number
Lesson 1 – 3	1, 9, 11, 13
Lesson 4	4, 8, 10
Lesson 5	6, 7, 14
Lesson 6	3, 12
Lesson 7	2, 5, 15

GED REVIEW 1

Directions: Read the following passage. Using the rules you have learned in this chapter, answer the items that follow. Not all of the sentences have errors.

<u>Items 1 to 10</u> are based on the following passage.

(1) Local officials are encouraging us to store supplys in our homes in case of an emergency. (2) Does the people in your house have what they need to survive? (3) One of the most important survival items are water. (4) For a three-day supply, everybody in your home need at least three gallons of water for drinking and washing. (5) A crescent wrench or a pipe wrench is a useful tool for turning off gas and water valves. (6) In case of power outages, both a battery-powered radio and several flashlights is helpful. (7) It is always a good idea to store at least a one-week supply of food for every person living in your home. (8) Food requiring little preparation, such as a can of beans or a package of freeze-dried eggs, are an excellent choice. (9) However, children and pregnant womans may need special types of foods. (10) Other items bringing an increase in safety and comfort are blankets, toiletries, and plastic forks, knifes, and spoons.

1. Sentence 1: **Local officials are encouraging us to store supplys in our homes in case of an emergency.**

   What correction should be made to this sentence?

   (1) change <u>officials</u> to <u>officiales</u>
   (2) change <u>are</u> to <u>is</u>
   (3) change <u>store</u> to <u>stores</u>
   (4) change <u>supplys</u> to <u>supplies</u>
   (5) change <u>emergency</u> to <u>emergencys</u>

2. Sentence 2: **Does the people in your house have what they need to survive?**

   What correction should be made to this sentence?

   (1) change <u>Does</u> to <u>Do</u>
   (2) change <u>people</u> to <u>peoples</u>
   (3) change <u>have</u> to <u>has</u>
   (4) change <u>need</u> to <u>needs</u>
   (5) change <u>survive</u> to <u>survives</u>

3. Sentence 3: **One of the most important survival items are water.**

What correction should be made to this sentence?

(1) change <u>One</u> to <u>Ones</u>
(2) change <u>items</u> to <u>itemes</u>
(3) change <u>are</u> to <u>is</u>
(4) change <u>survival</u> to <u>survives</u>
(5) no correction is necessary

4. Sentence 4: **For a three day supply, everybody in your home need at least three gallons of water for drinking and washing.**

What correction should be made to this sentence?

(1) change <u>day</u> to <u>days</u>
(2) change <u>day</u> to <u>daies</u>
(3) change <u>need</u> to <u>needs</u>
(4) change <u>gallons</u> to <u>gallon</u>
(5) no correction is necessary

5. Sentence 5: **A crescent wrench or a pipe wrench is a useful tool for turning off gas and water valves.**

What correction should be made to this sentence?

(1) replace <u>or</u> with <u>and</u>
(2) change <u>is</u> to <u>are</u>
(3) change <u>tool</u> to <u>tools</u>
(4) change <u>valves</u> to <u>valvs</u>
(5) no correction is necessary

6. Sentence 6: **In case of power outages, both a battery-powered radio and several flashlights is helpful.**

What correction should be made to this sentence?

(1) change <u>radio</u> to <u>radioes</u>
(2) change <u>and</u> to <u>or</u>
(3) change <u>flashlights</u> to <u>flashlight</u>
(4) change <u>is</u> to <u>are</u>
(5) no correction is necessary

7. Sentence 7: **It is always a good idea to store at least a one-week supply of food for every person living in your home.**

What correction should be made to this sentence?

(1) change <u>It</u> to <u>They</u>
(2) change <u>is</u> to <u>are</u>
(3) change <u>store</u> to <u>stores</u>
(4) change <u>person</u> to <u>people</u>
(5) no correction is necessary

8. Sentence 8: **Food requiring little preparation, such as a can of beans or a package of freeze-dried eggs, are an excellent choice.**

What correction should be made to this sentence?

(1) change <u>can</u> to <u>cans</u>
(2) change <u>eggs</u> to <u>egges</u>
(3) change <u>are</u> to <u>is</u>
(4) change <u>choice</u> to <u>choices</u>
(5) no correction is necessary

9. Sentence 9: **However, children and pregnant womans may need special types of foods.**

What correction should be made to this sentence?

(1) change <u>children</u> to <u>childs</u>
(2) change <u>womans</u> to <u>women</u>
(3) change <u>womans</u> to <u>womens</u>
(4) change <u>need</u> to <u>needs</u>
(5) no correction is necessary

10. Sentence 10: **Other items bringing an increase in safety and comfort are blankets, toiletries, and plastic forks, knifes, and spoons.**

What correction should be made to this sentence?

(1) change <u>are</u> to <u>is</u>
(2) change <u>blankets</u> to <u>blanketes</u>
(3) change <u>toiletries</u> to <u>toiletrys</u>
(4) change <u>knifes</u> to <u>knives</u>
(5) no correction is necessary

Answers are on page 326.

CHAPTER 2
VERB TENSE

Preview

Directions: Edit the following sentences to correct all errors in verb tense. Not all of the sentences have errors.

1. The Julian calendar is developed in 46 B.C. by Julius Caesar.
2. The diameter of the moon is about 2,160 miles, and its surface area was 14,650,000 square miles.
3. Richard Byrd spent many years exploring Antarctica.
4. Beethoven had write nine symphonies before his death in 1827.
5. Tomorrow we learn about Sir John A. Macdonald, the first prime minister of Canada.

Check your answers. Correct answers are on page 327. If you have all five answers correct, do the Chapter 2 Review on page 64. If you have fewer than five answers correct, study Chapter 2 beginning with Lesson 1.

Lesson 1
The Principal Parts of a Verb

What do you notice about each of the verbs in the following sentences?

The pilot <u>looks</u> at the instrument panel.

The pilot <u>looked</u> at the instrument panel five minutes ago.

The pilot <u>has looked</u> at the instrument panel frequently during the last hour.

The form of the verb in each sentence changed to express a different meaning. These various forms are called **tenses.** Tenses are formed using the principal parts of a verb. Every verb has three principal parts—the <u>present,</u> the <u>past,</u> and the <u>past participle</u>.

The **present form** is used to show that something happens in the present. Think of completing the sentence <u>Now I...</u>

The **past form** is used to show that something happened and was completed in the past. Think of completing the sentence <u>Yesterday I...</u>

The **past participle** is used with a helping verb to make a verb phrase. Think of completed these sentences: <u>Often, I have..., Often, I had...,</u> or <u>Often, he/she has...</u>

Principal Parts of Regular Verbs

Verbs known as **regular verbs** follow a certain pattern to form their past and past participle forms.

Look at these examples of regular verbs.

Present	Past	Past Participle
need	needed	needed
agree	agreed	agreed
join	joined	joined
vanish	vanished	vanished
desire	desired	desired

Both the past and the past participle forms are the same. These verbs are called *regular verbs* because the past and past participle forms are formed by adding *-d* or *-ed* to the present tense form.

Principle Parts of Irregular Verbs

Verbs known as **irregular verbs** use endings other than -d or -ed to form the past and the past participle. Compare the present and past forms of the verbs in the pairs of sentences below.

The wind <u>shakes</u> the leaves of the tree.

The wind <u>shook</u> the leaves of the tree.

The noise <u>grows</u> louder.

The noise <u>grew</u> louder.

Chart 1 is a list of commonly used verbs that have irregular past and past participle forms.

Chart 1 Irregular Verbs		
Present	**Past**	**Past Participle**
be (am, is, are)	was, were	been
become	became	become
begin	began	begun
bite	bit	bitten
blow	blew	blown
break	broke	broken
bring	brought	brought
built	built	built
burst	burst	burst
buy	bought	bought
choose	chose	chosen
come	came	come
dive	dived or dove	dived
do	did	done
draw	drew	drawn
drink	drank	drunk
drive	drove	driven
eat	ate	eaten
fall	fell	fallen
fly	flew	flown
forget	forgot	forgotten
freeze	froze	frozen
get	got	got or gotten
give	gave	given
go	went	gone
grow	grew	grown

Chart 1 Irregular Verbs (cont'd.)		
Present	**Past**	**Past Participle**
hide	hid	hidden
know	knew	known
lay (put)	laid	laid
leave	left	left
lie (recline)	lay	lain
ride	rode	ridden
ring	rang	rung
rise (go up)	rose	risen
run	ran	run
say	said	said
see	saw	seen
set (put)	set	set
shake	shook	shaken
shrink	shrank or shrunk	shrunk or shrunken
sing	sang	sung
sink	sank or sunk	sunk
sit	sat	sat
speak	spoke	spoken
spend	spent	spent
spring	sprang or sprung	sprung
stand	stood	stood
steal	stole	stolen
swim	swam	swum
take	took	taken
teach	taught	taught
tear	tore	torn
throw	threw	thrown
wake	woke or waked	waked or woken
wear	wore	worn
write	wrote	written

Directions: Write the correct form of the verb in parentheses in the space provided.

1. (begin) The Supreme Court _____ each term on the first Monday in October.
2. (draw) Chester Gould _____ the popular cartoon "Dick Tracy" for many years.
3. (build) A bird _____ its nest using many different materials.
4. (happen) In years past, most tornadoes _____ in the central section of the country.
5. (do) Scientists have _____ many experiments to determine the mineral composition of the moon.
6. (break) Germany _____ its treaty with the Soviet Union in 1941.
7. (say) The president of the company had _____ that the hiring freeze was temporary.
8. (teach) Native Americans _____ the early colonists how to grow corn.
9. (write) Many people have _____ to their representatives about the proposed law.
10. (swim) Currently, Anita _____ ten laps each day as part of her fitness program.

Answers are on page 327.

Verb Tenses

Read these sentences. When does the action of each of these sentences take place?

Carla <u>works</u> from 8:30 A.M. to 5:30 P.M. every day.

She <u>finished</u> an important project yesterday morning.

She <u>will</u> <u>report</u> her findings to her boss tomorrow.

In the first sentence, the action takes place in the present; in the second sentence, the action took place in the past; in the third sentence, the action will take place in the future. The **tense** of the verb in each sentence shows the time of the action described.

Verbs change forms to form different tenses. Sometimes a verb phrase is needed to show a tense. In the third sentence, a helping verb *will* is added to *report* to form the verb phrase *will report.*

The Three Simple Tenses

The three simple tenses are <u>present</u>, <u>past</u>, and <u>future</u>.

Use the **simple present tense** for things that happen now or are true now, for things that are generally true all the time, and for actions that are performed regularly.

Tim <u>rides</u> to work with Al and Marta.

Ms. Reynolds <u>is</u> the director of personnel.

Mike <u>visits</u> his grandmother every Saturday.

Use the **simple past tense** for things that were true in the past or for actions that happened at a specific time in the past.

> Mr. Goldhamer <u>was</u> my supervisor last year.

> Sarah <u>finished</u> the book yesterday.

Use the **simple past tense** for things that will be true in the future or for actions that will happen in the future.

> Jason <u>will be</u> eight years old on his next birthday.

> Samatha <u>will mail</u> the letter this afternoon.

Chart 2 explains how to form the three simple tenses.

Chart 2 The Simple Tenses		
Tense	**Form**	**Examples**
Present	Add <u>-s</u> or <u>-es</u> when used with singular nouns or with <u>he,</u> <u>she,</u> or <u>it.</u> No ending when used with plural nouns or with <u>I,</u> <u>you,</u> <u>we,</u> or <u>they.</u>	The plane descends. It lands. The planes descend. They land.
Past	For regular verbs, add <u>-d</u> or <u>-ed</u> to the present part. For irregular verbs, see your dictionary.	The plane descended. We arrived.
Future	Add <u>will</u> to the present tense.	We will arrive.

Continuing Verbs

Some actions happen at a certain point in time; others occur over time. A **continuing verb** shows that the action of a sentence continues over a period of time in either the present, past, or future.

Present Continuing: The baby <u>is sleeping</u> soundly.
Past Continuing: He <u>was working</u> in the storeroom yesterday.
Future Continuing: They <u>will be visiting</u> us in July.

A continuing verb is formed using one or more helping verbs and the present part of the main verb plus <u>ing.</u> Chart 3 will help you form continuing verbs correctly.

Chart 3 Continuing Verbs			
Tense	**If the subject of the sentence is...**	**Use...**	
Present Continuing	I	am	With the present part + -ing
	singular noun, he, she, or it	is	
	plural noun, we, you, or they	are	
Past Continuing	singular noun, I, he, she, or it	was	
	plural noun, we, you, or they	were	
Future Continuing	any noun or pronoun	will be	

Passive Verbs

Think about this sentence:

Sam <u>broke</u> the expensive camera yesterday.

The subject of the sentence is *Sam.* The verb is *broke,* the past tense form of the verb *break.*

This sentence contains much of the same information:

The expensive camera <u>was broken</u> yesterday.

However, the subject of the sentence is now the word *camera.* You cannot tell who broke the camera from this sentence. This second example contains a passive verb.

When a sentence has a **passive verb**, the action of the sentence happens to the subject. Someone or something else besides the subject does the action.

Passive verbs can be used with any tense.
Present Passive: This memo <u>is dated</u> January 15.
Past Passive: The letter <u>was addressed</u> to Max Singer.
Future Passive: The best salesperson <u>will be given</u> a $50 bonus.

A passive verb is written using one or more helping verbs and the past participle. Chart 4 will help you form passive verbs correctly.

Chart 4 Passive Verb Forms			
Tense	If the subject of the sentence is...	Use...	
Present Passive	I	am	With the past participle
	singular noun, he, she, or it	is	
	plural noun, we, you, or they	are	
Past Passive	singular noun, I, he, she, or it	was	
	plural noun, we, you, or they	were	
Future Passive	any noun or pronoun	will be	

Adding Endings to Regular Verbs

These rules will help you make correct spelling choices as you form the many tenses and forms of verbs.

Rule 1. When the present part of a verb ends in y preceded by a consonant, change the y to i before adding ed. However, do not change the y to add ing.

carry	carried	carrying
copy	copied	copying

Rule 2. When the present part of a verb ends with a silent e, drop the e before adding ing. Add only a d to form the past part.

live	lived	living
care	cared	caring

Rule 3. When the present part of a verb ends with a vowel-consonant pattern, and when the accent falls on the last, or only, syllable of the verb, double the final consonant before adding ed or ing.

drop	dropped	dropping
wrap	wrapped	wrapping

Rule 4. In all other situations involving regular verbs, simply add ed or ing to the present part.

watch	watched	watching
open	opened	opening
work	worked	working

Directions: Edit the following items to correct all verb tense errors. Not all of the items have errors.

1. Ms. Jemison called the office next Monday.
2. Risa gives Margo the message yesterday.
3. Mary was working from 9 A.M. until 1:30 P.M. for the next week.
4. Mr. Garcetti attends the conference every year.
5. The election results will be announced an hour ago.

Answers are on page 327.

The Perfect Tenses

The three perfect tenses are present perfect, past perfect, and future perfect. These tenses allow us to show the time relationship between two events or times.

The **present perfect tense** is used in three situations:

(1) When something started in the past and continues into the present.

Janice <u>has lived</u> in Seattle since 1990.

(2) When something started in the past and has just been completed.

I <u>have finished</u> my class project finally.

(3) When something happened in the past and is likely to continue happening.

That customer <u>has complained</u> about our refund policy more than once.

The present perfect tense is formed by adding either *has* or *have* to the past participle of the verb.

The **past perfect tense** is used when something that took place in the past was completed before a specific time in the past.

Bill <u>had driven</u> 200 miles before he stopped for gas.

By 11 A.M. I <u>had made</u> 15 telephone calls.

The past perfect tense is formed by adding *had* to the past participle of the verb.

The **future perfect tense** is used when an action will be completed before a specific time in the future.

> Kate <u>will have finished</u> school by next summer.

> I <u>will have done</u> the work before my boss gets here.

The future perfect tense is formed by adding *will have* to the past participle of the verb.

Chart 5 summarizes the process used in forming the three perfect tenses.

Chart 5 The Perfect Tenses		
Tense	**Form**	**Examples**
Present Perfect	Add <u>has</u> to the past participle when the subject is a singular noun or <u>he</u>, <u>she</u>, or <u>it</u> Add <u>have</u> to the past participle when the subject is a plural noun or <u>I</u>, <u>you</u>, <u>we</u>, or <u>they</u>.	She <u>has worked</u> in the stockroom since May. I <u>have asked</u> this question many times.
Past Perfect	Add <u>had</u> to the past participle. For irregular verbs, see your dictionary.	She <u>had mailed</u> the letter before last Monday.
Future Perfect	Add <u>will have</u> to the past participle.	We <u>will have arrived</u> by then.

Lesson 3 Exercise

Directions: Edit the following items to correct all verb tense errors. Not all of the items have errors.

1. Cynthia works for MarketCom Inc. since 1985.
2. Mrs. Garcia will complete the project by the end of the day tomorrow.
3. Mr. Graham has attended the Dodgers' opening game every year for the past twenty years.
4. Before last Friday, Bob will have made only 8 sales.
5. By the time Ms. Anderson arrives in Nashville next week, Jim had finished the plans.

Answers are on page 327.

Lesson 4

Word Clues to Tense in Sentences

Many sentences contain words that answer the question *When?* These words tell when something is occurring, has occurred, or will occur. Here are some examples of words that indicate the time of an event.

Present	Past	Future	Perfect Tenses
currently	in the past	tomorrow	by that time
today	yesterday	later	before then
now	recently	next month	since
at the moment	last Friday		for

You can use these kinds of words as clues to help you determine if the tense of a verb is correct. For example, read the following sentence.

> Currently there were more cars in Los Angeles than people.

Currently tells you that the action is taking place now. However, *were* is in the past tense. To correctly edit the sentence, change the tense of the verb to match the clue word or words given in the sentence.

> Currently there <u>are</u> more cars in Los Angeles than people.

Also look for words that give you time references.

> The world population in the year 6000 B.C. was approximately 5 million people.

The words "in the year 6000 B.C." tell you that the action is in the past. Therefore, the past tense verb *was* is correct.

Occasionally, a word that usually indicates the present may be used in a sentence that concerns an event in the future.

> Today, he will buy his first car.

Today in this sentence means "later today." Therefore, the use of the future tense verb is correct.

Directions: Edit these sentences to correct all errors in verb tense. Not all of the sentences have errors.

1. The first depression in the United States happens at the end of the Revolutionary War.
2. Right now, we imported more goods than we exported.
3. During the next decade, new kinds of heart surgery are developed.
4. Recently historians learned that the Egyptians invented the sailboat.
5. The last survivor of the *Mayflower* is John Alden.

Answers are on page 327.

Using Tense Consistently

Some sentences have more than one verb. Read the following sentences. Which one uses verb tenses consistently?

1. Many people *are* not athletic, but they *enjoyed* watching sports events.

2. Thousands of visitors *go* to national parks each year and *will enjoy* hiking and camping.

3. People *looked* for shelter as the lightning storm *began.*

The verb in the first part of sentence 1 — *are* — is a clue that can help you determine if the verb in the second part of the sentence is in the correct tense. *Are* is a present tense verb, but the verb in the second part of the sentence — *enjoyed* —is a past tense verb. Verb tenses, therefore, have not been used consistently in sentence 1. Sentence 2 is also incorrect because the action shifts from the present (*go*) to the future (*will enjoy*). Sentence 3 describes a sequence of events that took place in the past. Both verbs — *looked* and *began* — are past tense verbs. Sentence 3, therefore, is correct.

Directions: Edit the following sentences for correct use of tenses. Underline the correct verb form from the choices in parentheses.

1. The light from a laser is very powerful and (travels, traveled) in one direction.
2. The hospital receptionist paged the doctor while the patient's father (completes, completed) the forms.
3. Mr. Gonzalez is scheduled to work 40 hours next week, whereas Ms. Morgan (is, was) scheduled to work only 30 hours.
4. The company profits were higher last January than they (are, were) in July of the previous year.
5. The person who said "If you can't stand the heat, get out of the kitchen" (is, was) Harry Truman.

Answers are on page 328.

Word Clues to Tense in Paragraphs

When you take the GED test, you will be asked to read paragraphs. In order to complete some of the questions about the paragraph, you will need to determine whether the action of the paragraph is in the present, the past, or the future. Then you will be able to figure out if a particular sentence is written in the correct tense.

Tenses should be used consistently throughout a paragraph. In other words, the tense of a paragraph should stay the same unless there is a definite reason for changing the tense. Read the paragraph below and notice the verb tenses used.

> (1) Lizards *are* reptiles that *range* in size from a few inches to ten feet long. (2) Because lizards *are* cold blooded, most of them *live* in the tropics and other areas with warm climates. (3) When the temperature *became* too warm, they *moved* to the shade or *buried* themselves under the sand. (4) Lizards *defend* themselves in a variety of interesting ways. (5) The Australian frilled lizard *frightened* its enemies by unfolding the large frill that *encircled* its head.

This paragraph provides a general description of lizards and therefore should be written in the present tense. The first two sentences are written in the present tense, but the third sentence describes the behavior or lizards in the past tense. The fifth sentence also incorrectly shifts to the past tense to describe the behavior of the Australian frilled lizard. It is difficult to follow the meaning of a paragraph when tenses are not used consistently.

Here is the correctly edited paragraph. Notice that the present tense is consistently used.

> (1) Lizards *are* reptiles that *range* in size from a few inches to ten feet long. (2) Because lizards *are* cold blooded, most of them *live* in the tropics and other areas with warm climates. (3) When the temperature *becomes* too warm, they *move* to the shade or *bury* themselves under the sand. (4) Lizards *defend* themselves in a variety of interesting ways. (5) The Australian frilled lizard *frightens* its enemies by unfolding the large frill that *encircles* its head.

Directions: The following paragraph uses verb tenses inconsistently. Rewrite the paragraph in the proper tense. Not all of the sentences will have to be changed.

> Joseph Priestley, an eighteenth-century chemist, made several discoveries through his mistakes. For example, he invents seltzer quite by accident. While he is performing an experiment, he added gas to water. Priestley was amazed at the new taste that will result from the combination. During another experiment, he studied a certain type of tree sap. Some of the substance falls onto a piece of paper. He noticed the sap makes pencil marks on the paper disappear. This leads to the development of what we now call the *eraser.*

Answers are on page 328.

CHAPTER 2 REVIEW

Directions: Edit the following sentences to correct all errors in verb usage. Not all of the sentences have errors.

1. The new version of the software was available in March of next year.
2. In 1804, Lewis and Clark begin their expedition to the Northwest.
3. Tomorrow the president discusses the new tax bill with several of his advisors.
4. The deepest lake in the world is Lake Baikal in Siberia which measured almost a mile deep in some places.
5. This month five employees have written letters complaining about the new policy.
6. Charles F. Carlson invented the photocopy machine, although he has difficulty finding financial support.
7. The words "Mankind must put an end to war or war will put an end to mankind" were spoke by John Kennedy.
8. Millions of years ago, glaciers had covered parts of North America.
9. Ms. Carter had saw the results before Mr. Langley made the announcement.
10. The Puritans think soap and water were bad for one's health.
11. <u>Lochner v. New York</u> was a Supreme Court case that gives employees and employers the right to decide hours and wages without government interference.
12. John will have visited four of our branch offices by the end of this week.
13. In 1930, Sinclair Lewis became the first American author who wins the Nobel prize for literature.
14. The Larsen project was began two years ago.
15. The first American to fly in space is Alan Shepard, and he flies for a total of 15 minutes.

Check your answers. Correct answers are on pages 328-329. If you have all 15 answers correct, go on to Chapter 3. If you have any answers incorrect, find the item number on the chart below and review that lesson before you go on.

Review...	If you missed Item Number ...
Lesson 1 & 2	1, 2, 3, 7, 9, 10, 14
Lesson 3	5, 12
Lessons 4 & 6	1, 3, 8
Lesson 5	4, 6, 11, 13, 15

GED REVIEW 2

Directions: Read the following passage. Using the rules you have learned so far, answer the items that follow. Not all of the sentences have errors.

Items 1 to 10 are based on the following passages.

(1) Brian Calton is here next Friday to teach us about the new copy machine. (2) He taught the inservice last month on the FAX machine. (3) If you has any questions about the copier, please ask him on Friday. (4) The company that sold us the equipment is offering a 10% discount to any of our employees who want to buy a home computer. (5) I had bought a computer from them last year, and I was very pleased with the quality of service they provided.

(6) On another note, we is having problems in the parking lot again. (7) Some people were not parking in their assigned places. (8) Unless the parking attendant recognizes your car, he or she cannot notify you if there are a problem. (9) Effective immediately, every car needs an identification sticker. (10) Next month, we had reviewed the situation, and we will establish further procedures at that time, if necessary.

1. Sentence 1: **Brian Calton is here next Friday to teach us about the new copy machine.**

   What correction should be made to this sentence?

   (1) change is to are
   (2) change is to was
   (3) change is to will be
   (4) change is to had been
   (5) no correction is necessary

2. Sentence 2: **He taught the inservice last month on the FAX machine.**

   Which of the following is the best way to write the underlined portion of this sentence? If you think the original is the best way, choose option (1).

   (1) He taught
   (2) He teached
   (3) He will teach
   (4) He teaches
   (5) He has taught

3. Sentence 3: **If you has any questions about the copier, please ask him on Friday.**

What correction should be made to this sentence?

   (1) change has to have
   (2) change has to will have
   (3) change has to is having
   (4) change ask to will ask
   (5) change ask to asked

4. Sentence 4: **The company that selled us the equipment is offering a 10% discount to any of our employees who want to buy a home computer.**

What correction should be made to this sentence?

   (1) change selled to will sell
   (2) change selled to sold
   (3) change is offering to are offering
   (4) change want to wants
   (5) change want to is wanting

5. Sentence 5: **I had bought a computer from them last year, and I was very pleased with the quality of service they provided.**

Which of the following is the best way to write the underlined portion of this sentence? If you think the original is the best way, choose option (1).

   (1) I had bought
   (2) I have bought
   (3) I am buying
   (4) I bought
   (5) I will buy

6. Sentence 6: **On another note, <u>we is having</u> problems in the parking lot again.**

Which if the following is the best way to write the underlined portion of this sentence? If you think the original is the best way, choose option (1).

   (1) we is having
   (2) we are having
   (3) we will have
   (4) we had been having
   (5) we was having

7. Sentence 7: **Some people were not parking in their assigned places.**

What correction should be made to this sentence?

   (1) change people to peoples
   (2) change were to is
   (3) change were to are
   (4) change were to will be
   (5) change parking to parked

8. Sentence 8: **Unless the parking attendant recognizes your car, he or she cannot notify you if there are a problem.**

What correction should be made to this sentence?

   (1) change recognizes to recognize
   (2) change recognizes to recognized
   (3) change notify to notified
   (4) change are to will be
   (5) change are to is

9. Sentence 9: **Effective immediately, every car needs an identification sticker.**

   If you rewrote sentence 9 beginning with

   <u>By the beginning of next month, every car</u>

   the next word(s) should be

   (1) need
   (2) needed
   (3) will need
   (4) had needed
   (5) was needing

10. Sentence 10: **Next month, we had reviewed the situation, and we will establish further procedures at that time, if necessary.**

    What correction should be made to this sentence?

    (1) change <u>had</u> to <u>have</u>
    (2) change <u>had reviewed</u> to <u>will review</u>
    (3) change <u>had reviewed</u> to <u>reviews</u>
    (4) change <u>will establish</u> to <u>establishes</u>
    (5) change <u>will establish</u> to <u>established</u>

    Answers are on page 329.

CHAPTER 3
PRONOUN REFERENCE

Preview

Directions: Edit the following sentences to correct all errors in pronoun reference. Not all of the sentences have errors. There may be more than one way to correct a sentence.

1. Either salt or pepper can improve the taste of food when it is used in moderation.
2. Joseph will ride home with Samantha and I after the game.
3. We benefit from studying history because it helps you learn from past mistakes.
4. Plants and flowers, who are often given to people in the hospital, may have a healing effect on chronically ill patients.
5. Michelle did not see Diane again after she changed jobs.

Check your answers. Correct answers are on page 329. If you have all five answers correct, do the Chapter 3 Review on page 82. If you have fewer than five answers correct, study Chapter 3 beginning with Lesson 1.

Lesson 1

Personal Pronouns

Nouns name people, places, or things. Pronouns are words that take the place of nouns. Read the following two sentences. Which one sounds better?

> When Jeff parked in the garage this morning, Jeff accidentally locked Jeff's keys in the car.

> When Jeff parked in the garage this morning, **he** accidentally locked **his** keys in the car.

The first sentence sounds awkward because the noun *Jeff* is repeated so often. The second sentence has exactly the same meaning as the first, but its uses pronouns to eliminate repetition of the noun. In other words, the pronouns substitute for the nouns.

Personal pronouns change form depending on their use in a sentence. Notice how the pronouns change in this paragraph.

> Jane and Luis Rodriguez bought **their** home computer from Computer Club Warehouse. **They** wanted a color monitor and an enhanced keyboard. The salesperson sold **them** the right computer for a good price.

The pronouns *their*, *they*, and *them* all refer to Jane and Luis Rodriguez.

Chart 1 shoes how the personal pronouns are organized by form.

Chart 1 The Forms of Personal Pronouns			
Subject Pronouns	Object Pronouns	Possessive Pronouns	
		before a noun	after a verb
I	me	my	mine
you	you	your	yours
he	him	his	his
she	her	her	hers
it	it	its	its
we	us	our	ours
you	you	your	yours
they	them	their	theirs

It is fairly easy to know when you need a possessive pronoun. Possessive words show ownership or belonging. Use the first set of possessive pronouns when the possessive word comes before the noun that is owned.

Monica loves <u>her</u> job.

Leslie and Bob signed <u>their</u> lease on May 1.

Use the second set of possessive pronouns when the possessive word comes after the verb.

The red convertible is <u>mine.</u>

The office by the water fountain is <u>his.</u>

You have already learned to find the subject of a sentence. Subject pronouns are used as the subject of a sentence.

<u>I</u> listened to the debate intently.

<u>She</u> expressed her point of view eloquently.

Object pronouns usually come after the verb. They are never used as subjects.

Rosa gave <u>us</u> tickets to the Dodgers game.

She left <u>them</u> on my desk at noon.

Compound subjects and objects may make pronoun choices seem difficult. Which of these sentences is correct?

Linda invited Sam and <u>I</u> to the barbeque.

Linda invited Sam and <u>me</u> to the barbeque.

Although the first sentence may sound okay, you know that Linda is the subject of the sentence, so an object pronoun is needed. The second sentence is correct. To test your answer, cross out the words <u>Sam and.</u>

Linda invited ~~Sam and~~ <u>I</u> to the barbeque.

Linda invited ~~Sam and~~ <u>me</u> to the barbeque.

Now the second sentence definitely "sounds correct."

To avoid confusion when working with any sentence, always find all the subjects and verbs in the sentence before you edit the pronoun usage.

Directions: Edit the following sentences to correct all errors in personal pronoun usage. Not all of the sentences have errors.

1. Ms. Warnick ordered four tickets for they.
2. We gave Mr. Franco and she the opportunity to express their opinions.
3. Bill and her will be going to the job fair in Sacramento.
4. Julie recommended hers friend for the job.
5. Dennis and I plan to visit his cousin on our trip through Arkansas.

Answers are on pages 329-330.

Pronoun-Antecedent Agreement

In a sentence, the word that a pronoun replaces or refers to is called its **antecedent.** Read the sentence below. To what does the word *their* refer?

> The Stamp Act was repealed after nine colonies expressed their opposition to taxation without representation.

The antecedent of the pronoun *their* is the word *colonies.* A pronoun must agree with its antecedent in number (singular or plural) and gender (masculine or feminine). Follow these rules for correct pronoun-antecedent agreement. The rules for pronoun-antecedent agreement are similar to the rules for subject-verb agreement.

Rule 1: A singular antecedent requires a singular pronoun.

> Eleanor Roosevelt wrote a newspaper column during <u>her</u> husband's presidency.

Note: When a singular antecedent does not specify a certain gender (or sex), use <u>his or her</u> to agree with the antecedent or rewrite the sentence so that the antecedent is plural.

> INCORRECT: Everyone should bring <u>their</u> resume to the interview.

> CORRECT: Everyone should bring <u>his or her</u> resume to the interview.

> CORRECT: The <u>applicants</u> should bring their resumes to the interview.

Rule 2: A plural antecedent requires a plural pronoun.

The people gave up some of <u>their</u> land to build a recreation center and library.

Rule 3: When two antecedents are joined by *or* or *nor*, the pronoun should agree with the closer antecedent.

Neither Greg nor the office clerks agreed to work on <u>their</u> day off.

Neither the office clerks nor Greg agreed to work on <u>his</u> day off.

Rule 4: When two antecedents are joined by *and*, the result is plural and a plural pronoun is needed.

Frank and Marjorie saved most of <u>their</u> money to buy a new car.

Lesson 2 Exercise

Directions: Edit the following sentence to correct all errors in pronoun-antecedent agreement. Not all of the sentences have errors.

1. Each person has to learn their lessons the hard way.
2. A new cosmetic or drug must be tested before they can be sold to the public.
3. Neither the manager nor the salespeople picked up their time cards on Monday.
4. Both Mr. Gordon and Mr. Sjue park his cars in the lot on the corner.
5. Harry Truman became President of the United States, but they did not attend college.

Answers are on page 330.

Avoiding Pronoun Shifts

Pronouns must agree in number with their antecedents. They also must agree in person. **Person** refers to the difference between the *person speaking* (first person), the *person spoken to* (second person), and the *person or thing spoken about* (third person).

First Person: <u>I</u> am giving a party for Karen and Ricco on Tuesday.
Second Person: Will <u>you</u> be able to come?
Third Person: <u>It</u> will start at 7 P.M.

Chart 2 shows how the personal pronouns are organized by person.

Chart 2 Personal Pronouns	
First-person pronouns	I, me, my, mine, we, us, our, ours
Second-person pronouns	you, your, yours
Third-person pronouns	he, him, his, she, her, hers, it, its, they, them, theirs

The following example contains a shift in person.

> If <u>we</u> do not limit salt intake in the diet, <u>your</u> chance of getting heart disease increases.

This sentence is confusing because it shifts from the first person (*we*) to the second person (*your*). There are two ways this sentence could be correctly edited.

> If <u>we</u> do not limit salt intake in the diet, <u>our</u> chance of getting heart disease increases.

OR

> If <u>you</u> do not limit salt intake in the diet, <u>your</u> chance of getting heart disease increases.

Singular and plural nouns and other kinds of pronouns can also be antecedents. Except for the first- and second-person personal pronouns, all other antecedents are third person.

Avoid confusing shifts in person by deciding which person is appropriate to the meaning of the sentence and then using that person consistently throughout the sentence.

Lesson 3 Exercise

Directions: Edit the following sentences to correct all errors in pronoun shift. Not all of the sentences have errors.

1. I exercise daily because physical exercise helps you maintain good health.
2. Whenever you buy merchandise, you should find out the return policy of the store.
3. When we are nervous, your pulse may quicken.
4. It is important for one to understand the new tax law before filing your tax returns.
5. People are more likely to be injured while they are at home than while we are riding in a car.

Answers on page 330.

Relative Pronouns

Find the pronoun in the following sentence.

> The Leaning Tower of Pisa, which leans 17 feet to the right,
> has a foundation only 10 feet deep.

If you chose *which,* you were correct. The word *which* is used as a relative pronoun. A *relative pronoun* introduces a group of words that describe a noun or a pronoun. In the example above, *which leans 17 feet to the right* describes or refers to *Leaning Tower of Pisa. Leaning Tower of Pisa* is the antecedent of the relative pronoun *which.*

The following words are used as relative pronouns.

which   that   who   whom

A common error in the use of pronouns is choosing an incorrect relative pronoun. The choose the correct relative pronoun, remember the following.

Who and whom refer to people or animals.

Which refers to animals, places, or things.

That refers to people, animals, places, or things.

> Blackbird, <u>who</u> was a chief of the Omaha Indian tribe, was buried sitting on his horse.

> A dog <u>that</u> is trained to guide the blind cannot tell the difference between a red and a green light.

> Himalayan cats, <u>which</u> are a cross between Siamese and Persian cats, are a rare breed.

The word *what* is sometimes used incorrectly as a relative pronoun. The pronoun *what* should never be used in this way.

> INCORRECT: The books what I enjoy most are science fiction.

> CORRECT: The books that I enjoy most are science fiction.

To choose correctly between *who* and *whom,* use your knowledge of subject and object pronouns. The pronoun *who* is a subject pronoun. To see if *who* is the correct choice in a sentence, try another subject pronoun (*I, we, he, she,* or *they*) in its place.

> Benjamin Franklin, (**who, whom**) was one of the signers of the Declaration of Independence, was also a talented inventor.

Think: *He was one of the signers of the Declaration of Independence.* Since the subject pronoun *he* is correct in this situation, you know that the correct relative pronoun is *who.*

To see if *whom* is the correct choice, try another object pronoun (*us, me, him,* or *her*) in its place. You may have to rearrange the words slightly.

> The only president (**who, whom**) Congress impeached was Andrew Johnson.

Think: Congress impeached *him.* Since the object pronoun *him* is correct in this situation, you know that the correct relative pronoun is *whom.*

Lesson 4 Exercise

Directions: Edit the following sentences to correct all errors in relative pronoun usage. Not all of the sentences have errors.

1. Only drivers which are licensed may drive in the United States.
2. The elephant is the only animal that has four knees.
3. Ants and humans are the only two animal species what wage war on their own kind.
4. The state who uses the phrase "Land of Lincoln" on its license plates is Illinois.
5. The first American astronaut whom orbited Earth was John Glenn.

Answers are on page 330.

Avoiding Vague Pronoun References

In order for the meaning of a sentence to be clear, a pronoun must have a clear antecedent. Read the following sentences.

> UNCLEAR: The workers walked off the job, which is why there is a backlog of orders.

> CLEAR: There is a backlog of orders because the workers walked off the job.

In the first sentence above, the relative pronoun *which* is used. There is no clear antecedent for *which* in the sentence, however. The clearly written version of the sentence eliminates the vague or unclear pronoun reference by eliminating the pronoun *which*.

The example below shows you how vague pronoun references can be eliminated by replacing a pronoun with a noun.

> UNCLEAR: You should buy your ticket early because they are always crowded during holidays.

> CLEAR: You should buy your ticket early because the air lines are always crowded during holidays.

In the first version of the sentence, the pronoun *they* does not have a clear antecedent. If the writer's subject is airline tickets, then the meaning of the sentence can be clarified by using a noun — *airlines* — instead of the pronoun *they*.

Directions: Edit the following sentences to correct all errors in vague pronoun references. You may need to rewrite the sentence to make it clearer. There may be more than one way to correct a sentence.

1. The machinist did not wear safety goggles, which was against the company's policy.
2. On last night's weather forecast, they said there was an 80 percent chance of rain.
3. Helium contracts the vocal chords, which causes the pitch of the voice to rise.
4. It says that ten inches of snow equals one inch of rain.
5. They predict that during the next decade the price of housing will triple.

Answers are on page 330.

Avoiding Ambiguous Pronoun References

You have seen that a pronoun depends on other words for its meaning. In the last lesson, you studied examples of sentences that were unclear because they included pronouns that did not have specific antecedents. Sometimes a writer uses a pronoun that may refer to more than one word in the sentence, which makes the pronoun reference ambiguous. Read the following sentence.

> UNCLEAR: The New York Mets and the Boston Red Sox were tied after the sixth game, but they finally won the last game.

Did you understand this sentence? Who won the game—the Mets or the Red Sox? Because the pronoun, *they,* might refer to either team, the meaning of the sentence is not clear. Read the edited version below.

> CLEAR: The New York Mets and the Boston Red Sox were tied after the sixth game, but the Mets finally won the last game.

On the GED Test, you will need to look for ambiguous pronoun references. If a sentence is unclear because a pronoun may refer to more than one noun, reword the sentence to eliminate the ambiguous pronoun.

> UNCLEAR: The staff members told the directors that they could not attend today's meeting.

> CLEAR: The staff members told the directors, "We cannot attend today's meeting."

OR

The directors were told that the staff members could not attend today's meeting.

Directions: Edit the following sentences to correct all errors in ambiguous pronoun reference. There may be more than one way to correct a sentence.

1. Because the discussion leader and the secretary were responsible for the minutes of the meeting, he was told to make accurate notes.
2. When she returned from vacation, the supervisor gave the employee additional responsibilities.
3. The student asked the teacher if she could change the assignment.
4. If a child has an allergic reaction to a certain food, throw it away.
5. Mike told Randy that he was the starting pitcher for tomorrow's game.

Answers are on pages 330-331.

CHAPTER 3 REVIEW

Directions: Edit the following sentences to correct all errors in pronoun usage. Not all of the sentences have errors. There may be more than one way to correct a sentence.

1. A mosquito cannot beat their wings in temperatures below 60 degrees.
2. Vince and me are looking for someone to join our carpool group.
3. A man which is at rest breathes about 16 times per minute.
4. Neither potato chips nor candy bars give us the nutrition you need to stay healthy.
5. The president told the adviser that she should cancel the press conference.
6. Nancy gave Ms. Prow and he two copies of her résumé.
7. Anyone that uses the metric system is using a mathematical system developed by the French.
8. Mr. Garrett told Phil that he would be getting a promotion.
9. Whales use its tails to make slapping sounds on the surface of the ocean.
10. Frank Lloyd Wright was an architect whom designed houses with low, horizontal shapes.
11. Animals living in cold climates have smaller ears than its cousins in warmer climates.
12. Rick, who he wanted for the job, is not longer available.
13. The legends what are told about King Arthur may be based on historical facts.
14. The letter was addressed to they.
15. After World War II, the housing supply could not keep up with the demand because it grew so rapidly.

Check your answers. Correct answers are on page 331. If you have all 15 answers correct, go on to Test-Taking Strategies 1. If you have any answers incorrect, find the item number on the chart below and review that lesson before you go on.

Review...	If you missed Item Number ...
Lesson 1	2, 6, 14
Lesson 2	1, 9, 11, 15
Lesson 3	4
Lesson 4	3, 7, 10, 12, 13
Lessons 5 & 6	5, 8

GED REVIEW 3

Directions: Read the following passages. Using the rules you have learned so far, answer the items that follow. Not all of the sentences have errors.

Items 1 to 5 are based on the following passage.

(1) In a recent election, voters showed strong support for several women candidates and her policies. (2) Linda K. Nelson, whom ran for the only vacant seat on the city council, was encouraged by the results. (3) Ms. Nelson said, "The people of our city have expressed a desire for change, and my staff and I plan to give it to them." (4) If anyone has a problem or suggestion for Ms. Nelson, you should call her office directly. (5) Ms. Nelson and her assistants told reporters that they care deeply about the voters' needs.

1. Sentence 1: **In a recent election, voters showed strong support for several women candidates and her policies.**

   What correction should be made to this sentence?

   (1) change <u>showed</u> to <u>show</u>
   (2) change <u>her</u> to <u>hers</u>
   (3) change <u>her</u> to <u>their</u>
   (4) change <u>policies</u> to <u>policys</u>
   (5) no correction is necessary

2. Sentence 2: **Linda K. Nelson, whom ran for the only vacant seat on the city council, was encouraged by the results.**

   What correct should be made to this sentence?

   (1) change <u>whom</u> to <u>which</u>
   (2) change <u>whom</u> to <u>who</u>
   (3) change <u>was</u> to <u>were</u>
   (4) change <u>was</u> to <u>are</u>
   (5) no correction is necessary

3. Sentence 3: **Ms. Nelson said, "The people of our city have expressed a desire for change, and my staff and I plan to give it to them."**

   What correction should be made to this sentence?

   (1) change <u>my</u> to <u>mine</u>
   (2) change <u>I</u> to <u>me</u>
   (3) change <u>I</u> to <u>us</u>
   (4) change <u>them</u> to <u>they</u>
   (5) no correction is necessary

4. Sentence 4: **If anyone has a problem or suggestion for Ms. Nelson, you should call her office directly.**

What correction should be made to this sentence?

(1) replace <u>you</u> with <u>they</u>
(2) replace <u>you</u> with <u>he or she</u>
(3) change <u>has</u> to <u>have</u>
(4) replace <u>her</u> with <u>their</u>
(5) no correction is necessary

5. Sentence 5: **Ms. Nelson and her assistants told reporters that they care deeply about the voters' needs.**

What correction should be made to this sentence?

(1) change <u>they</u> to <u>them</u>
(2) replace <u>they</u> with <u>we</u>
(3) replace <u>they</u> with <u>she and her staff</u>
(4) change <u>care</u> to <u>cares</u>
(5) no correction is necessary

<u>Items 6 through 10</u> refer to the following passage.

(1) The computer literacy class, who was originally scheduled to be held in Room 114, has been moved to Room 118. (2) Each employee interested in taking the class needs to sign their name on the class list on the bulletin board in the staff lounge. (3) If anyone needs a textbook, we can buy our books from one of the teachers, either Mike Goldhamer or Stephanie Utley. (4) Mike and her will give us any other materials we need during the first class. (5) Mike said, "The employees who finish the class will get a certificate signed by Stephanie and I."

6. Sentence 1: **The computer literacy class, <u>who was</u> originally scheduled to be held in Room 114, has been moved to Room 118.**

Which if the following is the best way to write the underlined portion of this sentence? If you think the original is the best way, choose option (1).

(1) who was
(2) who were
(3) which was
(4) that were
(5) which are

7. Sentence 2: **Each employee interested in taking the class needs to sign their name on the class list on the bulletin board in the staff lounge.**

What correction should be made to this sentence?

(1) change <u>needs</u> to <u>need</u>
(2) change <u>needs</u> to <u>has needed</u>
(3) replace <u>their</u> with <u>his or her</u>
(4) replace <u>their name</u> with <u>our names</u>
(5) replace <u>their</u> with <u>your</u>

8. Sentence 3: **If anyone needs a textbook, we can buy our books from one of the teachers, either Mike Goldhamer or Stephanie Utley.**

If you rewrote Sentence 3 beginning with

<u>If you need a textbook,</u>

the next word should be

(1) we
(2) anyone
(3) they
(4) you
(5) us

9. Sentence 4: **Mike and her will give us any other materials we need during the first class.**

What correction should be made to this sentence?

(1) change <u>her</u> to <u>she</u>
(2) change <u>her</u> to <u>hers</u>
(3) change <u>us</u> to <u>we</u>
(4) replace <u>we</u> with <u>they</u>
(5) change <u>need</u> to <u>needed</u>

10. Sentence 10: **Mike said, "The employees who finish the class will get a certificate signed by Stephanie and I."**

What correction should be made to this sentence?

(1) change <u>who</u> to <u>whom</u>
(2) replace <u>who</u> with <u>which</u>
(3) change <u>finish</u> to <u>finishes</u>
(4) change <u>will get</u> to <u>got</u>
(5) change <u>I</u> to <u>me</u>

Answers are on pages 331-332.

TEST-TAKING STRATEGIES 1

In Unit 1 you have been dealing with errors in usage. On the GED Test, your understanding of usage will be tested using three types of multiple-choice test items. These items show how well you can proofread sentences.

Proofreading is the skill of recognizing and correcting errors within sentences. The GED Test will require that you do four basic tasks:

1. Read paragraphs.
2. Proofread sentences.
3. Evaluate suggested answers.
4. Select answers that illustrate effective writing.

As you read a paragraph, you will see that each sentence is numbered. These numbers correspond to multiple-choice test items that follow each paragraph. For example, a test item might look like this:

> (1) Have you ever wondered how a magician succeeds at the trick of sawing a woman in half? (2) The illusion really involves two women. (3) One is already hidden in the table. (4) She climbs into the box through a trap-door in the table and sticks her feet out of the end of the box. (5) The other woman draw her knees up to her chin. (6) An empty space results, and it is here that the magician begins to saw the box in half.

Sentence 5: **The other woman draw her knees up to her chin.**

What correction should be made to this sentence?

(1) change woman to women
(2) change draw to draws
(3) change draw to drew
(4) change her knees to hers knees
(5) no correction is necessary

The sentence to be corrected is repeated in the multiple-choice test item. The five suggested alternatives (or answers) follow. They are presented in the order in which they occur in the sentence. The alternatives may suggest different kinds of changes: spelling, verb tense, pronoun reference, subject-verb agreement, and so on.

Remember, however, that there is a maximum of one error per sentence. This means that only one of the choices can be correct. Sometimes there is no error in the sentence. In this case, the correct choice reads *(5) no correction is necessary.*

Look at the sample paragraph and test item again. Which answer would you choose to correct sentence 5? If you chose alternative 2, you were correct. This sentence has an error in subject-verb agreement.

The Three Types of Test Items

There are three types of multiple-choice items on the Writing Skills Test. All test your knowledge of sentence structure, usage, spelling, punctuation, and capitalization. Approximately 50 percent of the questions will be **sentence-correction items**. This type of test item repeats a sentence from the paragraph and asks what correction is needed.

Sentence 3: **The people which live in Hawaii tend to live about four years longer than Americans who live in other states.**

What correction should be made to this sentence?

(1) change <u>people</u> to <u>peoples</u>
(2) change <u>which</u> to <u>who</u>
(3) change <u>which live</u> to <u>which lives</u>
(4) change <u>who</u> to <u>which</u>
(5) no correction is necessary

After you read the sentence, review each alternative carefully. In this example, alternative (2) is the correct choice because the relative pronoun *which* should not be used to refer to people.

The second type of question will be **sentence-revision items.** In these items, part of the sentence will be underlined. This underlined portion may or may not contain an error. These items also have five alternatives. The first alternative will be the same as the original sentence. The other alternatives suggest possible changes.

Sentence 2: **In ancient Greece, a woman counted her age from the date <u>on which she were married.</u>**

Which of the following is the best way to write the underlined portion of this sentence? If you think the original is the best way, choose option (1).

(1) on which she were married.
(2) on who she were married.
(3) on which she are married.
(4) on which she was married.
(5) on which they were married.

Which answer would you choose? This sentence contains a problem with subject-verb agreement. The subject of the underlined portion *she* is singular. The singular verb *was* is needed to agree with the singular subject. Alternative (4) is the correct choice.

Construction-shift items are the third type of test item. In these items, you will be given a sentence that is awkward or unclear. The item will then show how the sentence might be changed. You will be given a portion of the rewritten sentence and be asked to choose which word should come next from the five alternatives.

Sentence 7: **Everyone must realize that they cannot walk alone at night in any large city without taking a great risk.**

If you rewrote sentence 7 beginning with

People must realize that,

the next word would be

(1) you
(2) everyone
(3) they
(4) anyone
(5) we

In this type of item, you will need to decide which alternative suggests the best way to write the sentence without changing its meaning. In this example, the sentence contains an awkward person shift. In the new sentence, the subject *People* is third person and plural; as a result, the correct pronoun choice is the third person, plural pronoun *they*. Choice (3) is correct.

The 5-R Method of Editing

Proofreading for errors in written material can help produce more effective writing. In addition to checking for errors, it is important to check for correct meaning and word choice. This combination of skills is called **editing.** When you edit, you

- **evaluate written material**

- **correct errors**

- **increase understanding**

- **transmit effectively written material**

Following a process will help you work through each multiple-choice item on the GED Test and concentrate on the content of each question.

The 5-R method of editing is an effective process for answering items on the GED Test. In this method you will

Read   Reflect   Revise   Reread   Record

To use this method, complete each step in this order.

Step 1 Read   Read the paragraph quickly for its meaning and writing style.

Step 2 Reflect   Reflect by looking for any errors within the paragraph.

Step 3 Revise   Read the first test item and its alternatives. Decide which alternative identifies and corrects the error.

Step 4 Reread   Read the revised sentence with the selected correction. If you are satisfied with the answer, go on to the next step. If you are not satisfied, go back to Step 3.

Step 5 Record   Mark the number of the alternative that you have chosen. Then, move on to the next item. Continue using Steps 3 through 5 until you complete the items for that paragraph.

In Unit 1 you have been learning about usage rules. Your knowledge of usage will be tested in about 35 percent of the questions on Part I of the GED Writing Skills Test.

To answer usage questions effectively, use the 5-R method of editing. As you *reflect* in Step 2, ask yourself these questions.

1. **Do the subjects agree with the verbs?**

   INCORRECT: One of the letters have been received.

   CORRECT: One of the letters has been received.

2. **Are the verbs in the correct tense?**

   INCORRECT: I had wrote to him two weeks ago.

   CORRECT: I had written to him two weeks ago.

3. **Are the pronouns used correctly and clearly?**

   INCORRECT: One of the letters had too little postage on them.

   CORRECT: One of the letters had too little postage on it.

As you practice the 5-R method, you will gain confidence in using it. Eventually, you will not need to write anything down as you do a step. You will be able to answer an item by just thinking about it.

Directions: Read the following paragraph. It contains errors in usage. No sentence contains more than one error. Use the 5-R method of editing to find the correct response to each item. Put a check by each step after you have completed it.

Items 1 to 5 are based on the following passage.

(1) The first microwave oven produced for home use was introduced in 1945. (2) Since then, the use of these ovens is increased because of the speed with which they cook food. (3) Food in these ovens is cooked by friction. (4) Short radio waves, called microwaves, travel through a metal tube who scatters them throughout the oven. (5) They bounce off the oven's walls and enter the food. (6) They cause the food's molecules to vibrate. (7) The resulting motion produce heat, which cooks the food. (8) These waves can pass through glass, cardboard, or china. (9) Therefore, containers made of these materials will be safe to use in this type of oven.

1. Sentence 2: **Since then, the use of these ovens is increased because of the speed with which they cook food.**

   What correction should be made to this sentence?

(1) change <u>is</u> to <u>are</u>	**Step 1.** Read: _____
(2) change <u>is</u> to <u>have</u>	**Step 2.** Reflect: _____
(3) change <u>is</u> to <u>has</u>	**Step 3.** Revise: _____
(4) change <u>they</u> to <u>it</u>	**Step 4.** Reread: _____
(5) change <u>cook</u> to <u>cooks</u>	**Step 5.** Record: _____

2. Sentence 4: **Short radio waves, called microwaves, travel through a metal tube who scatters them throughout the oven.**

   What correction should be made to this sentence?

(1) change <u>travel</u> to <u>travels</u>	**Step 1.** Read: _____
(2) change <u>who</u> to <u>that</u>	**Step 2.** Reflect: _____
(3) change <u>scatters</u> to <u>scatter</u>	**Step 3.** Revise: _____
(4) change <u>them</u> to <u>it</u>	**Step 4.** Reread: _____
(5) no correction is necessary	**Step 5.** Record: _____

3. Sentence 5 & 6: **They bounce off the oven's walls and enter the food. They cause the food's molecules to vibrate.**

The most effective combination of sentences 5 and 6 would include which of the following groups of words?

(1) enter the food, which causes their molecules   **Step 1.** Read: _____

(2) enter the food, which causes its molecules   **Step 2.** Reflect: _____

(3) enter the food, which causes they molecules   **Step 3.** Revise: _____

(4) enter the food, which causes your molecules   **Step 4.** Reread: _____

(5) enter the food, which causes our molecules   **Step 5.** Record: _____

4. Sentence 7: **The resulting motion produce heat, which cooks the food.**

What correction should be made to this sentence?

(1) change <u>produce</u> to <u>produces</u>   **Step 1.** Read: _____

(2) change <u>which</u> to <u>who</u>   **Step 2.** Reflect: _____

(3) change <u>cooks</u> to <u>cook</u>   **Step 3.** Revise: _____

(4) change <u>cooks</u> to <u>cooked</u>   **Step 4.** Reread: _____

(5) no correction is necessary   **Step 5.** Record: _____

5. Sentence 9: **Therefore, containers made of these <u>materials will be safe to use in this type of oven.</u>**

Which of the following is the best way to write the underlined portion of this sentence? If you think the original is the best way, choose option (1).

(1) materials will be safe   **Step 1.** Read: _____

(2) materials were safe   **Step 2.** Reflect: _____

(3) materials is safe   **Step 3.** Revise: _____

(4) materials are safe   **Step 4.** Reread: _____

(5) materials had been safe   **Step 5.** Record: _____

Answers are on page 332.

UNIT 1 REVIEW

Directions: The items in this review are based on paragraphs that contain numbered sentences. Some of the sentences contain errors in usage. A few sentences, however, may be correct as written. Read each paragraph and then answer the items that follow it.

Items 1 to 4 are based on the following passage.

(1) Married women is entering the labor force because of economic need. (2) Nearly three million working women have husbands which are not working. (3) Inflation has caused families to rely on a second income to maintain its standard of living. (4) If this situation continues, voters must insist that government leaders have given more attention to the availability of high-quality day care.

1. Sentence 1: **Married women is entering the labor force because of economic need.**

   Which of the following is the best way to write the underlined portion of this sentence? If you think the original is the best way, choose option (1).

   (1) is entering
   (2) was entering
   (3) are entering
   (4) were entering
   (5) had been entering

2. Sentence 2: **Nearly three million working women have husbands which are not working.**

   What correction should be made to this sentence?

   (1) change <u>have</u> to <u>has</u>
   (2) change <u>have</u> to <u>had</u>
   (3) change <u>which</u> to <u>who</u>
   (4) change <u>is</u> to <u>are</u>
   (5) no correction is necessary

3. Sentence 3: **Inflation has caused families to rely on a second income to maintain its standard of living.**

   What correction should be made to this sentence?

   (1) change <u>has</u> to <u>was</u>
   (2) change <u>has</u> to <u>have</u>
   (3) change <u>its</u> to <u>our</u>
   (4) change <u>its</u> to <u>your</u>
   (5) change <u>its</u> to <u>their</u>

4. Sentence 4: **If this situation continues, voters must insist that government <u>leaders have given</u> more attention to the availability of high-quality day care.**

   Which of the following is the best way to write the underlined portion of this sentence? If you think the original is the best way, choose option (1).

   (1) leaders have given
   (2) leaders give
   (3) leaders are giving
   (4) leaders will give
   (5) leaders had given

Items 5 to 8 are based on the following paragraph.

(1) Rick Barry was always a top scorer during his basketball career. (2) His ability is apparent even in high school, when more than 30 colleges offered him basketball scholarships. (3) After he became a leading scorer for the University of Miami, he was chose to play for the San Francisco Warriors. (4) In 1965, he averaged more than 25 points a game and was named Rookie of the Year by the nation's sportswriters. (5) The next year he will score 40 points in the All-Star game. (6) He was named the game's Most Valuable Player.

5. Sentence 2: **His ability is apparent even in high school, when more than 30 colleges offered him basketball scholarships.**

What correction should be made to this sentence?

(1) change <u>is</u> to <u>were</u>
(2) change <u>is</u> to <u>are</u>
(3) change <u>is</u> to <u>was</u>
(4) change <u>offered</u> to <u>offers</u>
(5) change <u>him</u> to <u>he</u>

6. Sentence 3: **After he became a leading scorer for the University of Miami, <u>he was chose</u> to play for the San Francisco Warriors.**

Which of the following is the best way to write the underlined portion of this sentence? If you think the original is the best way, choose option (1).

(1) he was chose
(2) he was chosen
(3) he is chose
(4) he is chosen
(5) he were chosen

7. Sentence 4: **In 1965, he averaged more than 25 points a game and was named Rookie of the Year by the nation's sportswriters.**

If you rewrote sentence 4 beginning with

<u>After Rick averaged more than 25 points a game in 1965, the nation's sportswriters named</u>

the next word should be

(1) he
(2) his
(3) him
(4) they
(5) them

8. Sentence 5: **The next year he will score 40 points in the All-Star game.**

What correction should be made to this sentence?

(1) change <u>he</u> to <u>him</u>
(2) change <u>will score</u> to <u>scores</u>
(3) change <u>will score</u> to <u>scored</u>
(4) change <u>will score</u> to <u>had scored</u>
(5) no correction is necessary

Items 9 to 12 are based on the following paragraph.

(1) Did you know that salt is added to canned vegetables, soups, ice cream, cheese, frozen dinners, pizza, crackers, and cereals? (2) In fact, salt is in almost every prepared food on grocery store shelves. (3) Eating too many of these foods is dangerous for us, and your health may suffer. (4) Excessive salt intake can lead to high blood pressure. (5) In fact, one in every five Americans have high blood pressure. (6) Patients which have hypertension can be treated successfully. (7) They can control the amount of salt they eat.

9. Sentence 2: **In fact, salt is in almost every prepared food on grocery store shelves.**

   If you rewrote Sentence 2 beginning with

   Almost every prepared food on grocery store shelves

   the next words would be

   (1) contain salt.
   (2) contains salt.
   (3) containing salt.
   (4) was containing salt.
   (5) is salt.

10. Sentence 3: **Eating too many of these foods is dangerous for us, and your health may suffer.**

    What correction should be made to this sentence?

    (1) change is to are
    (2) change is to has been
    (3) change us to we
    (4) change us to you
    (5) change us to them

11. Sentence 5: **In fact, one in every five Americans have high blood pressure.**

    What correction should be made to this sentence?

    (1) change have to has
    (2) change have to had
    (3) change have to was having
    (4) change have to are having
    (5) no correction is necessary

12. Sentence 6: **Patients which have hypertension can be treated successfully.**

    Which of the following is the best way to write the underlined portion of this sentence? If you think the original is the best way, choose option (1).

    (1) which have
    (2) which has
    (3) which had
    (4) who have
    (5) who has

Answers are on pages 332-333.

UNIT 2 – SENTENCE STRUCTURE

Credit: © Eugene Gordon

Objective

In this unit, you will learn to

- write complete sentences

- correct faulty sentence structure

- combine sentences

- express ideas clearly

Unit II Progress Chart

Sentence Structure

Use the following chart to keep track of your work. When you complete a lesson, circle the number of questions you anwered correctly in the Lesson Exercise. The numbers in color represent scores at a level of 80% or better.

Lesson	Page	
		CHAPTER 1: Complete Sentences
1	98	Eliminating Sentence Fragments 1 2 3 4 5
2	100	Eliminating Run-on Sentences 1 2 3 4 5
3	102	Compound Sentences 1 2 3 4 5 6 7 8 9 10 11 12 13 14 15
4	107	Complex Sentences 1 2 3 4 5
5	111	Combining Sentences 1 2 3 4 5
	114	**Chapter 1 Review** 1 2 3 4 5 6 7 8 9 10 11 12 13 14 15
		CHAPTER 2: Clear Sentences
1	121	Clarity of Thought 1 2 3 4 5
2	123	Proper Placement of Modifiers 1 2 3 4 5
3	125	Parallel Structure 1 2 3 4 5
	127	**Chapter 2 Review** 1 2 3 4 5 6 7 8 9 10

CHAPTER 1
COMPLETE SENTENCES

Preview

Directions: Edit the following items to correct all errors in sentence structure. There may be more than one correct way to edit some sentences. Not all of the items have errors.

1. There are 206 bones in the human body the thigh bone is the longest.

2. The movie was not successful, the book on which it was based was a bestseller for six months.

3. The total shown on the receipt.

4. Although their first flight took place in 1903, the Wright brothers did not receive public recognition for their "flying machine" until 1908.

5. William Henry Harrison was president of the United States for only 31 days; as a result, he died of pneumonia in 1841.

Check your answers. Correct answers are on page 334. If you have all five answers correct, do the Chapter 1 Review on page 114. If you have fewer than five answers correct, study Chapter 1 beginning with Lesson 1.

Eliminating Sentence Fragments

People write because they want to communicate an idea, a fact, or a feeling. To communicate clearly, a sentence must have a subject and a verb, and it must express a complete thought.

Each of the following items is missing some necessary piece of information.

1. All of the boxes on this shelf. (*What is being said about all of the boxes?*)

2. Traded in his camera for a better one. (*Who traded in his camera?*)

3. When the president signed the bill into law. (*What happened when the president signed the bill?*)

Items 1 to 3 are called **sentence fragments**. Item 1 is missing a verb. To correct the error in item 1, add a verb and any other words that are needed to complete the thought.

All of the boxes <u>belong</u> on this shelf.

OR

All of the boxes on this shelf <u>are dusty</u>.

Item 2 needs a subject in order to express a complete thought.

<u>Stan Mulroy</u> traded in his camera for a better one.

Item 3 has both a subject (*president*) and a verb (*signed*), but it does not express a complete thought. To correct this type of sentence-fragment error, add words to make the meaning clear.

> When the president signed the bill into law, he thanked Congress for passing the bill.

OR

> Reporters were present when the president signed the bill into law.

Notice that there may be many ways of correcting a sentence-fragment error.

Lesson 1 Exercise

Directions: Edit the following items to correct all sentence-fragment errors. Not all of the sentences have errors. There may be more than one way to correct a sentence.

1. Some cash registers are actually computers.
2. Even though I missed my usual train.
3. Stood and cheered the home team's victory.
4. The treasurer of the Hikers' Club.
5. Tomatoes that are grown in hothouses.

Answers are on page 334.

Eliminating Run-on Sentences

Sometimes two complete ideas are incorrectly combined as if they were one sentence. Read the following example:

The sun was very hot we decided to sit in the shade.

These are two complete thoughts—*the sun was very hot* and *we decided to sit in the shade.* When two or more complete thoughts are joined without any or the correct punctuation, the result is a **run-on sentence**. One way to correct a run-on is to write each complete idea as a separate sentence.

The sun was very hot. We decided to sit in the shade.

Notice that a period ends the first sentence and that the second sentence begins with a capital letter.

Another kind of run-on sentence occurs when two complete ideas are separated by only a comma.

Milk is a good source of calcium, nonfat milk is also low in calories.

This type of run-on sentence is called a **comma splice**. Again, the error can be corrected by writing two separate sentences.

Milk is a good source of calcium. Nonfat milk is also low in calories.

Sentences with Compound Verbs

To decide if a sentence is a run-on, identify each complete thought. For example, the following sentence expresses only one complete thought. This is not a run-on:

> Mr. Sherman wrote a letter to his cousin and sent it by Air Mail.

The second part of this sentence (*sent it by Air Mail*) is not a complete idea. Notice that the sentence has two verbs, *wrote* and *sent,* but only one subject, *Mr. Sherman.* Two verbs that have the same subject in a sentence are called **compound verbs**.

In this lesson you have learned to correct run-on sentences by writing two separate sentences. In Lesson 3, you will learn other ways to correct run-on sentences.

Lesson 2 Exercise

Directions: Edit the following items to correct all run-on sentences. Not all of the sentences have errors.

1. Woodrow Wilson was our 28th president he was the only president who had a Ph.D. degree.
2. The Nineteenth Amendment to the Constitution gave women the right to vote, it was adopted in 1920.
3. Congress established the first U.S. mint it was located in Philadelphia.
4. The Western states are bigger than the states in the East and are less densely populated.
5. The state flag of Alaska was chosen in a competition the winner was only 13 years old.

Answers are on page 334.

Compound Sentences

A **compound sentence** is a sentence that expresses two or more complete thoughts. Run-ons and comma splices are incorrect ways of writing compound sentences. In Lesson 2 you learned to correct run-ons and comma splices by writing the ideas as two separate sentences.

You can also correct run-ons and comma splices by joining the two ideas in a compound sentence using one of these methods:

1. **Use a comma and a coordinating conjunction to join two complete ideas.** A compound sentence expresses two or more complete ideas that are of equal importance. The words used to connect the ideas in a compound sentence are called **coordinators**. The conjunctions that may be used with a comma are *and, but, or, nor, so, for,* and *yet*.

Coordinators have different meanings, and each can be used to show a relationship between the ideas that are connected. Chart 1 shows the meaning of the seven coordinate conjunctions.

Chart 1	
Coordinate Conjunctions	**Purpose**
and	connects related ideas
but, yet	contrasts one idea with another
or	expresses choice between ideas
nor	negates a choice
for	shows a cause
so	shows a result

The following compound sentences show the correct use of the coordinate conjunctions.

Janice works in Personnel, <u>and</u> Shane works in Customer Service.

Janice enjoys word processing, <u>but</u> Shane hates it.

Shane dislikes his computer class, <u>yet</u> he is doing well in it.

Janice plans to buy a computer, <u>or</u> she will lease one.

Shane does not own a computer, <u>nor</u> does he use one in his work.

Janice is learning new job skills, <u>for</u> she wants a promotion.

Janice wants a promotion, <u>so</u> she is learning new job skills.

2. **Use a semicolon to join two short and closely related sentences.**

   Mrs. Ortiz did not fly to Philadelphia, she went by train.

This comma splice can be corrected by changing the comma after *Philadelphia* to a semicolon.

   Mrs. Ortiz did not fly to Philadelphia; she went by train.

3. **Use a semicolon and a coordinating word or phrase followed by a comma to join closely related ideas.**

   Mrs. Ortiz did not fly to Philadelphia; <u>instead</u>, she went by train.

Chart 2 shows a list of some words and phrases that may be used after a semicolon to connect equal ideas in compound sentences.

Chart 2	
Coordinators Used with a Semicolon	**Purpose**
also, furthermore, moreover, besides, in addition, similarly, likewise	connects or adds on two related ideas
however, still, instead, nevertheless, nonetheless, on the contrary, on the other hand	contrasts one idea with another
afterward, later, meanwhile, next, then, finally, subsequently	shows time passing or shows a sequence
indeed, certainly, in fact, for example, for instance, that is	gives emphasis or shows a reason or an example
therefore, thus, hence, accordingly, as a result, consequently	shows a result or a conclusion

Several things are important to keep in mind in writing or editing compound sentences.

1. If a coordinator is used, it should be chosen to express the relationship between ideas. In the following sentence, the coordinator has a meaning of contrast, but the ideas are not really in contrast with each other.

> The worst earthquake in history occurred in 1556 in China; on the other hand, over 800,000 people died.

A correct coordinator would be *as a result* or *in fact*.

> The worst earthquake in history occurred in 1556 in China; as a result, over 800,000 people died.

2. Ideas that are not related should not be joined in a compound sentence. Is the following a correct compound sentence?

> The Cincinnati Reds are in first place, and I'm going to see the Dodgers play the Braves tonight.

Because the ideas are not closely related, they should be separate sentences. It is also possible to change the second idea to one that has some connection with the first, as in the following revision.

> The Cincinnati Reds are in first place, but the Dodgers are only 3 games behind them.

3. A sentence should not contain so many ideas or be so long that it becomes confusing.

> For many years the Empire State Building was the tallest building in the world; <u>later</u>, the World Trade Center in New York became the tallest; <u>however</u>, the Sears Tower in Chicago is now the tallest, <u>for</u> it stands at 1,451 feet and has 109 stories; <u>in addition</u>, the Sears Tower has 16,000 windows and 103 elevators.

This sentence should be divided into several shorter sentences, so that the ideas and the connections between them can be readily understood.

> For many years the Empire State Building was the tallest building in the world; <u>later</u>, the World Trade Center in New York became the tallest. <u>Now</u>, <u>however</u>, the Sears Tower in Chicago is the tallest. It stands at 1,451 feet and has 109 stories. <u>In addition</u>, the Sears Tower has 16,000 windows and 103 elevators.

Editing Compound Sentences

Remember, a compound sentence is a sentence that expresses two or more complete thoughts. The complete thoughts may be joined in any of the ways shown in this lesson.

Read the following sentences. Which ones are compound sentences? Are any of the sentences punctuated incorrectly?

1. Breeds of dogs are organized into groups; for example, there are 23 breeds of terriers.

2. Kabuki theater developed in Japan during the 1600s, and is still very popular today.

3. Detergents have many uses, yet they can harm the skin and eyes.

Sentences 1 and 3 are compound sentences and are correct as written. Sentence 2 is not a compound sentence. Although sentence 2 has compound verbs (*developed* and *is*), it does not express two complete ideas. The comma should be removed from this sentence.

Kabuki theater developed in Japan during the 1600s and is still very popular today.

Lesson 3 Exercise

Directions: Edit the following items to correct all run-on sentences and all errors in the use of coordinators. Use any of the methods described in this lesson or in Lesson 2. Not all of the sentences have errors.

1. Egyptians made candy over 4,000 years ago, they used dates and honey.

2. England and France fought the longest war it lasted from 1337 to 1453 and was called the Hundred Years' War.

3. The first African-American to become a Supreme Court justice was Thurgood Marshall he was appointed in 1967 by President Lyndon Johnson.

4. A deer's antlers fall off every winter and grow back in the summer.

5. This apartment needs some repairs, however, the rent is reasonable.

6. The United States is the world's largest producer of cheese, France is second.

7. The country with the largest number of doctors is not America, nor is it Japan.

8. The first government employee strike was the Boston police strike it happened in 1919.

9. Pluto takes 248 years to complete one orbit around the sun, many comets orbit beyond Pluto.

10. Pretzels were invented by a French monk, he shaped the dough to represent arms folded in prayer.

11. Irving Berlin wrote "White Christmas," the most popular song ever recorded; however, over 100 million copies have been sold.

12. The Great Wall of China is 1,684 miles long; on the other hand, it is the longest wall in the world.

13. O'Hare Airport in Chicago is the busiest in the world, and my aunt is a flight attendant.

14. The largest prison in the world is Kharkov Prison in Russia; in fact, it can hold 40,000 prisoners.

15. Jon Fitch designed the first steamboat, and it looked like a canoe but had steam-driven paddles; moreover, he also built a boat that had paddle wheels on the side, but he had difficulty finding people to back him financially, so his designs failed to be successful.

Answers are on pages 334-335.

Lesson 4

Complex Sentences

A compound sentence combines ideas of equal importance.

> The Dallas-Fort Worth Airport covers more than 18,000 acres, <u>and</u> it is the largest airport in the world.

Sometimes, though, you need to combine ideas while showing that one idea is more important than the other. To do this, you must change the wording to subordinate one of the ideas.

There are two ideas in the sentence above:
#1: The Dallas-Fort Worth Airport covers more than 18,000 acres.

#2: The Dallas-Fort Worth Airport is the largest airport in the world.

In the following sentence, the first idea is subordinate, or of lesser importance, than the second idea.

> <u>Because</u> the Dallas-Fort Worth Airport covers more than 18,000 acres, it is the largest airport in the world.

The word *because* makes the first idea subordinate. The subordinate idea becomes a sentence fragment; the more important idea remains a complete thought. This complete thought is called the **main idea** of the sentence.

The subordinate may also appear at the end of a sentence.

> In 1867, Congress was called the Billion Dollar Congress <u>because it passed a budget of over one billion dollars.</u>

> A sentence with a main idea and at least one subordinate idea is called a **complex sentence**.

Chart 3 shows the most common words used as **subordinators** to connect ideas of unequal importance in a sentence. They are grouped according to meaning.

Chart 3	
Subordinators	**Examples**
Time Relationships	
before after as as long as as soon as when whenever while until	<u>After</u> you left the store, we were swamped with customers. I won't make a decision <u>until</u> I hear from you. Al becomes angry <u>whenever</u> David calls in sick.
Contrast	
although even though though whereas	<u>Even though</u> her toothache was gone, she kept her dentist appointment.
Conditions	
if unless	We will hold the meeting at 10 A.M. <u>if</u> you can get an early flight.
Cause and Effect	
because in order that since so that	Please display your parking permit on your dashboard <u>so that</u> the attendant can identify your car in an emergency.
Similarity	
as if as though	Nita looks <u>as though</u> she could use a day off.
Placement	
where wherever	I put the scissors <u>where</u> they would be easy to find.

There are four rules to remember about using subordinators.

1. The two sentence ideas must have something in common. Do not combine unrelated ideas.

> INCORRECT: Unless we could get good seats, we were surprised at the price of tickets.

> CORRECT: Unless we could get good seats, we did not want to see the show.

2. One idea will be stated in a sentence fragment, and one idea will be a complete sentence.

> COORDINATED IDEAS: Lungfish have lungs and breathe air, <u>but</u> they also have gills.

> SUBORDINATED IDEAS: <u>Although</u> lungfish have lungs and breathe air, they also have gills.

> **NOTE:** The coordinator (*but*) is dropped when the subordinator (*Although*) is used.

3. If the subordinate idea comes first in the sentence, it is followed by a comma. When it comes after the main part of the sentence, no comma is used.

> INCORRECT: When goldfish are kept in a dark room they lose their color.

> CORRECT: When goldfish are kept in a dark room, they lose their color.

> CORRECT: Goldfish lose their color when they are kept in a dark room.

4. Only one subordinator should be used at a time.

> INCORRECT: <u>Because even though</u> he is a talented professional golfer, Sam Snead never won the U.S. Open.

> CORRECT: <u>Even though</u> he is a talented professional golfer, Sam Snead never won the U.S. Open.

The ideas in this sentence are related by contrast, not by cause and effect. Thus, *even though* is an appropriate subordinator.

Directions: Edit the following sentences to correct all subordination errors. Not all of the sentences have errors. There may be more than one way to correct a sentence.

1. As long as you don't overdo it, jogging is a healthful activity.
2. Even though some mushrooms are poisonous, but others can be eaten safely.
3. After when the stock market crashed in 1929, many people refused to put their money in banks.
4. When Shakespeare wrote his historical plays he sometimes altered the truth to fit his story lines.
5. Pollution will continue to be a major problem in many of our cities until people begin to read more.

Answers are on page 335.

Combining Sentences

Sometimes a sentence repeats words that were used in an earlier sentence. It is often possible to improve a paragraph by combining such sentences into one. Coordinators such as *and*, *or*, and *but* can be used for this purpose.

Liver is a good source of vitamin A.

Butter is a good source of vitamin A.

To avoid repeating the words *is a good source of vitamin A*, the sentences can be combined.

Liver <u>and</u> butter are good sources of vitamin A.

Notice that the compound subject, *liver and butter*, requires a plural verb, *are*.

Other parts of sentences besides subjects can be combined to eliminate needless repetitions.

Miss Rodgers may buy a station wagon.

Miss Rodgers may buy a van.

COMBINED: Miss Rodgers may buy a station wagon <u>or</u> a van.

There is a vaccine against measles.

There is a vaccine against mumps.

COMBINED: There are vaccines against measles <u>and</u> mumps.

Notice that some words may have to be made plural in the combined sentence.

The paired coordinators *either...or* and *neither...nor* can also be used to combine sentences. Other changes in wording may be necessary when these coordinators are used.

A salad would be good for dinner.

A casserole would be good for dinner.

COMBINED: <u>Either</u> a salad <u>or</u> a casserole would be good for dinner.

Hilary did not attend the meeting.

Wiley did not attend the meeting.

COMBINED: <u>Neither</u> Hilary <u>nor</u> Wiley attended the meeting.

Sentences found by combining in these ways are not compound sentences. They do not need commas unless the combined sentence lists a series of three or more items, as in the following example.

Liver and butter are good sources of vitamin A.

Milk is a good source of vitamin A.

COMBINED: Liver, butter, and milk are good sources of vitamin A.

Directions: Edit the following pairs of sentences to make them less repetitious. Combine sentences in any of the ways used in this lesson.

1. Seneca Lake is in western New York State. Cayuga Lake is in western New York State.
2. Mr. Wittenberg did not enjoy the concert. Mr. Bush did not enjoy the concert.
3. You can buy that book in a hardcover edition. You can buy that book in paperback.
4. Roberta is making a skirt. Roberta is making a blazer.
5. Eliot fixed the faucet with a wrench. Eliot fixed the faucet with a screwdriver.

Answers are on page 335.

Chapter 1 Review

Directions: Edit the following items to correct all errors in complete sentence structure. Combine sentences using any of the methods used in this lesson. Not all of the items have errors.

1. The most common hand injury is a smashed fingertip, a painful bruise often appears beneath the fingernail within hours.

2. Redness or swelling in a child's hand could be serious, and should be seen by a doctor.

3. May require a cast.

4. Wilt Chamberlain holds the record for scoring the most points in a basketball game he scored 100 points in a game against the New York Knicks.

5. During the last 10 minutes.

6. In the first three quarters on Saturday, the Jazz played near perfect basketball, however the team quickly lost momentum in the final quarter.

7. The wildest game I have ever seen.

8. Morale among employees is affected greatly by the mood of their employers; on the other hand, an argument between two bosses reduces the productivity of the employees in the office.

9. Whenever a new contract is being negotiated, and tension among employees increases.

10. Some company owners reward their employees for ideas that save the company money, but I plan to own my own business.

11. One concern that companies and families share is the high cost of utilities; as a result, energy costs are rising with each passing year.

12. In the public schools, children are taught the importance of recycling, however, many adults resist the extra work involved in sorting the trash.

13. When they are washing dishes or brushing their teeth many people waste water without realizing it.

14. Whenever it is possible, turn off unnecessary lights to help conserve energy.

15. Microwave ovens are very popular; in fact estimates show that at least three-quarters of American households now own one of these ovens; accordingly, food manufacturers are developing new lines of frozen microwave products for people who want quick, easy meals; for example, single-serving kid's meals are a new item that is selling well.

Check your answers. Correct answers are on pages 335-336. If you have all 15 answers correct, go on to Chapter 2. If you have any answers incorrect, find the item number on the following chart and review that lesson before you go on.

Review...	If you missed Item Number ...
Lesson 1	3, 5, 7
Lessons 2, 3, & 5	1, 2, 4, 6, 8, 10, 11, 12, 15
Lesson 4	9, 13, 14

GED REVIEW 4

Directions: The following items are based on paragraphs that contain numbered sentences. Some of the sentences contain errors in usage and sentence structure. A few sentences, however, may be correct as written. Read each paragraph and then answer the items that follow it.

Items 1 to 5 are based on the following passage.

(1) Rickets is a disorder of the bones caused by a lack of exposure to sunlight. (2) Because too little sunlight causes a Vitamin D deficiency. (3) A hundred years ago, rickets was the most common serious disease of children in Europe. (4) It was also the most common serious disease in America. (5) Because children worked indoors in windowless factories rickets reached epidemic proportions during the Industrial Revolution. (6) In addition, heavy air pollution caused by the factories blocks most of the sun's healthful ultraviolet rays. (7) Sunlight prevents rickets by converting a form of cholesterol in the body's tissues to Vitamin D. (8) Rickets can also be prevented by giving people small doses of Vitamin D.

1. Sentence 2: **Because too little sunlight causes a Vitamin D deficiency.**

   Which of the following is the best way to write the underlined portion of this sentence? If you think the original is the best way, choose option (1).

   (1) Because too little sunlight causes a Vitamin D deficiency.
   (2) Although too little sunlight causes a Vitamin D deficiency.
   (3) Too little sunlight causes a Vitamin D deficiency.
   (4) However, too little sunlight causes a Vitamin D deficiency.
   (5) When too little sunlight causes a Vitamin D deficiency.

2. Sentences 3 and 4: **A hundred years ago, rickets was the most common serious disease of children in Europe. It was also the most common serious disease in America.**

   The most effective combination of sentences 3 and 4 would include which of the following groups of words?

   (1) children in Europe; it
   (2) children in Europe; nevertheless, it
   (3) children in Europe, but it
   (4) children in Europe and America.
   (5) children in Europe and children of America.

3. Sentence 5: **Because children worked indoors in windowless <u>factories rickets reached</u> epidemic proportions during the Industrial Revolution.**

Which of the following is the best way to write the underlined portion of this sentence? If you think the original is the best way, choose option (1).

(1) factories rickets reached
(2) factories, rickets reached
(3) factories; rickets reached
(4) factories, and rickets reached
(5) factories, but rickets reached

4. Sentence 6: **In addition, heavy air pollution caused by the factories blocks most of the sun's healthful ultraviolet rays.**

What correction should be made to this sentence?

(1) change <u>caused</u> to <u>causes</u>
(2) change <u>factories</u> to <u>factorys</u>
(3) insert a comma after <u>factories</u>
(4) change <u>blocks</u> to <u>blocked</u>
(5) no correction is necessary

5. Sentences 7 and 8: **Sunlight prevents rickets by converting a form of cholesterol in the body's tissues to Vitamin D. Rickets can also be prevented by giving people small doses of Vitamin D.**

The most effective combination of sentences 7 and 8 would include which of the following groups of words?

(1) Vitamin D; instead, rickets
(2) Vitamin D, on the other hand, rickets
(3) Vitamin D; hence, rickets
(4) Vitamin D; besides, rickets
(5) Vitamin D, yet rickets

<u>Items 6 to 9</u> are based on the following passage.

(1) The Energy Child Development Center is a model child-care facility built largely through the efforts of Sheila Watkins. (2) In 1989, President George Bush named her husband, James D. Watkins, secretary of energy. (3) A few days later Mrs. Watkins was touring the Department of Energy and she noticed that there was no child-care facility on the site. (4) She immediately announced her plan to build an ecologically sound child-care center. (5) The building occupies the space formerly used for employee volleyball games it is one of the few existing buildings designed specifically for child care. (6) The building features toddler-height windows, and soft mats in play areas. (7) The center is energy efficient since three giant solar panels provide most of the center's hot water. (8) The panels also provide most of the center's lighting.

6. Sentence 3: **A few days later Mrs. Watkins was touring the Department of Energy and she noticed that there was no child-care facility on the site.**

What correction should be made to this sentence?

(1) change <u>was touring</u> to <u>will be touring</u>
(2) change <u>was touring</u> to <u>were touring</u>
(3) insert a comma after <u>Energy</u>
(4) insert a semicolon after <u>Energy</u>
(5) no correction is necessary

7. Sentence 5: **The building occupies the space formerly used for employee volleyball <u>games it is one</u> of the few existing buildings designed specifically for child care.**

Which of the following is the best way to write the underlined portion of this sentence? If you think the original is the best way, choose option (1).

(1) games it is one
(2) games, but it is one
(3) games unless it is one
(4) games; therefore, it is one
(5) games. It is one

8. Sentence 6: **The building features toddler-height <u>windows, and soft mats</u> in play areas.**

Which of the following is the best way to write the underlined portion of this sentence? If you think the original is the best way, choose option (1).

(1) windows, and soft mats
(2) windows and soft mats
(3) windows; in addition, soft mats
(4) windows; soft mats
(5) windows, or soft mats

9. Sentences 7 and 8: **The center is energy efficient since three giant solar panels provide most of the center's hot water. The panels also provide most of the center's lighting.**

The most effective combination of sentences 7 and 8 would include which of the following groups of words?

(1) energy and giant solar panels
(2) giant solar panels and hot water
(3) giant solar panels and lighting
(4) hot water and lighting
(5) the center and the panels

Items 10 to 12 are based on the following passage.

(1) Living in outer space for extended periods of time poses unique challenges. (2) Emergencies that would be handled easily on earth present special difficulties in a weightless environment. (3) Astronauts who have conducted experiments to check the effect of gravity on smoldering foam and overheated wires. (4) A fire needs oxygen, fuel, and heat. (5) There is very little air in space to replenish the oxygen supply to a fire. (6) A fire in space does not go out immediately. (7) It smolders, and grows hotter because hot air does not rise in space. (8) Even a small fire aboard a spacecraft can do a great deal of damage to wiring and equipment. (9) Scientists hope these experiments will lead to safer methods of fire control in space.

10. Sentence 3: **Astronauts who have conducted experiments to check the effect of gravity on smoldering foam and overheated wires.**

What correction should be made to this sentence?

   (1) insert a comma after <u>Astronauts</u>
   (2) change <u>who</u> to <u>that</u>
   (3) remove <u>who</u>
   (4) replace <u>have conducted</u> with <u>conduct</u>
   (5) no correction is necessary

11. Sentences 5 and 6: **There is very little air in space to replenish the oxygen supply to a fire. A fire in space does not go out immediately.**

The most effective combination of sentences 5 and 6 would include which of the following groups of words?

   (1) fire; afterward, a fire in space
   (2) fire; for example, a fire in space
   (3) fire; that is, a fire in space
   (4) fire; besides, a fire in space
   (5) fire; however, a fire in space

12. Sentence 7: **It <u>smolders, and grows hotter</u> because hot air does not rise in space.**

Which of the following is the best way to write the underlined portion of this sentence? If you think the original is the best way, choose option (1).

   (1) smolders, and grows hotter
   (2) smolders; and grows hotter
   (3) smolders and grows hotter
   (4) smolders, yet grows hotter
   (5) smolders yet grows hotter

Answers are on pages 336-337.

CHAPTER 2
CLEAR SENTENCES

Preview

Directions: Edit these sentences to correct all errors in clarity. Not all of the sentences have errors.

1. At last we finally had all the boxes packed and sealed.
2. Good reading skills will help you enjoy literature and learn more about our world.
3. With happiness, Ms. Fischer gladly accepted the promotion.
4. Flown from sunrise to sunset, the White House displays the U.S. flag every day.
5. Reading the newspaper, the dog waited patiently to go for a walk.

Check your answers. Correct answers are on page 337. If you have all five answers correct, do the Chapter 2 Review on page 127. If you have fewer than five answers correct, study Chapter 2 beginning with Lesson 1.

Lesson 1

Clarity of Thought

A sentence may be free of grammatical errors but still not be understandable. Such a sentence lacks clarity, or clearness.

> I ate nachos before I rode the roller coaster, which made me sick to my stomach.

Is the meaning of this sentence clear? *What* made me sick to my stomach? The nachos? Or the roller coaster? Or both? It is difficult to tell by the wording of the sentence.

Unclear writing can result from any of the following problems.

1. Unclear choice of words. Whenever possible, a sentence should express an idea in clear, simple words. Long words and complicated sentences do not necessarily help to make an idea understandable. In fact, they may confuse the reader. Effective sentences make every word count.

> UNCLEAR: The employee reconciled himself to a reduction of his salary in order to prevent his impending termination.

> CLEAR: The employee agreed to take a pay cut to prevent losing his job.

> UNCLEAR: You might expect an irritation to the epidermis from prolonged exposure to normal yard coverings.

> CLEAR: You might get a rash from lying in the grass.

2. Use of unnecessary words. If a writer uses more words than are needed to express an idea, the result is called wordiness. Sometimes wordiness is caused by unclear word choice, as the examples above show. At other times, a writer may turn to clichés or important sounding phrases that actually say very little. Avoid unnecessary repetition and overuse of words by simple getting to the point.

WORDY: You shiver on account of the fact that your body is attempting to try to increase heat within the body.

CLEAR: You shiver because your body is trying to create heat within itself.

WORDY: Mr. Addington should be in the vicinity of Fairfax and Wilshire at the present time.

CLEAR: Mr. Addington should be near Fairfax and Wilshire now.

Most wordy sentences are long; however, short sentences can also be wordy.

WORDY: There are four employees who can work overtime tonight.

CLEAR: Four employees can work overtime tonight.

WORDY: The soldiers advanced forward.

CLEAR: The soldiers advanced.

Because *advance* means "move forward," it is unnecessary to write *advanced forward.*

Lesson 1 Exercise

Directions: Edit the following sentence to correct all errors in clarity. Not all of the sentences have errors.

1. It is Mr. Marshall's belief that his back injury was due to the fact that he chose to lift boxes that were heavy.
2. Her supervisors plan to combine together all the ideas from the meeting.
3. I warned Diane to be punctual for the job interview.
4. Last year we spent last summer in Florida.
5. In a rage, the furious driver shouted angrily.

Answers are on page 337.

2 Proper Placement of Modifiers

The meaning of a sentence can also be unclear if its parts are not in logical order or if a needed part is missing.

> Hoping and praying, the plane landed safely after all.

> Containing 12,000 words and 40,000 definitions, Noah Webster compiled the first American-English language dictionary.

In both sentences, the meaning is uncertain. The first sentence seems to say that the plane is hoping and praying, which does not make sense. The second sentence seems to state that Noah Webster contains 12,000 words and 40,000 definitions. Neither sentence expresses the writer's meaning well.

The following versions have been edited to state clearly what the writer means.

1. Hoping and praying, we saw the plane land safely after all.

2. Noah Webster compiled the first American-English language dictionary, which contained 12,000 words and 40,000 definitions.

A **modifier** is a word or phrase that explains or describes another word in a sentence. In sentence 1, *hoping* and *praying* are modifiers that describe *we*. In sentence 2, the words *which contained 12,000 words and 40,000 definitions* explain, or modify, *dictionary.*

A modifier should be placed as close as possible to the word it describes. If the modifier is too far from this word, the sentence becomes confusing. The result is called a **misplaced modifier.**

1. Dangling modifiers. A modifier must clearly and logically explain another word in the sentence. If there is no word that can logically be modified or described, the result is a **dangling modifier**.

> Exhausted after a long day, a hot bath sounded good.

This sentence seems to be saying that the bath was exhausted. However, it is not logical for *exhausted* to modify *bath*. The sentence can be corrected by introducing a word that *exhausted* can modify:

> Exhausted after a long day, I thought a hot bath sounded good.

Sometimes it is possible to reword the dangling modifier as a separate idea introduced by a subordinator.

> Because I was exhausted after a long day, a hot bath sounded good.

2. Misplaced modifiers. In this example, the modifying phrase is placed too far from the word it describes.

> Lake Victoria is located in Africa, which is 270 feet deep.
> *(This sentence seems to say that Africa is 270 feet deep.)*

To correct this sentence, rearrange the words. Place the misplaced modifier as close as possible to the word it modifies.

> Lake Victoria, which is 270 feet deep, is located in Africa.
> *(This sentence states that Lake Victoria is 270 feet deep.)*

Lesson 2 Exercise

Directions: Edit the following sentences to correct all modification errors. Not all of the sentences have errors.

1. Running into the end zone, the winning touchdown was scored.
2. Wishing to become an expert chess player, Ernest practices every day.
3. A rainbow from an airplane can be seen as a complete circle.
4. Michelangelo painted the ceiling of the Sistine Chapel on his back.
5. The detective watched the suspect's house wearing a disguise.

Answers are on page 337.

Parallel Structure

The following sentence tells about a person's interests.

> Art's hobbies are hiking, sketching, and gardening.

Notice the form of the words that name Art's hobbies: each is the -ing form of a verb. Because all of the activities are being mentioned as a person's hobbies, they all play similar roles in the sentence. Ideas that have similar roles in a sentence should be worded with similar, or parallel, structures.

Do the following sentences have parallel structure? Decide whether or not related ideas are worded in similar ways.

> On my vacation, I plan to read romance novels, see all this summer's blockbuster movies, and taking frequent naps.

In this sentence, the three activities I plan to engage in are not listed in the same form. Two activities begin with the present form of the verb but the third does not. Parallel structure requires the word *taking* to be changed to present form as well.

> On my vacation, I plan to read romance novels, see all this summer's blockbuster movies, and take frequent naps.

Can you find the error in this sentence?

> Alexander Graham Bell was a painter, teacher, and he invented things.

In this sentence, two nouns describe Alexander Graham Bell; however, the third idea uses a verb, *invented*. To give the sentence parallel structure, change the words *he invented things* to a noun.

> Alexander Graham Bell was a painter, teacher, and inventor.

Use this method when you look for errors in parallel structure:

1. See if the sentence includes a listing of at least two nouns, verbs, or descriptive words. The connecting words *and*, *or*, *nor*, or *but also* are often used in listings.
2. Decide if all items in the listing have been written in the same form.
3. If there is an error in parallel structure, select one form and use it consistently throughout the listing.

Lesson 3 Exercise

Directions: Edit the following sentences to correct all errors in parallel structure. Not all of the sentences have errors.

1. A U.S. senator must be at least 30 years old, be a U.S. citizen for a minimum of 9 years, and to live in the state in which he or she seeks election.
2. Activities that strengthen the heart muscle include swimming, jogging, and to ride a bike.
3. I enjoy sports that are challenging, fast-paced, and don't cost much money.
4. Is the birthstone of those born in July a ruby, sapphire, or is it the diamond?
5. The American Hospital Association believes that every patient has a right to be treated with dignity and to be given an explanation of the bill.

Answers are on page 337.

CHAPTER 2 REVIEW

Directions: Edit the following sentences to correct all errors in clarity. Not all of the sentences have errors.

1. The museum will be closed for remodeling for all days and nights during the month of July.
2. There are many people who use computers in their jobs.
3. What I need is for you to sign the form and return it to me in the envelope that I enclosed with this memo.
4. While taking a shower, the telephone rang.
5. Margaret enjoyed singing and dancing more than to act.
6. After Greg thoroughly scrutinized the letter for errors, he retyped it.
7. The doctor explained the patient's symptoms, diagnosis, and what treatment would be used.
8. After studying for three days, I thought the test was easy.
9. Excited and anxious, the birthday gifts were quickly unwrapped.
10. The stories of Edgar Allan Poe are unusual, exciting, and they have suspense.

Check your answers. Correct answers are on pages 337-338. If you have all 10 answers correct, go on to Test-Taking Strategies 2. If you have any answers incorrect, find the item number on the chart below and review that lesson before you go on.

Review...	If you missed Item Number ...
Lesson 1	1, 2, 3, 6
Lesson 2	4, 8, 9
Lesson 3	5, 7, 10

GED REVIEW 5

Directions: The following items are based on paragraphs that contain numbered sentences. Some of the sentences contain errors in usage and sentence structure. A few sentences, however, may be correct as written. Read each paragraph and then answer the items that follow it.

Items 1 to 4 are based on the following passage.

(1) The Eastside Inn has several affordable summer specials that will fit within your family budget. (2) The popular Family Plan includes a luxury room for a family of four and the use of the tennis courts and swimming pools. (3) Camp Eastside is our popular kids' program for children ages 3 to 14. (4) Activities are planned on weekdays from Monday through Friday. (5) The playground for your children are located at the west end of the recreation field. (6) The Camp Eastside fee is only $15 per child, per day. (7) If you like swimming, sunbathing, and to play tennis, make Eastside Inn part of your family's summer.

1. Sentence 1: **The Eastside Inn has several affordable summer specials that will fit within your family budget.**

   What correction should be made to this sentence?

   (1) change has to have
   (2) remove affordable
   (3) change that to which
   (4) change that to who
   (5) replace will fit with fit

2. Sentence 4: **Activities are planned on weekdays from Monday through Friday.**

   Which of the following is the best way to write the underlined portion of this sentence? If you think the original is the best way, choose option (1).

   (1) are planned on weekdays from Monday through Friday.
   (2) is planned on weekdays from Monday through Friday.
   (3) was planned on weekdays from Monday through Friday.
   (4) were planned on weekdays from Monday through Friday.
   (5) are planned on weekdays from Monday through Friday.

3. Sentence 5: **The playground for <u>your children are located</u> at the west end of the recreation field.**

Which of the following is the best way to write the underlined portion of this sentence? If you think the original is the best way, choose option (1).

(1) your children are located
(2) your children is located
(3) your children was located
(4) your children which are located
(5) your children that are located

4. Sentence 7: **If you like swimming, sunbathing, <u>and to play tennis, make</u> Eastside Inn part of your family's summer.**

Which of the following is the best way to write the underlined portion of this sentence? If you think the original is the best way, choose option (1).

(1) and to play tennis, make
(2) and play tennis, make
(3) and playing tennis, make
(4) and to play tennis make
(5) and to play tennis; make

<u>Items 5 to 9</u> are based on the following passage.

(1) Osteoporosis is a condition in which bones deteriorate rapidly. (2) Routine regular checkups for older women commonly include tests to detect this condition. (3) Bone is constantly broken down, and then rebuilt in the body. (4) Until about age 35, the amount of bone formed is greater than the amount lost. (5) After a woman reaches age 35, her bones may begin to deteriorate. (6) Some women are more at risk than others. (7) Those who smoke cigarettes or drink excessive amounts of alcohol are at high risk. (8) To reduce the risk of osteoporosis, doctors recommend exercising regularly, taking calcium supplements, and to cut down on drinks that contain caffeine.

5. Sentence 2: **Routine regular checkups for older women commonly include tests to detect this condition.**

What correction should be made to this sentence?

(1) remove <u>regular</u>
(2) change <u>women</u> to <u>womans</u>
(3) remove <u>commonly</u>
(4) replace <u>include</u> with <u>will include</u>
(5) change <u>include</u> to <u>included</u>

6. Sentence 3: **Bone is constantly broken down, and then rebuilt in the body.**

What correction should be made to this sentence?

(1) change <u>is</u> to <u>are</u>
(2) remove <u>constantly</u>
(3) remove the comma after <u>down</u>
(4) change <u>rebuilt</u> to <u>rebuilded</u>
(5) no correction is necessary

7. Sentence 5: **After a woman <u>reaches age 35, her</u> bones may begin to deteriorate.**

Which of the following is the best way to write the underlined portion of this sentence? If you think the original is the best way, choose option (1).

(1) reaches age 35, her
(2) reached age 35, her
(3) reach age 35, her
(4) reaches age 35 her
(5) reaches age 35; her

8. Sentences 6 and 7: **Some women are more at risk than others. Those who smoke cigarettes or drink excessive amounts of alcohol are at high risk.**

The most effective combination of sentences 6 and 7 would include which of the following groups of words?

(1) others, or those
(2) others, for those
(3) others even though those
(4) others; nevertheless, those
(5) others; for example, those

9. Sentence 8: **To reduce the risk of osteoporosis, doctors recommend exercising regularly, taking calcium supplements, and to cut down on drinks that contain caffeine.**

What correction should be made to this sentence?

(1) change <u>recommend</u> to <u>recommends</u>
(2) replace <u>exercising</u> with <u>to exercise</u>
(3) replace <u>taking</u> with <u>to take</u>
(4) replace <u>to cut</u> with <u>cutting</u>
(5) change <u>that</u> to <u>which</u>

Items 10 to 12 are based on the following passage.

(1) Ever since money has been used, people have tried to counterfeit it. (2) Plastic credit cards have become the world's newest form of currency, and counterfeiting is a major problem. (3) One major card company reported losses in excess of $57 million over one year alone. (4) Banks and card companies have added holograms, magnetic strips, and invisible watermarks to cards to deter counterfeiters; therefore, nothing works for long. (5) Knowing the same technology, the cards are copied within a short period of time. (6) Someday, cards may carry photographs, embedded computer chips, or bar codes.

10. Sentence 2: **Plastic credit cards have become the world's newest form of currency, and counterfeiting is a major problem.**

   Which of the following is the best way to write the underlined portion of this sentence? If you think the original is the best way, choose option (1).

   (1) currency, and counterfeiting
   (2) currency and counterfeiting
   (3) currency, for counterfeiting
   (4) currency, or counterfeiting
   (5) currency; for example, counterfeiting

11. Sentence 4: **Banks and card companies have added holograms, magnetic strips, and invisible watermarks to cards to deter counterfeiters; therefore, nothing works for long.**

   Which of the following is the best way to write the underlined portion of this sentence? If you think the original is the best way, choose option (1).

   (1) counterfeiters; therefore, nothing works
   (2) counterfeiters; in fact, nothing works
   (3) counterfeiters; however, nothing works
   (4) counterfeiters, and nothing works
   (5) counterfeiters, for nothing works

12. Sentence 5: **Knowing the same technology, the cards are copied within a short period of time.**

   If you rewrote sentence 5 beginning with

   Because they know the same technology,

   the next word(s) should be

   (1) the cards
   (2) the police
   (3) the card companies
   (4) the counterfeiters
   (5) the holograms

Answers are on page 338.

TEST-TAKING STRATEGIES 2

Your knowledge of sentence structure will be tested in about 35 percent of the questions on Part I of the GED Writing Skills Test. All three types of multiple-choice questions discussed in Test-Taking Strategies 1 will be used.

To answer these questions effectively, you will need to organize your thinking. Follow the 5-R method of editing:

Step 1	**Read**	Read the paragraph quickly for its meaning and writing style.
Step 2	**Reflect**	Reflect by looking for any errors within the paragraph.
Step 3	**Revise**	Read the first test item and the five choices. Decide which alternative identifies and corrects the error.
Step 4	**Reread**	Read the revised sentence with the selected correction.
Step 5	**Record**	Mark the number of the alternative that you have chosen. Then, move on to the next item.

To answer sentence structure questions effectively, ask yourself these questions as you *reflect* in Step 2.

1. **Do all groups of words that begin with a capital letter and end with a period express a complete thought?**

    INCORRECT: Carving wooden ducks by hand.

    CORRECT: Mark enjoys carving wooden ducks.

2. **Are all compound sentences written in proper form?** (Check for run-ons and comma splices. If a sentence contains more than one complete idea, the ideas must be properly connected and punctuated.)

    INCORRECT: On Tuesday John went to the doctor, he went to the dentist on Wednesday.

    CORRECT: On Tuesday John went to the doctor, and he went to the dentist on Wednesday.

3. **Are the sentences clearly written and logically organized?** (Check for repetition of words and ideas within a sentence.)

    INCORRECT: The dog chased the cat barking noisily up the tree.

    CORRECT: Barking noisily, the dog chased the cat up the tree.

4. Are the ideas, items, or actions in each sentence expressed using parallel structure?

INCORRECT: After the meeting, Susan took two aspirins, drank a cup of tea, and she took a long nap.

CORRECT: After the meeting, Susan took two aspirins, drank a cup of tea, and took a long nap.

Read the following paragraph. As you *read* and *reflect*, apply the four sentence-structure questions that are listed above.

(1) Video games have become a big business. (2) Over 14 million game consoles have been installed in U.S. homes, over 75 million game cartridges have been sold. (3) Each year, over $5 billion spent playing video machines in video arcades. (4) Why are people intent on spending so much money on these games? (5) Video games provide a source of stimulation, a temporary escape from the real world, and break up the feeling of boredom. (6) Because as long as people feel this need to add excitement to their lives, they will continue to spend money on this form of entertainment.

You should have found one comma-splice sentence (sentence 2), one sentence that is a fragment (sentence 3), one sentence that lacks parallel structure (sentence 5), and one sentence that had a subordination error (sentence 6). If you had difficulty finding these errors, you may need to review Unit 2 before doing the exercise for this lesson.

Directions: Read the following paragraph. As you read, ask yourself the four basic questions that are used when editing for sentence structure. No sentence contains more than one error. Use the 5-R method of editing as you work through each question.

(1) Everyone at some time faces the task of looking for a job. (2) However, job seekers often limit themselves. (3) They only look in the want-ad section of the newspaper. (4) Where this will give you a start, it's not the only source to use. (5) Some people have actually run their own ads. (6) They list their skills, the type of work they are seeking, and telling their phone number. (7) Another good idea is to check library bulletin boards they frequently display job listings. (8) A third idea is to choose a field of employment that interests you, locate employers in the Yellow Pages of the telephone book, and call a few, asking if they need additional help. (9) Last, such job sources don't overlook as school alumni associations, employment agencies, and government personnel offices.

1. Sentences 2 and 3: **However, job seekers may limit themselves. They only look in the want-ad section of the newspaper.**

   The most effective combination of sentences 2 and 3 would include which of the following groups of words?

   (1) themselves besides they only look
   (2) themselves, but they only look
   (3) themselves if they only look
   (4) themselves, yet they only look
   (5) themselves although they only look

2. Sentence 4: **Where this will give you a start, it's not the only source to use.**

   What correction should be made to this sentence?

   (1) remove <u>Where</u>
   (2) replace <u>Where</u> with <u>Although</u>
   (3) remove the comma after <u>start</u>
   (4) insert a semicolon after <u>start</u>
   (5) no correction is necessary

3. Sentence 6: **They list their skills, the type of work they are <u>seeking, and telling their phone number.</u>**

Which of the following is the best way to write the underlined portion of this sentence? If you think the original is the best way, choose option (1).

(1) seeking, and telling their phone number.
(2) seeking and telling their phone number.
(3) seek, and tell their phone number.
(4) seek and their phone number.
(5) seeking, and their phone number.

4. Sentence 7: **Another good idea is to check library bulletin <u>boards they frequently display</u> job listings.**

Which of the following is the best way to write the underlined portion of this sentence? If you think the original is the best way, choose option (1).

(1) boards they frequently display
(2) boards who frequently display
(3) boards; they frequently display
(4) boards, employers frequently display
(5) boards, who frequently display

5. Sentence 9: **Last, <u>such job sources don't overlook</u> as school alumni associations, employment agencies, and government personnel offices.**

Which of the following is the best way to write the underlined portion of this sentence? If you think the original is the best way, choose option (1).

(1) such job sources don't overlook
(2) such sources do not overlook
(3) overlook such sources
(4) don't overlook such job sources
(5) don't overlook, such job sources

Answers are on pages 338-339.

UNIT 2 REVIEW

Directions: The items in this review are based on paragraphs that contain numbered sentences. Some of the sentences contain errors in usage. A few sentences, however, may be correct as written. Read each paragraph and then answer the items that follow it.

Items 1 to 4 are based on the following paragraph.

(1) Braille is a system for reading and writing used by and for blind people. (2) This system was invented by Louis Braille which has 63 characters made up of one to six raised dots. (3) Louis Braille was blinded accidentally at the age of three, he was playing with a tool in his father's workshop. (4) When Louis entered a school for the blind in 1819, he learned of a system of writing using dots that was invented by Captain Charles Barbier, an army officer. (5) Barbier developed his 12-dot system for sending messages during battles at night. (6) Wanting to simplify the system, only six dots were used by Louis Braille. (7) Braille was only 15 years old when he invented his system; however, it was not widely used by the blind until 1854.

1. Sentence 2: **This <u>system was invented by Louis Braille which has</u> 63 characters made up of one to six raised dots.**

   Which of the following is the best way to write the underlined portion of this sentence? If you think the original is the best way, choose option (1).

   (1) system was invented by Louis Braille which has
   (2) system, was invented by Louis Braille, which has
   (3) system were invented by Louis Braille, which has
   (4) system, which was invented by Louis Braille, has
   (5) system, invented by Louis Braille, which has

2. Sentence 3: **Louis Braille was blinded accidentally at the age of <u>three, he was playing</u> with a tool in his father's workshop.**

   Which of the following is the best way to write the underlined portion of this sentence? If you think the original is the best way, choose option (1).

   (1) three, he was playing
   (2) three while he was playing
   (3) three although he was playing
   (4) three, and he was playing
   (5) three; as a result, he was playing

3. Sentence 6: **Wanting to simplify the system, only six dots were used by Louis Braille.**

If you rewrote sentence 6 beginning with

Because he wanted to simplify the system,

the next word should be

(1) the
(2) only
(3) that
(4) who
(5) Louis

4. Sentence 7: **Braille was only 15 years old when he invented his system; however, it was not widely used by the blind until 1854.**

Which of the following is the best way to write the underlined portion of this sentence? If you think the original is the best way, choose option (1).

(1) his system; however, it was
(2) his system, and it was
(3) his system. It was
(4) his system, but it was
(5) his system; in fact, it was

Items 5 to 8 are based on the following passage.

(1) People who care about their health are concerned about the presence of chemical additives in their foods. (2) Chemicals are added to foods to prevent flavor and color changes, to enhance flavors, and for keeping liquids and soft foods well mixed. (3) Most additives that we eat and drink are safe for consumption. (4) However, some have been poorly tested or are unsafe if they are eaten in large amounts. (5) Of special concern is the color dyes added primarily to beverages, candy, and baked goods. (6) Most artificial colorings are synthetic chemicals that do not occur in nature. (7) Avoiding unsafe dyes is difficult because they do not require them to be listed by name on food labels. (8) Most cancer-causing additives have been outlawed, but suggestions of cancer risk have been associated with most coloring agents. (9) Until these chemicals have been proven safe, they should be avoided whenever possible.

5. Sentence 2: **Chemicals are added to foods to prevent flavor and color changes, to enhance flavors, and for keeping liquids and soft foods well mixed.**

What correction should be made to this sentence?

(1) replace to prevent with that prevent
(2) remove the comma after changes
(3) replace to enhance with enhancing
(4) replace for keeping with to keep
(5) no correction is necessary

6. Sentence 3: **Most <u>additives that we eat and drink are safe</u> for consumption.**

Which of the following is the best way to write the underlined portion of this sentence? If you think the original is the best way, choose option (1).

(1) additives that we eat and drink are safe
(2) additives that we ate and drank are safe
(3) additives that we eat and drink is safe
(4) additives that are eaten and drunk are safe
(5) additives are safe

7. Sentence 5: **Of special concern is the color dyes added primarily to beverages, candy, and baked goods.**

What correction should be made to this sentence?

(1) change <u>is</u> to <u>are</u>
(2) change <u>is</u> to <u>was</u>
(3) insert <u>which</u> after <u>dyes</u>
(4) insert <u>to</u> after <u>and</u>
(5) no correction is necessary

8. Sentence 7: **Avoiding unsafe dyes is difficult <u>because they do not require them to be listed</u> by name on food labels.**

Which of the following is the best way to write the underlined portion of this sentence? If you think the original is the best way, choose option (1).

(1) because they do not require them to be listed
(2) although they do not require them to be listed
(3) because they are not listed
(4) because they do not list them
(5) because you do not list them

<u>Items 9 to 12</u> are based on the following passage.

(1) One of the most exciting years in the history of baseball was 1941. (2) The New York Yankees won the American League pennant by 17 games over the Boston Red Sox. (3) The Brooklyn Dodgers won a tight race for the National League pennant. (4) The first Dodgers-Yankees World Series lasted only five games; meanwhile, it was probably the most competitive five-game Series in history. (5) Each team won one of the first two games. (6) Then Brooklyn lost Game 3 of the Series when pitcher Freddie Fitzsimmons left the game with a fractured kneecap after pitching seven scoreless innings. (7) The Dodgers lost Game 4 when catcher Mickey Owens let a third strike get by him in the ninth inning with two out. (8) His error let the Yankees back in the game and they finally won it 7 to 4. (9) The next day Tiny Bonham who pitched a four-hitter to clinch the Series for the Yankees.

9. Sentences 2 and 3: **The New York Yankees won the American League pennant by 17 games over the Boston Red Sox. The Brooklyn Dodgers won a tight race for the National League pennant.**

The most effective combination of sentences 2 and 3 would include which of the following groups of words?

(1) Boston Red Sox, but the Brooklyn Dodgers
(2) Boston Red Sox, for the Brooklyn Dodgers
(3) Boston Red Sox while the Brooklyn Dodgers
(4) Boston Red Sox because the Brooklyn Dodgers
(5) Boston Red Sox; therefore, the Brooklyn Dodgers

10. Sentence 4: **The first Dodgers-Yankees World Series lasted only <u>five games; meanwhile, it was probably</u> the most competitive five-game Series in history.**

Which of the following is the best way to write the underlined portion of this sentence? If you think the original is the best way, choose option (1).

(1) five games; meanwhile, it was probably

(2) five games; therefore, it was probably

(3) five games; finally, it was probably

(4) five games; in addition, it was probably

(5) five games; nonetheless, it was probably

11. Sentence 8: **His error let the Yankees back in the game and they finally won it 7 to 4.**

What correction should be made to this sentence?

(1) insert a comma after <u>game</u>

(2) change <u>and</u> to <u>yet</u>

(3) replace <u>they</u> with <u>the Dodgers</u>

(4) replace <u>won</u> with <u>had won</u>

(5) replace <u>it</u> with <u>the game</u>

12. Sentence 9: **The next day Tiny Bonham who pitched a four-hitter to clinch the Series for the Yankees.**

What correction should be made to this sentence?

(1) change <u>who</u> to <u>which</u>

(2) remove <u>who</u>

(3) change <u>pitched</u> to <u>will pitch</u>

(4) insert a comma after <u>four-hitter</u>

(5) no correction is necessary

Answers are on page 339.

UNIT 3 – MECHANICS

Credit: Courtesy Apple Computers

Objective

In this unit, you will learn to

- **capitalize appropriate words within a sentence**

- **use commas properly in different kinds of sentences**

- **use apostrophes to form possessive words and contractions**

- **recognize the differences between closely related words**

- **improve your spelling using several suggested techniques**

Unit III Progress Chart

Mechanics

Use the following chart to keep track of your work. When you complete a lesson, circle the number of questions you anwered correctly in the Lesson Exercise. The numbers in color represent scores at a level of 80% or better.

Lesson	Page		
		CHAPTER 1: Capitalization	
1	143	Proper Nouns and Proper Adjective	1 2 3 4 5
2	146	Titles of People and Addresses	1 2 3 4 5
3	149	Time, Dates, Seasons, Special Events and	
		Historical Eras	1 2 3 4 5
	151	**Chapter 1 Review**	1 2 3 4 5 6 7 8 9 10 11 12 13 14 15
		CHAPTER 2: Punctuation	
1	157	Ending Punctuation	1 2 3 4 5
2	158	Commas between Items in a Series	1 2 3 4 5
3	161	Commas and Semicolons in Compound Sentences	1 2 3 4 5
4	163	Commas After Introductory Elements	1 2 3 4 5
5	166	Commas with Sentence Interrupters	1 2 3 4 5
6	168	Avoiding Overuse of Commas	1 2 3 4 5
	170	**Chapter 2 Review**	1 2 3 4 5 6 7 8 9 10 11 12 13 14 15
		CHAPTER 3: Spelling	
1	177	Basic Spelling Rules	1 2 3 4 5
2	179	Contractions	1 2 3 4 5
3	181	Possesives	1 2 3 4 5
4	184	Homonyms	1 2 3 4 5 6 7 8 9 10
5	191	Spelling List	1 2 3 4 5 6 7 8 9 10
	199	**Chapter 3 Review**	1 2 3 4 5 6 7 8 9 10 11 12 13 14 15

Chapter 1
Capitalization

Proper Nouns and Proper Adjectives

A word is "capitalized" if it begins with a capital letter. The first word of a sentence is always capitalized to show that it is the beginning of a sentence. Other words in a sentence may also be capitalized, as illustrated in the following sentence.

Niagara Falls, a famous landmark located between the United States and Canada, recedes about 2 1/2 feet each year.

All of the underlined words in this sentence are nouns. Some of these nouns are capitalized, whereas, others are not.

Rule 1: A noun that does not name a specific person, place, or thing is called a **common noun**. Do not capitalize a common noun.

Rule 2: A noun that names a specific person, place, or thing is called a **proper noun**. Capitalize all proper nouns.

Chart 1 gives examples of common and proper nouns.

Chart 1 Common and Proper Nouns		
Category	**Common Noun**	**Proper Noun**
People	generals	George C. Marshall Omar Bradley
	presidents	Ronald Reagan Gerald Ford
	actresses/actors	Jane Fonda Bill Cosby
	races of people	African-American Caucasian (Note: do not capitalize color distinction: blacks, whites)
	nationalities of people	Mexican Japanese
	languages of people	Spanish English
	religions of people	Lutheran Catholic

Chart 1 Common and Proper Nouns (cont'd)		
Category	**Common Noun**	**Proper Noun**
Places	states	Minnesota Oregon
	countries	Germany Brazil
	cities	Atlanta London
	continents	South America Asia
	islands	Hawaiian Islands Greenland
	bodies of water	Lake Michigan Mississippi River
	mountains	Atlas Mountains Alps
	sections of the country	the West the Midwest (Note: Do not capitalize these words when they indicate direction: We were traveling west.)
Things	awards	Emmy Award Pulitzer Prize
	buildings	White House Sears Tower
	clubs, organizations, and associations	Chicago Bears American Dental Association
	government departments and agencies	Senate Defense Department
	businesses and companies	American Airlines International Business Machines (Note: Capitalize abbreviations: IBM)
	boats, trains, airplanes, and spacecraft	*Concorde* *U.S.S. Arizona*
	newspapers and magazines	*Chicago Tribune* *Time*
	movies, books, television shows, plays, and songs	*The Scarlet Letter* *Romancing the Stone*

A proper noun may have more than one word, as shown by some of the examples in Chart 1. Capitalize all the words naming a particular thing, place, or person.

NOTE: Short words (such as *the, a, in,* and *of)* are not capitalized, unless they are the first or last word of a title.

<u>Of</u> Mice and Men (novel)

Strait <u>of</u> Magellen (body of water)

<u>The</u> Sound <u>of</u> Music (movie title)

In addition to proper nouns, certain kinds of adjectives should always be capitalized. An adjective is a word that describes, or modifies, a noun or pronoun.

Rule 3: When an adjective is formed from a proper noun, it is called a **proper adjective**. Always capitalize a proper adjective.

Proper Noun:	Proper Adjective:
Africa	African tribe
China	Chinese food
the South	Southern hospitality
Greece	Greek mythology

NOTE: The proper adjective is capitalized but not the common noun that it modifies.

Marie Curie was a French <u>scientist</u> famous for her work on radioactivity.

Lesson 1 Exercise

Directions: Edit the following sentences to correct all capitalization errors. Not all of the sentences have errors.

1. The Mediterranean Sea is part of the atlantic ocean.
2. Louisa May Alcott is the American author of *Little Women*.
3. The presidential medal of freedom was established in 1963.
4. In 1865 a Steamboat explosion on the Mississippi River killed 1,653 people.
5. Using his research ship *calypso*, Jacques Cousteau explored the oceans.

Answers are on page 340.

Titles of People and Addresses

A person's name is always capitalized because it is a proper noun. Another word that is always capitalized is the pronoun *I* because it refers to one particular person—the person who is speaking or writing.

> John and <u>I</u> plan to visit every baseball stadium in the country over the next five years.

A person's title is almost as important as a person's name. In certain situations, the titles of people are capitalized.

Rule 1: Capitalize a title when it is used as part of a person's name.

> A famous book about raising children was written by <u>Doctor</u> Benjamin Spock.

> <u>President</u> Paula Larsen will be the keynote speaker this evening.

Do not capitalize a title if it is not used as part of a person's name.

> The <u>doctor</u> who wrote a famous book about raising children was Benjamin Spock.

> Paula Larsen, <u>president</u> of Datacom Inc., will be the keynote speaker this evening.

However, a title that refers to the highest official of a country is always capitalized.

> Franklin D. Roosevelt, the 32nd <u>President</u> of the United States, was reelected to the presidency three times.

Rule 2: Capitalize family titles, words such as *aunt*, *uncle*, *mother*, and *father* when they are used as part of a person's name. Also, capitalize these titles when they are used alone in place of the person's name.

We borrowed <u>Uncle Ray's</u> fishing equipment for the weekend.

Is <u>Dad</u> planning to attend the family reunion?

Do not capitalize words that indicate family relationships when they are not part of a person's name.

Our <u>uncle</u> has an expensive collection of rods and reels.

I have two <u>sisters</u> and one <u>brother</u>.

An address is the name of a specific place. Because proper names of places are capitalized, the words that make up an address are also capitalized.

Rule 3: The names of streets and highways (and their abbreviations) in a specific address are capitalized.

Common Noun:	Proper Noun:
street	Madison St.
freeway	Marquette Fwy.
avenue	Greenfield Ave.
road	Barker Rd.

The president lives on <u>Pennsylvania Avenue</u> in Washington D.C.

The <u>street</u> was closed for repairs.

Rule 4: Capitalize the words *north*, *south*, *east*, and *west* when used as part of an address or when referring to a particular region of a country or state.

The package was sent to 343 <u>East</u> 600 <u>North</u>, Provo, Utah.

Bob's parents live in <u>Northern California</u>.

Mike and Lee Ann will go to Disneyworld when they travel through the <u>South</u> this summer.

NOTE: Do not capitalize *north*, *south*, *east*, *west* when they refer to direction.

We will travel <u>east</u> this winter to visit relatives.

Directions: Edit the following sentences to correct all capitalization errors. Not all of the sentences have errors.

1. The first woman to be appointed to the Supreme Court was justice Sandra Day O'Conner.
2. Carnegie Hall is located at Seventh avenue and fifty-seventh street in New York City.
3. My doctor received his medical degree from Harvard Medical School.
4. While he was president of the United States, Herbert Hoover gave all of his paychecks to charity.
5. Our new offices are located at 5310 south gardner road.

Answers are on page 340.

Time, Dates, Seasons, Special Events, and Historical Eras

Rule 1: Use small capital letters for the abbreviations A.D. and B.C. in reference to a specific date. Also use small capital letters for the abbreviations A.M. and P.M., which show the time of day.

In A.D. 600 the Arabs used coffee beans as a medicine.

The first American satellite lifted off the launchpad at 1:44 P.M. on December 6, 1957.

Rule 2: Capitalize the months of the year, the days of the week, holidays, and special events.

Memorial Day is celebrated on the last Monday in May.

Many communities hold special programs during Fire Prevention Week.

NOTE: The names of the seasons are not capitalized.

A winter vacation is a good way to renew your energy.

There is nothing imaginary about spring fever.

Rule 3: Capitalize the names of historical periods and events.

The Renaissance produced a revival of art, literature, and learning in Europe.

During World War I the United States and Russia were allies.

NOTE: A numerical designation of a historical period is not capitalized.

Two of the most tumultuous decades in the twentieth century were the twenties and the sixties.

Directions: Edit the following sentences to correct all capitalization errors. Not all of the sentences have errors.

1. The word "monday," referring to the second day of the week, was taken from an Old English word that meant "moon's day."
2. The first day of Winter is usually on December 21.
3. Socrates, the famous Greek philosopher, died in 399 B.C., but his ideas had a major influence on the philosophers of the christian era.
4. Babe Ruth Day was held on april 27, 1947, at Yankee Stadium.
5. Charles Dickens was one of the most popular novelists of the nineteenth century.

Answers are on page 340.

Chapter 1 Review

Directions: Edit the following sentences to correct all capitalization errors. Not all of the sentences have errors.

1. Cary Grant never won an academy award.
2. Cleopatra was an egyptian queen born in 69 B.C.
3. Peter O'Toole starred in the 1962 movie *Lawrence Of Arabia.*
4. Old Kent Road and Park Lane are two of the squares in the british version of Monopoly.
5. Thanksgiving Day was designated as a national holiday by President Abraham Lincoln.
6. I asked my brother where he was going this Summer for his vacation.
7. The Tokyo World Lanes Bowling Center in japan has 252 lanes.
8. Sherlock Holmes's landlady was mrs. Hudson.
9. The *Apollo 11* landed on the moon at 4:17 p.m. on July 20, 1969.
10. Lucas Santomee was the first known Black doctor in the United States.
11. The sneak preview of Kevin Costner's new movie will be shown on friday.
12. Janice Williams, our union representative, will be here on may 17 to discuss the new retirement plan.
13. Drive south six blocks until you come to Westlake road.
14. Marc Golov, one of the supervisors of the sales staff, invited professor Scott Pierpont to present a workshop on customer service.
15. Desmond Tutu of south Africa won the Nobel Peace Prize in the year 1984.

Check your answers. Correct answers are on pages 340-341. If you have all 15 answers correct, go on to Chapter 2. If you have any answers incorrect, find the item number on the chart below and review that lesson before you go on.

Review...	If you missed Item Number ...
Lesson 1	1, 2, 3, 4, 7, 10
Lesson 2	8, 13, 14, 15
Lesson 3	5, 6, 9, 11, 12

GED REVIEW 6

Directions: The following items are based on paragraphs that contain numbered sentences. Some of the sentences contain errors in usage, sentence structure, and mechanics. A few sentences, however, may be correct as written. Read each paragraph and then answer the items that follow it.

Items 1 to 4 are based on the following passage.

(1) Iceland, a land of ice and volcanoes, is one of the five countries known to the world as scandinavia. (2) The others include, Norway, Sweden, Finland, and Denmark. (3) The high, rugged mountains of Iceland are covered with ice and snow. (4) Suprisingly, the country of Iceland is quite warm for a land so far North. (5) The average temperature in July is about 52 degrees while the January average is nearly 32 degrees. (6) Because conditions are harsh, more than half of the 250,000 people who live in the country are in southern Iceland in or near the city of Reykjavik. (7) The most important natural resource is Fish; as a matter of fact, the fishing industry employs between 15 and 20 percent of the work force.

1. Sentence 1: **Iceland, a land of ice and volcanoes, is one of the five countries known to the world as scandinavia.**

   What correction should be made to this sentence?

   (1) change <u>is</u> to <u>are</u>
   (2) change <u>countries</u> to <u>Countries</u>
   (3) change <u>world</u> to <u>World</u>
   (4) change <u>scandinavia</u> to <u>Scandinavia</u>
   (5) no correction is necessary

2. Sentence 4: **Surprisingly, the country of Iceland is quite warm for a land so far North.**

   What correction should be made to this sentence?

   (1) change <u>country</u> to <u>Country</u>
   (2) change <u>Iceland</u> to <u>iceland</u>
   (3) change <u>is</u> to <u>are</u>
   (4) change <u>land</u> to <u>Land</u>
   (5) change <u>North</u> to <u>north</u>

3. Sentence 6: **Because conditions are harsh, more than half of the 250,000 people who live in the <u>country are in southern Iceland in or near the city</u> of Reykjavik.**

Which of the following is the best way to write the underlined portion of this sentence? If you think the original is the best way, choose option (1).

(1) country are in southern Iceland in or near the city

(2) Country are in southern Iceland in or near the city

(3) country are in Southern Iceland in or near the city

(4) country are in southern iceland in or near the city

(5) country are in southern Iceland in or near the City

4. Sentence 7: **The most important natural resource is Fish; as a matter of fact, the fishing industry employs between 15 and 20 percent of the work force.**

What correction should be made to this sentence?

(1) replace <u>natural resource</u> with <u>Natural Resource</u>

(2) change <u>Fish</u> to <u>fish</u>

(3) change the semicolon after <u>Fish</u> to a comma

(4) replace <u>fishing industry</u> with <u>Fishing Industry</u>

(5) no correction is necessary

<u>Items 5 to 9</u> are based on the following passage.

(1) Ms. Wright is pleased to announce that our sales convention this Summer will be held in Los Angeles, California. (2) We will be staying at the Beverly Crest Hotel. (3) During the week, you will have plenty of time to see the sites. (4) As a group, we will be going to Dodger Stadium on Thursday evening. (5) The stadium is at 1000 Elysian Park Avenue, and the game starts at 7:35 p.m. (6) You can get there from our Hotel by driving east on Sunset Boulevard. (7) There are no meetings on Friday, but you are free to do whatever you wish. (8) Several of us are making plans to go to Disneyland in Anaheim. (9) If you would be interested in seeing a play, Mr. Lewis will be making ticket reservations to see *A Streetcar Named Desire* by Tennessee Williams.

5. Sentence 1: **Ms. Wright is pleased to announce that our sales convention this Summer will be held in Los Angeles, California.**

What correction should be made to this sentence?

(1) change <u>is</u> to <u>are</u>

(2) replace <u>sales convention</u> with <u>Sales Convention</u>

(3) change <u>Summer</u> to <u>summer</u>

(4) change <u>held</u> to <u>holded</u>

(5) no correction is necessary

6. Sentence 5: **The stadium is at 1000 Elysian Park Avenue, and the game starts at 7:35 p.m.**

What correction should be made to this sentence?

   (1) change <u>stadium</u> to <u>Stadium</u>
   (2) change <u>Avenue</u> to <u>avenue</u>
   (3) remove the comma after <u>Avenue</u>
   (4) change <u>p.m.</u> to <u>P.M.</u>
   (5) no correction is necessary

7. Sentence 6: **You can get there from <u>our Hotel by driving east on Sunset Boulevard.</u>**

Which of the following is the best way to write the underlined portion of this sentence? If you think the original is the best way, choose option (1).

   (1) our Hotel by driving east on Sunset Boulevard
   (2) our hotel by driving east on Sunset Boulevard
   (3) our Hotel, by driving east on Sunset Boulevard
   (4) our Hotel by driving East on Sunset Boulevard
   (5) our Hotel by driving east on sunset boulevard

8. Sentence 7: **There are no meetings on Friday, but you are free to do whatever you wish.**

What correction should be made to this sentence?

   (1) change <u>Friday</u> to <u>friday</u>
   (2) change the comma after <u>Friday</u> to a semicolon
   (3) remove the comma after <u>Friday</u>
   (4) change <u>but</u> to <u>so</u>
   (5) change <u>but</u> to <u>for</u>

9. Sentence 9: **If you would be interested in seeing a play, Mr. Lewis will be making ticket reservations to see *A Streetcar Named Desire* by Tennessee Williams.**

What correction should be made to this sentence?

   (1) change <u>play</u> to <u>Play</u>
   (2) remove the comma after <u>play</u>
   (3) replace <u>ticket reservations</u> with <u>Ticket Reservations</u>
   (4) change <u>A</u> to <u>a</u>
   (5) no correction is necessary

Items 10 to 12 are based on the following passage.

(1) Doctor Jerry L. Martin, a member of the American Medical association, will be at the parents' meeting on Wednesday to discuss the importance of measles immunizations. (2) The disease, which was once on the brink of extinction, has been making a comeback in the United States. (3) In a letter to all parents, Melissa Kronick, one of the directors of Midway hospital, emphasized the importance of the immunization program to keep health costs down. (4) Many parents choose not to vaccinate their children because full vaccination costs approximately $65. (5) Ms. Kronick emphasized that hospital care alone for a child with measles costs an average of $7,000. (6) It is a sad fact that a 2-year-old child living in mexico city is more likely to receive up-to-date immunizations than the same-age child living in the United States.

10. Sentence 1: **Doctor Jerry L. Martin, a member of the American Medical association, will be at the parents' meeting on Wednesday to discuss the importance of measles immunizations.**

What correction should be made to this sentence?

(1) change <u>member</u> to <u>Member</u>
(2) change <u>Medical</u> to <u>medical</u>
(3) change <u>association</u> to <u>Association</u>
(4) change <u>measles</u> to <u>Measles</u>
(5) no correction is necessary

11. Sentence 3: **In a letter to all parents, Melissa Kronick, one of the directors of Midway hospital, emphasized the importance of the immunization program to keep health costs down.**

What correction should be made to this sentence?

(1) change <u>parents</u> to <u>Parents</u>
(2) change <u>directors</u> to <u>Directors</u>
(3) change <u>hospital</u> to <u>Hospital</u>
(4) replace <u>immunization program</u> with <u>Immunization Program</u>
(5) no correction is necessary

12. Sentence 6: **It is a sad fact that a 2-year-old child living <u>in mexico city is more likely</u> to receive up-to-date immunizations than the same-age child living in the United States.**

Which of the following is the best way to write the underlined portion of this sentence? If you think the original is the best way, choose option (1).

(1) in mexico city is more likely
(2) in Mexico City is more likely
(3) in Mexico city is more likely
(4) in mexico city, is more likely
(5) in mexico city are more likely

Answers are on page 341.

Chapter 2
Punctuation

Preview

Directions: Edit the following sentences to correct all errors in punctuation. Not all of the sentences have errors.

1. The first passengers to ride in a hot-air balloon were, a duck, a sheep, and a rooster.
2. The Statue of Liberty has special meaning to the United States for, it was a gift from France.
3. Did you know that Memphis was also the name of an ancient city in Egypt.
4. Because it didn't fade, purple was the ancient color of royalty.
5. The honest, reliable, candidate got the job.

Check your answers. Correct answers are on page 341. If you have all five answers correct, do the Chapter 2 Review on page 170. If you have fewer than five answers correct, study Chapter 2 beginning with Lesson 1.

Ending Punctuation

A complete sentence has a subject and a verb and sounds complete. It also begins with a capital letter and ends with a mark of punctuation. The punctuation mark used at the end of the sentence depends on the kind of sentence.

A statement and most commands end with a period.

> There are more than 20,000 kinds of fish. (statement)

> General George Custer was 26 years old when he fought in the Civil War. (statement)

> Bring scratch paper and a pencil to the meeting. (command)

> Make two copies of the report. (command)

A question ends with a question mark.

> Will you be attending Mr. Renfro's retirement party?

> What movie did you see last night?

A statement or command that shows strong emotion ends with an exclamation point.

> I demand a cash refund immediately!

> Call for an ambulance!

Lesson 1 Exercise

Directions: Edit the following sentences to correct all errors in punctuation. Not all of the sentences have errors.

1. An evergreen tree keeps its leaves during the winter!
2. That woman needs a doctor immediately.
3. Do you already have your tickets?
4. Is Karl looking for a new job.
5. Do not send the letter until Ms. Martin reads it?

Answers are on pages 341-342.

Commas Between Items in a Series

A **series** is a list of similar things arranged one after another. Many sentences include words or phrases arranged in a series.

Whale oil is used to make <u>shampoos</u> <u>cosmetics</u> and <u>waxes</u>.

The underlined words are similar because they all name things that contain whale oil. When these items follow one another, commas are used to separate them. Here is the correctly punctuated sentence.

Whale oil is used to make shampoo<u>s,</u> cosmetic<u>s,</u> and waxes.

Rule 1: Use commas to separate three or more items in a series.

Because <u>dogs and cats</u> like garlic, it is added to most canned pet food.

(Because only two items are listed [*dogs and cats*], commas are not used.)

If you lived in a town named "Warren," you might live in Ohio<u>,</u> Pennsylvania<u>,</u> Illinois<u>,</u> Texas<u>,</u> or Arizona.

(Commas are used in this sentence because more than three items [*Ohio, Pennsylvania, Illinois, Texas,* or *Arizona*] are listed.)

Notice that commas are not placed before the first item or after the last item in a series.

INCORRECT: Lasers can, perform surgery, split gems, and scan prices, at grocery checkout counters.

CORRECT: Lasers can perform surgery, split gems, and scan prices at grocery checkout counters.

NOTE: When pairs of words are listed in a series, each pair of words is treated as one item.

> For dinner, the cafeteria offered <u>bread and butter</u>, <u>soup and salad</u>, <u>macaroni and cheese</u>, <u>pork and beans</u>, <u>apples and oranges</u>, and <u>cake and ice cream</u>.

Rule 2: When all the items in a series are joined by a connecting word such as <u>and</u>, <u>or</u>, or <u>nor</u>, do not use commas.

> Was Neptune <u>or</u> Mars <u>or</u> Zeus the Roman god of the sea?

> Thin people are more sensitive to the weather because they have less calciu<u>m and</u> wate<u>r and</u> fewer vitamins in their bodies.

Rule 3: A word that describes a noun is an **adjective**. When more than one adjective in a row describes a noun, commas are often used to separate the adjectives.

Use commas to separate adjectives in a row only if the sentence sounds "right" in these two circumstances:

- **if the order of the adjectives is changed, and**

- **if the word** *and* **is inserted between the adjectives.**

> Yesterday was a <u>cold, windy</u> day.

The sentence sounds "right" in both cases:

> Yesterday was a <u>windy, cold</u> day.

> Yesterday was a <u>cold and windy</u> day.

In this example, the adjectives should not be separated.

> Mike could not afford the insurance on the <u>red sports</u> car.

The sentence sounds "wrong" in both cases:

> Mike could not afford the insurance on the <u>sports red</u> car.

> Mike could not afford the insurance on the <u>red and sports</u> car.

Never put a comma between the last adjective and the noun it describes.

INCORRECT: Yesterday was a cold, windy, day.

CORRECT: Yesterday was a cold, windy day.

Lesson 2 Exercise

Directions: Edit the following sentences to correct all punctuation errors. Not all of the sentence have errors.

1. *Sputnik 5* orbited the earth with two dogs, and six mice aboard.
2. The tired hungry travelers could not find a motel room.
3. The colors of the flag of the United States are red and white and blue.
4. George Washington, Abraham Lincoln, and James Monroe, were descendants of England's King Edward I.
5. The five basic swimming strokes are, the crawl, the backstroke, the breaststroke, the butterfly, and the sidestroke.

Answers are on page 342.

Commas and Semicolons in Compound Sentences

Two sentences that express related ideas can be joined to form a **compound sentence**.

> SENTENCE 1: Every state has an official state bird.

> SENTENCE 2: New Mexico's state bird is the road runner.

> COMPOUND SENTENCE: Every state has an official state bird, and New Mexico's is the road runner.

In the last example, the word *and* is used to join the two separate sentences. Each part of the compound sentence is a complete idea.

Words that join the complete ideas in a compound sentence are called **coordinators**. In Unit 2, you learned three correct methods for joining the ideas in a compound sentence.

Method 1: Join two complete ideas with a coordinate conjunction (*and, but, or, nor, for,* or *yet*) preceded by a comma. The comma shows where the first complete idea ends.

> In 1816 the first glued postage stamp was issued, and it pictured Queen Victoria.

> In the United States, 1816 is known as "the year there was no summer," for it had one of the coldest summers on record.

For more information about the purpose and meaning of the coordinate conjunctions, see the chart on page 000.

Method 2: Join two complete, related sentences with only a semicolon.

> A mural is any kind of painting done on a wall; prehistoric murals of reindeer and bison have been found in Spain and France.

> Boston is the capital city of Massachusetts; it is also the nearest major U.S. seaport to Europe.

Method 3: Join two complete ideas with a semicolon and a coordinating word or phrase followed by a comma. Some examples of coordinators that can be used with a semicolon are *however, furthermore, meanwhile, indeed, in fact,* and *as a result.* For a more complete listing, see page 000.

> Jupiter is the largest planet in the solar system; in fact, it is larger than all the other planets combined.

> Erosion is caused by the movement of weathered particles of earth; for example, a river slowly carves out a valley as it moves soil and rock fragments.

Lesson 3 Exercise

Directions: Edit the following sentences to correct all punctuation errors. Not all of the sentences have errors.

1. Charles Dodgson wrote *Alice's Adventures in Wonderland* but he used the pen name Lewis Carroll.
2. Scientists count the number of times fish cough, for it helps scientists determine the amount of water pollution.
3. June is known as the month of romance and marriage however, it also has one of the highest crime rates.
4. Our universe contains billions of galaxies, the nearest is two billion light-years away.
5. Approximately fifty spacecraft have flown near the moon, or visited it since 1958.

Answers are on page 342.

Commas After Introductory Elements

The following sentences begin with a word or a phrase that introduces the sentence but is not part of the main idea. These words are called **introductory elements.**

Yes, a bank can provide the current exchange rate of a nation's currency.

In space travel terms, "burnout" is the point where a rocket in flight has used up its fuel.

Because temperatures of -127° F have been recorded there, Vostok in Antarctica is called "the coldest place in the world."

Introductory elements usually are followed by a comma. The following rules illustrate the kinds of introductory elements that require a comma after them.

Rule 1: Words such as *well, yes, no, why, still, oh, however, therefore, consequently, besides, yet,* and *nevertheless* that appear at the beginning of a sentence are followed by a comma.

Yes, it is possible to make oil from sawdust.

Oh, I didn't know that some plants can eat insects.

Therefore, some dolphins can jump higher than over 20 feet above the water.

However, the "lead" in a pencil is really "graphite."

Rule 2: When a writer uses *direct address*, he or she addresses remarks directly to a person or to a group of people. Names or expressions used in direct address are always followed by a comma.

<u>Ladies and gentlemen,</u> here is tonight's speaker.

<u>Gary,</u> did you reserve a room for Friday night?

Rule 3: Introductory elements are usually followed by a comma.

<u>Wanting to win the race,</u> the runner ran faster.

<u>As a matter of interest to those of us who like to put off things until tomorrow,</u> National Procrastination Week is the first week in March.

NOTE: If the introductory phrase is short (fewer than four words) and does not have a verb, the comma may be omitted unless the sentence would be misread without it. However, it is never wrong to put a comma after an introductory element.

<u>In 1849</u> Walter Hunt invented the safety pin.

<u>In the past,</u> age was respected.

In the first example above, a comma is not needed after *In 1849*. In the second example, a comma is needed after *In the past,* so that the word *past* is not misread as an adjective modifying the noun *age*.

Rule 4: A complex sentence has a main idea and a subordinate idea. The subordinate idea is a sentence fragment—it does not express a complete thought. When a subordinate idea appears at the beginning of the sentence, it is followed by a comma.

<u>Because Walter Hunt saw a need,</u> he invented the safety pin.

<u>Before milk bottles were invented,</u> customers had to provide their own containers.

When the subordinate idea comes after the main idea, do not use a comma to separate the two ideas.

The critics hated the movie <u>because it ran over three hours.</u>

Don't make the announcement <u>until Ms. Porter hears the news.</u>

Directions: Edit the following sentences to correct all punctuation errors. Not all of the sentences have errors.

1. When it began in 1860 the Pony Express mail service took ten days to deliver a letter from Missouri to California.
2. Linda the meeting is about to begin.
3. No she did not realize that the package arrived this morning.
4. To explain our new billing procedures we will send letters to our regular customers.
5. In 1962 John Glenn became the first American to orbit the earth.

Answers are on page 342.

Commas with Sentence Interrupters

Words other than adjectives sometimes are used to explain or describe nouns and pronouns in a sentence.

> The Marianas Trench, <u>the lowest spot on the ocean floor,</u> measures 36,200 feet below sea level.

The phrase, <u>the lowest spot on the ocean floor,</u> describes the proper noun, *Marianas Trench.* The phrase is not essential to the meaning of the sentence, but it provides additional information about the noun that is the subject of the sentence. Phrases that "interrupt" a sentence in this way are set off by commas from the rest of the sentence.

If the interrupting phrase is omitted, the sentence still can express a complete idea.

> The Marianas Trench measures 36,200 feet below sea level.

If a word or phrase that describes a noun in a sentence is essential to the meaning of the sentence, it is not set off by commas.

> The condition <u>bronchitis</u> often develops in children after a cold or a sore throat.

> The employee <u>who has the highest sales total for the weekend</u> will receive a $100 bonus.

The name of the condition *bronchitis* is needed to make the meaning of the first sentence clear. Without it, you would not know which condition the sentence is about. Similarly, the meaning of the second sentence would be unclear without the words *who has the highest sales total for the weekend.* The phrase tells you which employee will receive a bonus. Because both interruptors are "needed," they are not set off by commas.

The main idea of a sentence may be interrupted also by an expression that simply adds a "pause" to the sentence.

> The White House, <u>incidentally,</u> has 132 rooms.

The word *incidentally* does not add information to the main idea of the sentence.

The following are some common expressions that are used as sentence inter-rupters.

I believe	on the contrary	after all
I think	on the other hand	by the way
I hope	incidentally	of course
I know	in my opinion	for example
I am sure	nevertheless	however

Many people, <u>I am sure,</u> take the course at night.

Your book, <u>by the way,</u> is selling very well.

Like other interrupters that are not essential to the main idea of the sen-tence, these expressions are set off by commas from the rest of the sentence.

NOTE: These expressions are only interrupters when they are not part of the main idea of the sentence. In the following sentence, *I know* is the subject and verb of the sentence, therefore, commas should not be used.

<u>I know</u> that chemicals inside a firefly's body make it glow.

Lesson 5 Exercise

Directions: Edit the following sentences to correct all punctuation errors. Not all of the sentences have errors.

1. Major earthquakes can cause dangerous side effects such as a tsunami a gigantic sea wave.
2. Landslides of course are also associated with earthquakes.
3. I believe, that most earthquakes occur along fractures in the earth's crust.
4. These fractures, also known as faults, are not always visible at the surface of the earth.
5. The Richter scale a system for measuring an earthquake's magnitude, was developed during the 1930s.

Answers are on page 342.

Avoiding Overuse of Commas

The comma is the most frequently misused punctuation mark. Many writers use commas unnecessarily or incorrectly. Lessons 2 through 5 presented several ways to use commas to punctuate sentences. This lesson will explain when not to use commas and will review the rules you learned in the previous lessons.

Chart 2 illustrates the most frequently made mistakes involving commas. Compare the underlined portions of the correct and incorrect samples sentences as you read each pair of sentences.

Chart 2 Frequent Comma Errors		
Rule	**Incorrect**	**Correct**
Do not use a comma between the subject and verb of a sentence.	The speed of a computer, is measured in billionths of a second called nanoseconds.	The speed of a computer is measured in billionths of a second called nanoseconds.
Do not use commas with compound subjects or verbs	Robert E. Peary, and his team reached the North Pole in 1909.	Robert E. Peary and his team reached the North Pole in 1909.
	The first U.S. oil gusher blew in 1901, and sent oil 200 feet into the air.	The first U.S. oil gusher blew in 1901 and sent oil 200 feet into the air.
Do not use a comma between two complete sentences that are not joined by a coordinator.*	John Philip Sousa was a famous bandmaster of the U.S. Marine Band, he wrote "The Washington Post March."	John Philip Sousa was a famous bandmaster of the U.S. Marine Band, and he wrote "The Washington Post March."
Do not use a comma after a coordinator that joins two complete sentences.	The United States possesses a large energy resource for, it has about one-third of the world's coal deposits.	The United States possesses a large energy resource, for it has about one-third of the world's coal deposits.

Chart 2 Frequent Comma Errors (cont'd.)		
Rule	**Incorrect**	**Correct**
Do not use a comma before the first item or after the last item in a series.	Biology is the branch of science that studies <u>the,</u> history, physical characteristics, and habits of plants and animals.	Biology is the branch of science that studies <u>the</u> history, physical characteristics, and habits of plants and animals.
	Two eggs, three cups of flour, one cup of sugar, and a teaspoon of baking soda<u>, were</u> needed for the recipe.	Two eggs, three cups of flour, one cup of sugar, and a teaspoon of baking soda <u>were</u> needed for the recipe.
Do not use a comma to separate an adjective from the noun it describes, or modifies.	A bassoon is a woodwind instrument with a long, curved<u>, mouth-piece.</u>	A bassoon is a woodwind instrument with a long, curved <u>mouth-piece.</u>
Do not use a comma before the word <u>because.</u>	Avoid eating fatty foods<u>, because</u> they can raise your cholesterol level.	Avoid eating fatty foods <u>because</u> they can raise your cholesterol level.

*NOTE: These ideas could also be written as separate sentences or joined by a semicolon.

Lesson 6 Exercise

Directions: Edit the following sentences to correct all punctuation errors. Not all of the sentences have errors.

1. In 1920 Elmer Smith of the Cleveland Indians, hit the first grand-slam home run in a World Series game.
2. Dave DeBusschere played basketball for the New York Knicks, and pitched for the Chicago White Sox.
3. While playing water polo, one team wears white caps, the opposing team wears blue caps.
4. The game of tennis may be played on grass, clay, asphalt, or wood.
5. Bruce Jenner, Bill Toomey, and Rafer Johnson, were all Olympic decathlon winners.

Answers are on pages 342-343.

Chapter 2 Review

Directions: Edit the following sentences to correct all punctuation errors. Not all of the sentences have errors.

1. Both the Bering Sea, and the Coral Sea are in the Pacific Ocean.
2. An owl can turn its head 270 degrees but, it cannot move its eyes.
3. In Thailand people give presents on their own birthdays rather than receive them.
4. The first, automobile license plates were required by the state of New York.
5. More dinosaur bones have been found in Canada by the way than in any other place in the world.
6. John please order six cartons of paper for the copier.
7. Some birds that live in high places are, condors, eagles, and hawks.
8. Is it true that more than 60,000 bees can live in a single hive.
9. The first space shuttle flight took place in 1981, and, John Young was the commander.
10. During the Middle Ages, Europeans thought garlic would frighten away vampires.
11. A scientist, who studies weather, is called a meteorologist.
12. One hot dog, or one ounce of cheese, or one chicken drumstick provides seven grams of protein.
13. Water is more dangerous than wind during a hurricane, ninety percent of all hurricane-related deaths are caused by storm surges and floods.
14. Deserts are found on every continent, in fact, deserts cover about one-third of the land area of the earth.
15. Pike's Peak, a famous tourist attraction in Colorado stands 14,110 feet high.

Check your answers. Correct answers are on page 343. If you have 15 answers correct, go on to Chapter 3. If you have any answers incorrect, find the item number on the chart below and review that lesson before you go on.

Review...	If you missed Item Number ...		
Lesson 1	8		
Lesson 2	4, 7, 12		
Lesson 3	2, 9, 13, 14		
Lesson 4	3, 6, 10		
Lesson 5	5, 11, 15		
Lesson 6	1		

GED REVIEW 7

Directions: The following items are based on paragraphs that contain numbered sentences. Some of the sentences contain errors in usage, sentence structure, and mechanics. A few sentences, however, may be correct as written. Read each paragraph and then answer the items that follow it.

Items 1 to 6 are based on the following passage.

(1) Doctors who provide health care for young children are concerned about the increasing number of low-weight births in the United States. (2) Low birth weight is linked to higher rates of, cerebral palsy, mental retardation, and respiratory problems. (3) Since it is the leading predictor of infant deaths researchers are anxious to identify the causes and find ways to prevent it. (4) One cause of low birth weight is drug use. (5) According to recent estimates, about 20 percent of the babies, born in major American cities, are affected by their mothers' drug use. (6) Drug use, however is not the chief cause of low birth weight. (7) Because low birth weight occurs more often among the poor, Doctors are convinced that the leading causes are the mother's poor health and inadequate care during pregnancy. (8) Advanced medical technology cannot prevent this common problem. (9) Resources must be spent on educating women about proper health care before and during pregnancy.

1. Sentence 2: **Low birth weight is linked to higher rates of, cerebral palsy, mental retardation, and respiratory problems.**

   What correction should be made to this sentence?

   (1) insert a comma after <u>Low</u>
   (2) change <u>is</u> to <u>are</u>
   (3) remove the comma after <u>of</u>
   (4) remove the comma after <u>retardation</u>
   (5) no correction is necessary

2. Sentence 3: **Since it is the leading predictor of infant deaths researchers are anxious to identify the causes and find ways to prevent it.**

   What correction should be made to this sentence?

   (1) insert a semicolon after <u>deaths</u>
   (2) insert a comma after <u>deaths</u>
   (3) insert a comma after <u>anxious</u>
   (4) insert a comma after <u>causes</u>
   (5) no correction is necessary

3. Sentence 5: **According to recent estimates, about 20 percent of the babies, born in major American cities, are affected by their mothers' drug use.**

Which of the following is the best way to write the underlined portion of this sentence? If you think the original is the best way, choose option (1).

(1) babies, born in major American cities, are
(2) babies, born in major american cities, are
(3) babies born in major American cities, are
(4) babies, born in major American cities are
(5) babies born in major American cities are

4. Sentence 6: **Drug use, however is not the chief cause of low birth weight.**

What correction should be made to this sentence?

(1) remove the comma after <u>use</u>
(2) change the comma after <u>use</u> to a semicolon
(3) insert a comma after <u>however</u>
(4) insert a comma after <u>chief</u>
(5) no correction is necessary

5. Sentence 7: **Because low birth weight occurs more often <u>among the poor, Doctors are convinced</u> that the leading causes are the mother's poor health and inadequate care during pregnancy.**

Which of the following is the best way to write the underlined portion of this sentence? If you think the original is the best way, choose option (1).

(1) among the poor, Doctors are convinced
(2) among the poor; Doctors are convinced
(3) among the poor, doctors are convinced
(4) among the poor Doctors are convinced
(5) among the poor Doctors, are convinced

6. Sentences 8 and 9: **Advanced medical technology cannot prevent this common problem. Resources must be spent on educating women about proper health care before and during pregnancy.**

The most effective combination of sentences 8 and 9 would include which of the following groups of words?

(1) problem, and resources
(2) problem, or resources
(3) problem; afterward, resources
(4) problem; instead, resources
(5) problem; for example, resources

Items 7 to 12 are based on the following passage.

(1) If you are a fan of American musicals, you probably know and appreciate the music of George Gershwin. (2) Gershwin's talents have long been celebrated, but few realize the role his older brother Ira played in his success. (3) Ira originally named Israel Gershvin, was born in 1896. (4) He began writing lyrics for his brother's music in 1918; however he used the name Arthur Francis at first in order not to capitalize on George's reputation. (5) Ira quickly made a name for himself. (6) He was the first song lyricist to win a Pulitzer Prize. (7) George and him shared the award in 1932 for the show *Of Thee I Sing*. (8) He collaborated with his brother on more than 20 Broadway musicals and motion pictures. (9) After George's dealth in 1937, Ira worked with many other composers including Jerome Kern, and Harold Arlen. (10) His last project, finished in 1983, involved writing lyrics to his brother's music used in the musical *My One And Only*.

7. Sentence 3: **Ira originally named Israel Gershvin, was born in 1896.**

   What correction should be made to this sentence?

   (1) insert a comma after Ira
   (2) remove the comma after Gershvin
   (3) change the comma after Gershvin to a semicolon
   (4) change was to were
   (5) no correction is necessary

8. Sentence 4: **He began writing lyrics for his brother's music in 1918; however he used the name Arthur Francis at first in order not to capitalize on George's reputation.**

   Which of the following is the best way to write the underlined portion of this sentence? If you think the original is the best way, choose option (1).

   (1) in 1918; however he used
   (2) in 1918, however he used
   (3) in 1918, however, he used
   (4) in 1918; however, he used
   (5) in 1918 however he used

9. Sentences 5 and 6: **Ira quickly made a name for himself. He was the first song lyricist to win a Pulitzer Prize.**

   The most effective combination of sentences 5 and 6 would include which of the following groups of words?

   (1) himself, so he was
   (2) himself, yet he was
   (3) himself; nevertheless, he was
   (4) himself; meanwhile, he was
   (5) himself; in fact, he was

10. Sentence 7: **George and him shared the award in 1932 for the show *Of Thee I Sing*.**

    What correction should be made to this sentence?

    (1) change him to he
    (2) change award to Award
    (3) insert a comma after 1932
    (4) change Of to of
    (5) no correction is necessary

11. Sentence 9: **After George's death in 1937, Ira worked with many other composers including Jerome Kern, and Harold Arlen.**

What correction should be made to this sentence?

(1) remove the comma after <u>1937</u>
(2) insert a comma after <u>many</u>
(3) change <u>composers</u> to <u>Composers</u>
(4) remove the comma after <u>Kern</u>
(5) insert a comma after <u>and</u>

12. Sentence 10: **His last project, finished in 1983, involved writing lyrics to his brother's music used in <u>the musical My One And Only.</u>**

Which of the following is the best way to write the underlined portion of this sentence? If you think the original is the best way, choose option (1).

(1) the musical *My One And Only*
(2) the Musical *My One And Only*
(3) the musical *my One And Only*
(4) the musical *My One and Only*
(5) the musical *My one and only*

Answers are on pages 343-344.

Chapter 3
Spelling

Basic Spelling Rules

It is often difficult to figure out the spelling of a word in English by listening to the way it is pronounced. However, some basic spelling rules can be used when changing the form of a word, such as changing a singular noun to a plural noun or a present-tense verb to a past-tense verb.

Noun Forms

Rule 1: In general, plural nouns are formed by adding *s* or *es* to the singular form. The *-es* ending is used with nouns that end in *s, x, ch,* or *sh.*

> bench/benches   box/boxes   crash/crashes

Rule 2: Singular nouns that end in *y* preceded by a consonant are pluralized by replacing the *y* with *i* and adding *es.*

> mystery/mysteries   party/parties   baby/babies

NOTE: Nouns that end in *y* preceded by a vowel usually form their plurals by the addition of *s.*

> key/keys   pulley/pulleys   turkey/turkeys

Rule 3: Some nouns are the same in the singular and the plural form.

> sheep/sheep   deer/deer   fish/fish

Rule 4: Many singular nouns that end in *f* are pluralized by changing the *f* to *v* and adding *es.*

> shelf/shelves   leaf/leaves   calf/calves

The plural of many nouns ending in *fe* is formed by changing the *f* to *v* and adding *s.*

> knife/knives   life/lives   wife/wives

Verb Forms

Rule 5: To form the *-ing* tense of a verb that ends in *e*, drop the final *e*.

        wave/waving   decide/deciding   precede/preceding

Rule 6: Many one-syllable verbs that end in a single consonant require doubling of the consonant in the past tense and in the *-ing* tense.

        wrap/wrapped/wrapping   pet/petted/petting

        fit/fitted/fitting   plot/plotted/plotting

        strum/strummed/strumming

    NOTE: This rule applies to words that contain short vowel sounds, as illustrated in the above examples.

Lesson 1 Exercise

Directions: Edit the following sentences to correct all errors in spelling. Not all of the sentences have errors.

1. Recent discoverys in medicine have changed the way people live.
2. In many citys, trolleys once ran along main streets.
3. The train was delayed for several hours before arriving at the station.
4. The candidates runing for office appeared to have similar views.
5. Many families are prepareing their children for school by helping them learn to read.

Answers are on page 344.

Contractions

A **contraction** is a word formed by combining two words into one and omitting one or more letters. An apostrophe is used to show where the letter or letters have been omitted in forming a contraction.

<u>Are not</u> Saturn and Uranus the two planets that have rings?

<u>Aren't</u> Saturn and Uranus the two planets that have rings?

<u>Do not</u> hide under a tree during a thunderstorm.

<u>Don't</u> hide under a tree during a thunderstorm.

Chart 3 lists frequently used contractions and the words that form them.

Chart 3 Contractions and the Words That Form Them					
is not	isn't	cannot	can't	could have	could've
are not	aren't	could not	couldn't	should have	should've
was not	wasn't	should not	shouldn't	must have	must've
		do not	don't		
		does not	doesn't		
he is	he's	she is	she's	it is	it's
he has	he's	she has	she's	it has	it's
he will	he'll	she will	she'll	it will	it'll
he would	he'd	she would	she'd	it would	it'd
you are	you're	we are	we're	they are	they're
you have	you've	we have	we've	they have	they've
you will	you'll	we will	we'll	they will	they'll
you would	you'd	we would	we'd	they would	they'd
I am	I'm	who is	who's		
I have	I've	let us	let's		
I will	I'll	of the clock	o'clock		
I would	I'd	what is	what's		

NOTE: When using contractions, be careful not to confuse them with possessive pronouns.

CONTRACTION: <u>It's</u> (it is) estimated that the average American uses the telephone 940 times a year.

POSSESSIVE PRONOUN: Because of <u>its</u> agility, an antelope can outrun a horse.

CONTRACTION: Cinnamon sticks are a unique spice, for <u>they're</u> (they are) rolls of bark from a tree.

POSSESSIVE PRONOUN: Spiders do not get caught in <u>their</u> own webs.

CONTRACTION: When you eat cauliflower, <u>you're</u> (you are) actually eating undeveloped flower blossoms.

POSSESSIVE PRONOUN: Eating fish can lower <u>your</u> chance of getting heart disease.

NOTE: When you use contractions, do not put the apostrophe in the wrong place. Remember that the apostrophe in a contraction always replaces the missing letter or letters.

INCORRECT: <u>Was'nt</u> Aristotle the first person to believe the earth was round?

CORRECT: <u>Wasn't</u> Aristotle the first person to believe the earth was round?

Lesson 2 Exercise

Directions: Edit the following sentences to correct all errors in contractions. Not all of the sentences have errors.

1. A person cant jump higher than a horse.
2. Kangaroos carry they're young in a pouch.
3. Although it drinks huge amounts of water, a camel does'nt sweat.
4. Its a fact that light travels about 186,000 miles per second.
5. Isn't a seven-sided figure called a heptagon?

Answers are on page 344.

Possessives

In this lesson, you will learn how to use an **apostrophe** ('), the punctuation mark that is used to show possession, ownership, or belonging.

A rainbow is made up of raindrops that reflect the <u>sun's</u> rays.

Weather <u>forecasters'</u> predictions are becoming more accurate.

<u>Jack's</u> apartment is under rent control.

The underlined words in the above sentences are called **possessive nouns**. They show that something belongs to something or someone else.

Follow the rules below when using apostrophes to form possessive nouns.

Rule 1: If a noun is singular, add an apostrophe and the letter *s* to form the possessive.

Singular Noun	Singular Possessive
catcher	catcher's mitt
driver	driver's license
boss	boss's office

NOTE: If a singular noun ends in *s*, the possessive is formed in the same way—by adding an apostrophe and the letter *s* to the noun. (See the last example given above.)

Rule 2: If a noun is plural and ends in *s*, add only the apostrophe after the *s* to form the possessive.

Plural Noun	Possessive Noun
players	players' uniforms
boys	boys' club
workers	workers' wages

Rule 3: If the noun is plural and does not end in *s*, add an apostrophe and the letter *s* to form the possessive.

Plural Noun	Possessive Noun
people	people's choice
men	men's suits
mice	mice's tails

Pronouns that show possession or ownership are called **possessive pronouns**. Notice the spelling of the underlined possessive pronouns in the sentence below.

Is this <u>your</u> sweater or <u>mine</u>?

The following is a list of possessive pronouns.

my	his	our
mine	her	ours
your	hers	their
yours	its	theirs

Rule 4: Never use an apostrophe with a possessive pronoun. The possessive pronoun *its* and *your* are frequently misspelled. Remember, if an apostrophe is used with a pronoun, the word is a contraction, not a possessive pronoun.

A camel stores fat in <u>its</u> hump.

<u>It's</u> possible for a deep sea clam to live more than 100 years.

The thickness of the vocal cords determine the pitch of <u>your</u> voice.

Be sure to see the Great Sandy Desert when <u>you're</u> in Australia.

In the above examples, *its* and *your* are possessive pronouns, and *It's* and *you're* are contractions.

Directions: Edit the following sentences to correct all errors in the spelling of possessive nouns and pronouns. Not all of the sentences have errors.

1. The only flag on the moon is our's.
2. American's spend over $1 billion on gum each year.
3. In 1897 girls' bicycles cost about $29.00 each.
4. The anaconda, the world's largest snake, squeezes it's prey to death and swallows it whole.
5. Beethovens' music teacher criticized him for not having musical talent.

Answers are on page 344.

Homonyms

Many words in the English language are pronounced the same way but are spelled differently and have different meanings. These words are called **homonyms**.

In writing, using the wrong homonym is considered a spelling error.

INCORRECT: Are you <u>already</u> to go?

CORRECT: Are you <u>all ready</u> to go?

In this example the word *already* means *previously*. This would not make sense in the sentence. The correct homonym is *all ready*, meaning *everyone ready* or *completely ready*.

Do not confuse the meaning of a sentence by choosing the wrong homonym. The following list of paired words contains homonyms that are frequently confused. Study the list carefully.

1. **a lot** very much (two words)
   allot to assign

   <u>A lot</u> of people don't like to eat liver.

   Each month I <u>allot</u> $50 for entertainment.

2. **already** previously
   all ready completely ready; everyone ready

   He had <u>already</u> seen that movie.

   They are <u>all ready</u> to sign the contract.

3. **all right** entirely correct
   alright no such word. Do not use.

   It is <u>all right</u> to borrow my car.

4. **altar** a table or stand in a church
   alter to change

   The candles were burning on the <u>altar</u>.

   We had to <u>alter</u> our vacation plans.

5. **altogether** completely or entirely
   all together everyone or everything in the same place

   She wasn't <u>altogether</u> unhappy with the job.

   The family was <u>all together</u> for the holidays.

6. **born** brought forth by birth
   borne carried or endured

   He was <u>born</u> in October.

   The hockey player has <u>borne</u> many injuries.

7. **bored** not interested
   board a piece of wood; a group of people who set policy

   I was <u>bored</u> with the conversation.

   He drove a nail into the <u>board</u>.

   The <u>board</u> will meet next Tuesday.

8. **brake** device used to stop a machine
   break to fracture or shatter

   The engineer pulled the <u>brake</u> to stop the train.

   Did you <u>break</u> the window?

9. **Capitol** the name of a building in Washington, D.C.
   capitol the name for a building in which a state legislature meets
   capital a city that is the official seat of government in a state

   The lobby in the <u>Capitol</u> is being repaired.

   The debate was held at the <u>capitol</u>.

   The <u>capital</u> of California is Sacramento.

10. **coarse** rough
    course part of a meal; subject studied in school; path or route

    The wallpaper had a coarse feel to it.

    We were served salad for the first course.

    My math course is difficult but challenging.

    We looked for a straight course home.

11. **complement** something that completes something else
    compliment a flattering remark

    Fresh spices can complement any dish.

    How well can you take a compliment?

12. **council** a group of people that gives advice or makes decisions
    counsel to give advice

    The council elected a new president.

    The teacher tried to counsel the disruptive student.

13. **dessert** the final course of a meal
    desert to leave; a dry region

    For health reasons, eat fresh fruit for dessert.

    Don't desert me now!

    The desert has many unusual kinds of plants.

14. **herd** a group of cattle
    heard the past tense of the verb *hear*

    The herd ran toward the river.

    I heard the violinist practicing.

15. **it's** contraction for "it is"
    its possessive pronoun

    It's only a matter of time.

    The company puts its symbol on every product it makes.

16. **lead** a metal; graphite in a pencil
    led the past tense of the verb *lead*

    Lead is a very heavy metal.

    I broke the lead in this pencil.

    The lost hunters were led to safety.

17. **miner** a worker in a mine
    minor of little importance; under legal age

    The miner wore a hard hat for protection.

    After a few minor repairs, my car was as good as new.

    A child is protected by laws because he or she is a minor.

18. **passed** the past tense of the verb *pass*
    past time that has gone by; beyond in position

    Yesterday I passed my driver's test.

    The team has not won many games in the past.

    He walked past me without saying a word.

19. **peace** the absence of war or strife
    piece a part of something

    He longed for some peace and quiet.

    She offered her guests a second piece of cake.

20. **plain** clear; ordinary; an expanse of level land
    plane a tool; an airplane

    She made her reasons for retiring very plain.

    The house was decorated with plain furniture.

    Cattle grazed on the open plain.

    We used a plane to smooth the door's edge.

    The plane landed on the runway.

21. **principal** head of a school; the most important, main
    principle a basic law or rule of action

    The <u>principal</u> enjoyed talking to the students.

    The <u>principal</u> character died at the end of the play.

    The experiment demonstrated the scientific <u>principle</u>.

22. **role** a part in a play
    roll to move by turning over and over; a list of names; a round piece of bread

    Who played the <u>role</u> of the butler?

    The children liked to <u>roll</u> down the steep hill.

    The teacher called the <u>roll</u> at the beginning of class.

    I like to eat a <u>roll</u> with my soup.

23. **sight** vision; range of vision; spectacle
    site a piece of land or location

    He valued his <u>sight</u> more than his hearing.

    There wasn't a gas station in <u>sight</u>.

    The parade was quite a <u>sight</u>.

    We looked for a quiet <u>site</u> for our picnic.

24. **stationery** writing paper
    stationary in a fixed or unmoving position

    Karen bought another box of <u>stationery</u>.

    The desks in the classroom were <u>stationary</u>.

25. **there** in that place; expletive
    their possessive pronoun (belonging to them)
    they're contraction for "they are"

    We are to wait for the bus over <u>there</u>.

    <u>There</u> is no newspaper today.

    <u>Their</u> dog has run away.

    <u>They're</u> home by now.

26. to indicates direction; used before a verb
too also; excessive
two the number 2

Go <u>to</u> the right at the corner.

I'm anxious <u>to</u> ride in your new car.

Do you like to eat cold pizza, <u>too</u>?

I was <u>too</u> excited to sleep.

Lunch costs <u>two</u> dollars in the cafeteria.

27. waist a part of the body
waste to squander; unused material

She wore a leather belt around her <u>waist</u>.

Be careful not to <u>waste</u> food.

A current problem is the disposal of toxic <u>waste</u>.

28. weak not strong
week period of seven days

I felt <u>weak</u> after surgery.

I'll call you next <u>week</u>.

29. weather the climate
whether if

The <u>weather</u> in Florida is usually warm.

I asked <u>whether</u> I should finish the work.

30. who's contraction meaning who is or who has
whose possessive pronoun showing ownership

<u>Who's</u> the best pitcher in the major leagues?

I'm not sure <u>whose</u> idea it was.

31. your possessive pronoun (belonging to you)
you're contraction for "you are"

Are these <u>your</u> car keys?

<u>You're</u> going to Jan's birthday party, aren't you?

Directions: Edit the following sentences to correct all homonym errors. Not all of the sentences have errors. Some sentences may have more than one error.

1. It is alright to smile when you receive a complement.

2. In the passed, I have always eaten dessert because I enjoy sweets a lot.

3. Whose car were you driving when you had that minor accident?

4. Next weak the counsel will decide what coarse of action to take.

5. Don't waist stationery because it is to expensive.

6. The policy board will meet altogether next Thursday.

7. Its my opinion that our principal goal should be to improve employee morale.

8. Your roll at the meeting will be to make sure everyone has a chance to speak.

9. I want to make it plain that we cannot afford to waist any time at the meeting.

10. Ms. Conover herd that the new site for our office had all ready been decided.

Answers are on pages 344-345.

Spelling List

Good spellers are made, not born. That means that practice is necessary if you want to become a better speller. The following are several ways you can eliminate spelling errors from your writing.

1. **Refer to your dictionary as you write.** Do not guess at the spelling of a word. If you are unsure of the spelling of a word, look it up. To do this, you must first decide how you think the word should be spelled. If the word does not appear in the dictionary according to your initial spelling, try a different spelling. Continue to do this until you find the right word.

2. **Proofread and edit your writing.** When you have finished writing, check your work for errors in capitalization, punctuation, and spelling. Read line by line, looking at each word separately. Concentrate on misused homonyms, troublesome words, incorrect contractions and possessive words, and wrong letters.

3. **Record the errors you make frequently.** Make a special spelling note-book. Divide a page into two columns. In the first column, record the error and underline the letters that were incorrect. In the second column, write the correct spelling of the word. In addition to your dictionary, use this notebook as a reference source when you write.

4. **Learn the spelling rules and devise memory tricks.** Study the spelling rules in this lesson carefully. Remember, however, that most spelling rules have exceptions. It helps to learn these exceptions by devising "memory tricks" for those words that you spell incorrectly most often. These words should also be recorded in your spelling notebook.

For example, let's say that you have difficulty remembering the spelling of the word *believe*. You wonder if it should be spelled bel*ie*ve or bel*ei*ve. When you locate this word in a dictionary, you will find its correct spelling is *believe*. To help you remember to write the *i* before the *e* you might say

Eve couldn't bel<u>ieve</u> her luck.

OR

Never bel<u>ie</u>ve a <u>lie</u>.

You have taken the word apart, found that it has a word within a word, and devised a memory trick to remember the spelling of this word.

5. As you learn to spell words, use this method:

See it
> **Say it**
>> **Try it**

To use this method, follow these steps:

1. Picture the word in your mind.
2. Say the word slowly, dividing it into its syllables (parts). Say it several times.

   su-per-in-ten-dent

3. Write the word without looking at a list or a dictionary. Check to make sure you have written the word correctly. Then write it several more times.

Study Chart 4, a list of frequently misspelled words. These words, and forms of these words, should be reviewed as part of your preparation for the GED Writing Skills Test.

Chart 4 The Master List of Frequently Misspelled Words

a lot	agree	arrange	bottle
ability	aisle	arrangement	bottom
absence	all right	article	boundary
absent	almost	artificial	brake
abundance	already	ascend	breadth
accept	although	assistance	breath
acceptable	altogether	assistant	breathe
accident	always	associate	brilliant
accommodate	amateur	attempt	building
accompanied	American	attendance	bulletin
accomplish	among	attention	bureau
accumulation	amount	audience	burial
accuse	analysis	August	buried
accustomed	analyze	author	bury
ache	angel	automobile	bushes
achieve	angle	autumn	business
achievement	annual	auxiliary	cafeteria
acknowledge	another	available	calculator
acquaintance	answer	avenue	calendar
acquainted	antiseptic	awful	campaign
acquire	anxious	awkward	capital
across	apologize	bachelor	capitol
appropriate	apparatus	balance	captain
address	apparent	balloon	career
addressed	appear	bargain	careful
adequate	appearance	basic	careless
advantage	appetite	beautiful	carriage
advantageous	application	because	carrying
advertise	apply	become	category
advertisement	appreciate	before	ceiling
advice	appreciation	beginning	cemetery
advisable	approach	being	cereal
advise	appropriate	believe	certain
aerial	approval	benefit	changeable
affect	approve	benefited	characteristic
affectionate	approximate	between	charity
again	argue	bicycle	chief
against	arguing	board	choose
aggravate	argument	bored	chose
aggressive	arouse	borrow	cigarette

Chart 4 The Master List of Frequently Misspelled Words (cont'd.)

circumstance	consistent	descent	earnest
congratulate	continual	describe	easy
citizen	continuous	description	ecstasy
clothes	controlled	desert	ecstatic
clothing	controversy	desirable	education
coarse	convenience	despair	effect
coffee	convenient	desperate	efficiency
collect	conversation	dessert	efficient
college	corporal	destruction	eight
column	corroborate	determine	either
comedy	council	develop	eligibility
comfortable	counsel	development	eligible
commitment	counselor	device	eliminate
committed	courage	dictator	embarrass
committee	courageous	died	embarrassment
communicate	course	difference	emergency
company	courteous	different	emphasis
comparative	courtesy	dilemma	emphasize
compel	criticism	dinner	enclosure
competent	criticize	direction	encouraging
competition	crystal	disappear	endeavor
compliment	curiosity	disappoint	engineer
conceal	cylinder	disappointment	English
conceit	daily	disapproval	enormous
conceivable	daughter	disapprove	enough
conceive	daybreak	disastrous	entrance
concentration	death	discipline	envelope
conception	deceive	discover	environment
condition	December	discriminate	equipment
conference	deception	disease	equipped
congratulate	decide	dissatisfied	especially
confident	decision	dissection	essential
conquer	decisive	dissipate	evening
conscience	deed	distance	evident
conscientious	definite	distinction	exaggerate
conscious	delicious	division	exaggeration
consequence	dependent	doctor	examine
consequently	deposit	dollar	exceed
considerable	derelict	doubt	excellent
consistency	descend	dozen	except

Chart 4 The Master List of Frequently Misspelled Words (cont'd.)

exceptional	government	indispensable	laid
exercise	governor	inevitable	language
exhausted	grammar	influence	later
exhaustion	grateful	influential	latter
exhilaration	great	initiate	laugh
existence	grievance	innocence	leisure
exorbitant	grievous	inoculate	length
expense	grocery	inquiry	lesson
experience	guarantee	insistent	library
experiment	guess	instead	license
explanation	guidance	instinct	light
extreme	half	integrity	lightning
facility	hammer	intellectual	likelihood
factory	handkerchief	intelligence	likely
familiar	happiness	intercede	literal
fascinate	healthy	interest	literature
fascinating	heard	interfere	livelihood
fatigue	heavy	interference	loaf
February	height	interpreted	loneliness
financial	heroes	interrupt	loose
financier	heroine	invitation	lose
flourish	hideous	irrelevant	losing
forcibly	himself	irresistible	loyal
forehead	hoarse	irritable	loyalty
foreign	holiday	island	magazine
formal	hopeless	its	maintenance
former	hospital	it's	maneuver
fortunate	humorous	itself	marriage
fourteen	hurried	January	married
fourth	hurrying	jealous	marry
frequent	ignorance	journal	match
friend	imaginary	judgment	material
frightening	imbecile	kindergarten	mathematics
fundamental	imitation	kitchen	measure
further	immediately	knew	medicine
gallon	immigrant	knock	million
garden	incidental	know	miniature
gardener	increase	knowledge	minimum
general	independence	labor	miracle
genius	independent	laboratory	miscellaneous

Chart 4 The Master List of Frequently Misspelled Words (cont'd.)

mischief	once	persistent	prescription
mischievous	operate	personal	presence
misspelled	opinion	personality	president
mistake	opportune	personnel	prevalent
momentous	opportunity	persuade	primitive
monkey	optimist	persuasion	principal
monotonous	optimistic	pertain	principle
moral	origin	picture	privilege
morale	original	piece	probably
mortgage	oscillate	plain	procedure
mountain	ought	playwright	proceed
mournful	ounce	pleasant	produce
muscle	overcoat	please	professional
mysterious	paid	pleasure	professor
mystery	pamphlet	pocket	profitable
narrative	panicky	poison	prominent
natural	parallel	policeman	promise
necessary	parallelism	political	pronounce
needle	particular	population	pronunciation
negligence	partner	portrayal	propeller
neighbor	pastime	positive	prophecy
neither	patience	possess	prophet
newspaper	peace	possession	prospect
newsstand	peaceable	possessive	psychology
nickel	pear	possible	pursue
niece	peculiar	post office	pursuit
noticeable	pencil	potatoes	quality
obedient	people	practical	quantity
obstacle	perceive	prairie	quarreling
occasion	perception	precede	quart
occasional	perfect	preceding	quarter
occur	perform	precise	quiet
occurred	performance	predictable	quite
occurrence	perhaps	prefer	raise
ocean	period	preference	realistic
o'clock	permanence	preferential	realize
offer	permanent	preferred	reason
often	perpendicular	prejudice	rebellion
omission	perseverance	preparation	recede
omit	persevere	prepare	receipt

Chart 4 The Master List of Frequently Misspelled Words (cont'd.)			
receive	seminar	studying	undoubtedly
recipe	sense	substantial	United States
recognize	separate	succeed	university
recommend	service	successful	unnecessary
recuperate	several	sudden	unusual
referred	severely	superintendent	useful
rehearsal	shepherd	suppress	usual
reign	sheriff	surely	vacuum
relevant	shining	surprise	valley
relieve	shoulder	suspense	valuable
remedy	shriek	sweat	variety
renovate	siege	sweet	vegetable
repeat	sight	syllable	vein
repetition	signal	symmetrical	vengeance
representative	significance	sympathy	versatile
requirements	significant	synonym	vicinity
resemblance	similar	technical	vicious
resistance	similarity	telegram	view
resource	sincerely	telephone	village
respectability	site	temperament	villain
responsibility	soldier	temperature	visitor
restaurant	solemn	tenant	voice
rhythm	sophomore	tendency	volume
rhythmical	soul	therefore	waist
ridiculous	source	thorough	weak
right	souvenir	through	wear
role	special	title	weather
roll	specified	together	Wednesday
roommate	specimen	tomorrow	week
sandwich	speech	tongue	weigh
Saturday	stationary	toward	weird
scarcely	stationery	tragedy	whether
scene	statue	transferred	which
schedule	stockings	treasury	while
science	stomach	tremendous	whole
scientific	straight	tries	wholly
scissors	strength	truly	whose
season	strenuous	twelfth	wretched
secretary	stretch	twelve	
seize	striking	tyranny	

Lesson 5 Exercise

Directions: In each set of words, one or more words are misspelled. Circle the misspelled words and write the correct spelling of each word in the exercise.

1. abundence — alright
   adress — antiseptic
2. ascend — benefitted
   auxilary — breadth
3. calender — committment
   cheif — conscientious
4. coroborate — deceive
   critisism — dependant
5. dissappoint — exersice
   entrence — exhileration
6. Febuary — freind
   financier — government
7. grammer — imaginary
   hankerchief — manuever
8. newstand — ommission
   occassion — parallel
9. perserverance — rhythm
   representative — shephard
10. syllable — vacuumm
    unecessary — wierd

Answers are on page 345.

Chapter 3 Review

Chapter 3 Review

Directions: Edit the following sentences to correct all spelling errors. Not all of the sentences have errors.

1. The flea can jump a distance that is 130 times the height of it's body.
2. Many lives were lost in the war for independance from England.
3. The children have swiming lessons on Monday and tennis lessons on Tuesday.
4. The Caterpillar Club is an organization who's members have used parachutes to save their lives.
5. Every effort was made to accommodate the new principal.
6. The candidate doubted the voters would approve a raise in taxs.
7. Many whether satellites take pictures of cloud formations that surround the earth.
8. Solar energy is an efficeint way to use the sun's energy.
9. The committee's decision was the same as your's.
10. The council proposed puting parking meters in the alleys from Fourth Street to Broadway Avenue.
11. More people are buying frozen convenience foods than they ever have before.
12. On a librarys' shelves, rare books can be found under the number 090.
13. The developement of the Popsicle is credited to an 11-year-old boy.
14. I am surprised that you did'nt know about the recent job opening.
15. There is the stationary you ordered last month.

Check your answers. Correct answers are on pages 345-346. If you have 15 answers correct, go on to Test-Taking Strategies 3. If you have any answers incorrect, find the item number on the chart below and review that lesson before you go on.

Review...	If you missed Item Number ...
Lesson 1	3, 6, 10
Lessons 2 & 3	1, 4, 9, 12, 14
Lesson 4	5, 7, 15
Lesson 5	2, 8, 11, 13

GED Review 8

Directions: The following items are based on paragraphs that contain numbered sentences. Some of the sentences contain errors in usage, sentence structure, and mechanics. A few sentences, however, may be correct as written. Read each paragraph and then answer the items that follow it.

Items 1 to 4 are based on the following passage.

(1) Companies that recieve a great many telephone calls often use automated answering systems called *telephone trees*. (2) When a call is placed, the line is answered by a computer. (3) A persons' voice, previously recorded, directs the caller to press a number if the caller is using a touchtone phone. (4) If the number is pushed, the voice gives additional instructions and choices to help route the call to the appropriate office or staff member. (5) Although telephone trees are desirable because their efficient, many callers are annoyed by the amount of time spent waiting to talk to a living person. (6) Whether you like them or not, these systems are bound to increase in popularity since they are successful in cuting costs for business owners.

1. Sentence 1: **Companies that recieve a great many telephone calls often use automated answering systems called *telephone trees*.**

   Which of the following is the best way to write the underlined portion of this sentence? If you think the original is the best way, choose option (1).

   (1) Companies that recieve
   (2) Companys that recieve
   (3) Companies which recieve
   (4) Companies, that recieve
   (5) Companies that receive

2. Sentence 3: **A persons' voice, previously recorded, directs the caller to press a number if the caller is using a touchtone phone.**

   What correction should be made to this sentence?

   (1) change persons' to person's
   (2) remove the comma after recorded
   (3) replace to press with too press
   (4) insert a comma after number
   (5) change using to useing

3. Sentence 5: **Although telephone trees are desirable because their efficient, many callers are annoyed by the amount of time spent waiting to talk to a living person.**

What correction should be made to this sentence?

(1) change <u>Although</u> to <u>Allthough</u>
(2) change <u>desirable</u> to <u>desireable</u>
(3) change <u>their</u> to <u>they're</u>
(4) change <u>living</u> to <u>liveing</u>
(5) no correction is necessary

4. Sentence 6: **Whether you like them or not, these systems are bound to increase in popularity since they are successful in cuting costs for business owners.**

What correction should be made to this sentence?

(1) change <u>Whether</u> to <u>Weather</u>
(2) remove the comma after <u>not</u>
(3) change <u>increase</u> to <u>increasce</u>
(4) change <u>successful</u> to <u>sucessful</u>
(5) change <u>cuting</u> to <u>cutting</u>

Items 5 to 8 are based on the following passage.

(1) Have you ever wondered what causes an eclipse? (2) An eclipse occurs when one heavenly body, such as the sun or the moon, produce a shadow causing our view of another heavenly body to disappear. (3) An eclipse of the moon occurs when the sun, Earth, and moon form a straight line so that the Earth's shadow covers the moon. (4) Because all heavenly bodys are in constant motion, eclipses rarely last for more than a few minutes altogether. (5) Scientists can predict eclipses because the future movements of the sun, Earth, and moon can be mathematically calculated. (6) There predictions are very reliable; in fact, they usually forecast the time and place of eclipses many years in advance. (7) For example, scientists have already determined that a total eclipse of the sun will take place on August 11, 1999. (8) This eclipse, which will be able to be viewed from Central Europe, the middle east, and India, will last an approximate 2 minutes 23 seconds.

5. Sentence 2: **An eclipse occurs when one heavenly body, such as the sun or the <u>moon, produce a shadow causing our view</u> of another heavenly body to disappear.**

Which of the following is the best way to write the underlined portion of this sentence? If you think the original is the best way, choose option (1).

(1) moon, produce a shadow causing our view
(2) moon produce a shadow causing our view
(3) moon, produces a shadow causing our view
(4) moon, produce a shadow causeing our view
(5) moon, produce a shadow causing our veiw

6. Sentence 4: **Because all heavenly bodies are in constant motion, eclipses rarely last for more than a few minutes altogether.**

What correction should be made to this sentence?

(1) change Because to Becuase
(2) change bodys to bodies
(3) remove the comma after motion
(4) change altogether to all together
(5) no correction is necessary

7. Sentence 6: **There predictions are very reliable; in fact, they usually forecast the time and place of eclipses many years in advance.**

What correction should be made to this sentence?

(1) change There to They're
(2) change There to Their
(3) change reliable to relaible
(4) change the semicolon to a comma
(5) remove the comma after in fact

8. Sentence 8: **This eclipse, which will be able to be viewed from Central Europe, the middle east, and India, will last an approximate 2 minutes 23 seconds.**

What correction should be made to this sentence?

(1) remove the comma after eclipse
(2) change which to who
(3) replace middle east with Middle East
(4) change approximate to approxamate
(5) no correction is necessary

Items 9 to 12 are based on the following passage.

(1) If you were the first person to arrive at the scene of an accident, would you know what to do? (2) You're impulse might be to move any victims away from the site of the accident, but moving an injured person can cause more problems. (3) In most cases, first aid in an emergency should be limited to only those procedures necessary to prevent further injury or save a life. (4) Unless you have no other choice, don't move the victim until a doctor or police officer or paramedic arrives. (5) If an accident is a miner one, you must still watch all victims' reactions carefully for signs of shock. (6) Shock is a natural reaction to severe stress, either physical or emotional. (7) It's symptoms include skin that is cold and clammy, a weak and rapid pulse, eyes that appear to stare, restless behavior, nausea, extreme thirst, and faintness. (8) If a victim shows signs of shock, position the victim so that the head is lower than the rest of the body and keep the victim comfortably warm.

9. Sentence 2: **You're impulse might be to move any victims away from the site of the accident, but moving an injured person can cause more problems.**

What correction should be made to this sentence?

(1) change You're to Your
(2) change site to sight
(3) change accident to accedent
(4) remove the comma after accident
(5) change the comma to a semicolon

10. Sentence 3: **In most cases, first aid in an emergency should be limited to only those procedures necessary to prevent further injury or save a life.**

What correction should be made to this sentence?

(1) remove the comma after <u>cases</u>
(2) change <u>emergency</u> to <u>emergensy</u>
(3) replace <u>limited to</u> with <u>limited too</u>
(4) change <u>procedures</u> to <u>proceedures</u>
(5) no correction is necessary

11. Sentence 5: **If an accident is a miner one, you must still watch all victims' reactions carefully for signs of shock.**

What correction should be made to this sentence?

(1) change <u>miner</u> to <u>minor</u>
(2) remove the comma after <u>one</u>
(3) change <u>victims'</u> to <u>victim's</u>
(4) change <u>victims'</u> to <u>victims</u>
(5) change <u>carefully</u> to <u>carfully</u>

12. Sentence 7: <u>**It's symptoms include skin that is cold and clammy,**</u> **a weak and rapid pulse, eyes that appear to stare, restless behavior, nausea, extreme thirst, and faintness.**

Which of the following is the best way to write the underlined portion of this sentence? If you think the original is the best way, choose option (1).

(1) It's symptoms include skin that is cold and clammy,
(2) Its symptoms include skin that is cold and clammy,
(3) It's symptoms includes skin that is cold and clammy,
(4) It's symptoms include skin that are cold and clammy,
(5) It's symptoms include skin that is cold and clammy

Answers are on page 346.

Test-Taking Strategies 3

Your knowledge of mechanics will be tested in about 30 percent of the questions on Part I of the GED Writing Skills Test. To effectively answer these questions, you will need to organize your thinking. Following the 5-R method of editing.

Step 1	**Read**	Read the paragraph quickly for its meaning and writing style.
Step 2	**Reflect**	Reflect by looking for and underlining any errors within the paragraph.
Step 3	**Revise**	Read the first test item and the five choices. Decide which alternative identifies and corrects the error.
Step 4	**Reread**	Read the revised sentence with the selected correction.
Step 5	**Record**	Mark the number of the alternative that you have chosen. Then, move on to the next item.

To answer mechanics questions effectively, ask yourself these questions as you *reflect* in Step 2.

1. Are all the appropriate words capitalized correctly?

INCORRECT: The white house is on pennsylvania avenue in washington, d.c.

CORRECT: The White House is on Pennsylvania Avenue in Washington, D.C.

2. Are all words and sentences punctuated correctly?

INCORRECT: Diane likes jazz country and heavy metal music.

CORRECT: Diane likes jazz, country, and heavy metal music.

INCORRECT: As a matter of fact either idea would solve the problem.

CORRECT: As a matter of fact, either idea would solve the problem.

3. Are all words spelled correctly?

> INCORRECT: The pilot announced that our flight was on scedule.

> CORRECT: The pilot announced that our flight was on schedule.

Read the following paragraph. As you read and reflect, apply the mechanics questions listed above.

> (1) Using a rocket-powered airplane, captain Charles E. Yeager was the first person to break the sound barrier. (2) Because of the speed of the airplane a sonic boom was created. (3) This sound is nothing more than a shock wave which is caused by differences in air pressure. (4) The sonic boom has been an important part of the further development of supersonic plains.

You should have found one capitalization error (sentence 1), one punctuation error (sentence 2), and one spelling error (sentence 4). If you had difficulty finding these errors, you may need to review Unit 3 before doing the exercise for this lesson.

Directions: Read the following paragraph. As you read, ask yourself the three basic questions that are used when editing for mechanical errors. No sentence contains more than one error. Use the 5-R method of editing as you work through each question.

Items 1 to 5 are based on the following paragraph.

(1) Television networks rely upon ratings to determine the popularity of they're shows. (2) The A.C. Nielsen company is one of the most important firms that provides this sevice. (3) The Nielsen service includes over 1,200 homes across the United States. (4) On the basis of Census Bureau figures, certain households are selected as representitive of certain locations. (5) An audimeter, a machine that measures all TV set usage is placed in these homes. (6) It records when a TV set is turned on and the length of time each channel is used. (7) The audimeter is connected to a special phone line that retrieves the stored information. (8) This information is then processed by the companys computer, and within a few hours the ratings are ready for publication.

1. Sentence 1: **Television networks rely upon ratings to determine the popularity of they're shows.**

   What correction should be made to this sentence?

   (1) change <u>rely</u> to <u>relies</u>
   (2) insert a comma after <u>ratings</u>
   (3) replace <u>to</u> with <u>too</u>
   (4) change <u>they're</u> to <u>their</u>
   (5) no correction is necessary

2. Sentence 2: **The A.C. Nielsen company is one of the most important firms that provides this service.**

   What correction should be made to this sentence?

   (1) change <u>company</u> to <u>Company</u>
   (2) insert a comma after <u>most</u>
   (3) replace <u>that</u> with <u>whom</u>
   (4) change <u>provides</u> to <u>provide</u>
   (5) change the spelling of <u>service</u> to <u>servise</u>

3. Sentence 4: **On the basis of Census Bureau figures, certain households are selected as representitive of certain locations.**

What correction should be made to this sentence?

(1) remove the comma after <u>figures</u>
(2) change <u>are</u> to <u>is</u>
(3) insert a comma after <u>selected</u>
(4) change the spelling of <u>representitive</u> to <u>representative</u>
(5) no correction is necessary

4. Sentence 5: **An audimeter, a machine that measures all TV <u>set usage is placed in</u> these homes.**

Which of the following is the best way to write the underlined portion of this sentence? If you think the original is the best way, choose option (1).

(1) set usage is placed in
(2) set usage; is placed in
(3) set,usage is placed in
(4) set usage, is placed in
(5) set usage is placed, in

5. Sentence 8: **This information is then processed by the <u>companys computer, and</u> within a few hours the ratings are ready for publication.**

Which of the following is the best way to write the underlined portion of this sentence? If you think the original is the best way, choose option (1).

(1) companys computer, and
(2) companys computer and
(3) companys computer and,
(4) company's computer and
(5) company's computer, and

Answers are on page 346.

UNIT 3 REVIEW

Directions: The items in this review are based on paragraphs that contain numbered sentences. Some of the sentences contain errors in usage, sentence structure, or mechanics. A few sentences, however, may be correct as written. Read each paragraph and then answer the items that follow it.

Items 1 to 6 are based on the following paragraph.

(1) Our society has become increasengly obsessed with height. (2) Recent studies have showed that our stature may influence the jobs we get and the salaries we earn. (3) The Wall Street Journal reported the results of a study done by David Kurtz a marketing professor. (4) His study revealed that when 140 job recruiters had to make a choice between two equally qualified applicants, the applicant who was over 6 feet tall was hired more often than the applicant who's height was significantly under 6 feet. (5) In fact, 72 percent of the recruiters hired the taller person. (6) Taller people also began with higher starting salaries and received larger raises. (7) These results have been interpreted as a possible source of prejudice and employment discrimination. (8) Whatever the interpretation, height can be an important factor in employment decisions. (9) U.S. News And World Report has said that height bias is ".. a reality most must face at one time or another in their working lives."

1. Sentence 1: **Our society has become increasengly obsessed with height.**

   What correction should be made to this sentence?

   (1) change <u>Our</u> to <u>Our'</u>
   (2) change <u>has</u> to <u>have</u>
   (3) change the spelling of <u>increasengly</u> to <u>increasingly</u>
   (4) insert a comma after <u>increasengly</u>
   (5) no correction is necessary

2. Sentence 2: **Recent studies have showed that our stature may influence the jobs we get and the salaries we earn.**

   What correction should be made to this sentence?

   (1) change the spelling of <u>studies</u> to <u>studys</u>
   (2) change <u>have showed</u> to <u>have shown</u>
   (3) insert a comma after <u>showed</u>
   (4) insert a comma after <u>get</u>
   (5) change <u>salaries</u> to <u>salary's</u>

3. Sentence 3: **The Wall Street Journal reported the results of a study done by David Kurtz a marketing professor.**

Which of the following is the best way to write the underlined portion of this sentence? If you think the original is the best way, choose option (1).

(1) by David Kurtz
(2) by David Kurtz.
(3) by, David Kurtz
(4) by David Kurtz,
(5) by, David Kurtz,

4. Sentence 4: **His study revealed that when 140 job recruiters had to make a choice between two equally qualified applicants, the applicant who was over 6 feet tall was hired more often than the applicant who's height was significantly under 6 feet.**

What correction should be made to this sentence?

(1) insert a comma after <u>that</u>
(2) change <u>between</u> to <u>among</u>
(3) change the spelling of <u>applicants</u> to <u>aplicants</u>
(4) remove the comma after <u>applicants</u>
(5) change <u>who's</u> to <u>whose</u>

5. Sentence 6: **Taller people also began with <u>higher starting salaries and received</u> larger raises.**

Which of the following is the best way to write the underlined portion of this sentence? If you think the original is the best way, choose option (1).

(1) higher starting salaries and received
(2) higher starting salarys and received
(3) higher starting salaries, and received
(4) higher starting salaries; and received
(5) higher starting salaries and recieved

6. Sentence 9: **U.S. News And World Report has said that height bias is "... a reality most must face at one time or another in their working lives."**

What correction should be made to this sentence?

(1) change <u>And</u> to <u>and</u>
(2) insert a comma after <u>Report</u>
(3) replace <u>has said</u> with <u>have said</u>
(4) change <u>height</u> to <u>hieght</u>
(5) change <u>their</u> to <u>there</u>

(1) One of the fastest-growing industries in our nation is the fast-food business. (2) The results of a study conducted by the Newspaper Advertising Bureau showed that the average american over 12 years old eats in a fast-food restaurant at least 9 times a month. (3) Researchers who study buying trends conclude that fast-food restaurants are profitable because they fill a need.

(4) People patronize these types of restaurants because they are convenient, inexpensive and fast. (5) McDonald's for example, attempts to serve a typical meal of a hamburger, french fries, and a shake in about 50 seconds. (6) Burger King can broil a hamburger in 80 seconds and can produce over 700 Whoppers in an hour!

(7) Will the fast-food business continue to grow? (8) In 1966 McDonald's billboards boasted, "2 billion sold." (9) In 1991 the same signs claimed, "Over 80 billion served." (10) Marketing forecasts show that fast-food sales will likely continue increasing at a rapid rate.

7. Sentence 2: **The results of a study conducted by the Newspaper Advertising Bureau showed that the average american over 12 years old eats in a fast-food restaurant at least 9 times a month.**

   What correction should be made to this sentence?

   (1) change <u>Advertising</u> to <u>Advertizing</u>
   (2) change <u>Advertising</u> to <u>Advertiseing</u>
   (3) change <u>american</u> to <u>American</u>
   (4) insert a comma after <u>old</u>
   (5) no correction is necessary

8. Sentence 3: **<u>Researchers who study buying trends conclude</u> that fast-food restaurants are profitable because they fill a need.**

   Which of the following is the best way to write the underlined portion of this sentence? If you think the original is the best way, choose option (1).

   (1) Researchers who study buying trends conclude
   (2) Researchers, who study buying trends conclude
   (3) Researchers, who study buying trends, conclude
   (4) Researchers who study buying trends, conclude
   (5) Researchers who study buying trends conclude,

9. Sentence 4: **People patronize these types of restaurants because they <u>are convenient, inexpensive and fast.</u>**

   Which of the following is the best way to write the underlined portion of this sentence? If you think the original is the best way, choose option (1).

   (1) are convenient, inexpensive and fast.
   (2) are convenient, inexpensive, and fast.
   (3) are convenient inexpensive and fast.
   (4) are, convenient, inexpensive and fast.
   (5) are convenient, inexpensive and; fast.

10. Sentence 5: **McDonald's for example, attempts to serve a typical meal of a hamburger, french fries, and a shake in about 50 seconds.**

What correction should be made to this sentence?

(1) insert a comma after McDonald's
(2) remove the comma after example
(3) change the spelling of attempts to attemps
(4) change attempts to attempt
(5) insert a comma after shake

11. Sentences 8 & 9: **In 1966 McDonald's billboards boasted, "2 billion sold." In 1991 the same signs claimed, "Over 80 billion served."**

The most effective combination of sentences 8 and 9 would include which of the following groups of words?

(1) because in 1991 they claimed
(2) while in 1991 they claimed
(3) so that in 1991 they claimed
(4) consequently in 1991 they claimed
(5) in fact claiming that

Items 12 to 16 are based on the following paragraph.

(1) The Summer months are the months when most people take their vacations. (2) Wherever you travel, you should always carry a first-aid kit. (3) Antibiotic cream, bandage strips, and gauze pads are some of the standard items you should have on hand. (4) Someone, who is allergic to insect stings, may also need special medications. (5) Hydrogen peroxide is also a good item to keep in the kit. (6) It can be used to clean a wound when soap and water aren't availible. (7) A well-stocked first-aid kit can keep accident's from ruining your vacation.

12. Sentence 1: **The Summer months are the months when most people take their vacations.**

What correction should be made to this sentence?

(1) replace The with A
(2) change Summer to summer
(3) insert a comma after are
(4) change take to took
(5) change their to they're

13. Sentence 2: **Wherever you travel, you should always carry a first-aid kit.**

Which of the following is the best way to write the underlined portion of this sentence? If you think the original is the best way, choose option (1).

(1) travel, you should always
(2) travel you should, always
(3) travel you should always
(4) travel. You should always
(5) travel, you should always,

14. Sentence 4: **Someone, who is allergic to insect stings, may also need special medications.**

Which of the following is the best way to write the underlined portion of this sentence? If you think the original is the best way, choose option (1).

(1) Someone, who is allergic to insect stings, may
(2) Someone who is allergic to insect stings, may
(3) Someone, who is allergic to insect stings may
(4) Someone who is allergic to insect stings may
(5) Someone who is allergic, to insect stings may

15. Sentence 6: **It can be used to clean a wound when soap and water aren't availible.**

What correction should be made to this sentence?

(1) change It to They
(2) change used to using
(3) insert a comma after wound
(4) change the spelling of aren't to are'nt
(5) change the spelling of availible to available

16. Sentence 7: **A well-stocked first-aid kit can keep accident's from ruining your vacation.**

What correction should be made to this sentence?

(1) insert a comma after well-stocked
(2) insert a comma after kit
(3) change accident's to accidents
(4) change your to our
(5) no correction is necessary

Answers are on pages 346-347.

Directions: The items in this test are based on paragraphs that contain numbered sentences. Some of the sentences may contain errors in usage, sentence structure, or mechanics. A few sentences, however, may be correct as written. Read each paragraph and then answer the items that follow it.

Items 1 to 8 are based on the following passage.

(1) Home computers and television has made a tremendous impact on our society. (2) While even though some would argue that electronic advances have aided the education of our youth, others point out that these machines represent the growing trend of passive activity. (3) A 1985 survey was conducted by the President's Council on Physical Fitness and Sports. (4) It showed the results of a lack of enough active participation in exercise. (5) A total of 18,857 boys and girls, ages 6 though 17, were studied. (6) Of these, 40 percent of the boys, and 70 percent of the girls could not do more than one pull-up. (7) In addition, About 50 percent of the girls and 30 percent of the boys, ages 6-12, couldn't run a mile in less than 10 minutes. (8) Medically, these results illustrate a problem because poor fitness in childhood increased the likelihood of heart attacks and other health-related problems in adulthood. (9) Accordingly, we need to educate our children's bodies as well as his mind.

1. Sentence 1: **Home computers and television has made a tremendous impact on our society.**

   What correction should be made to this sentence?

   (1) insert a comma after <u>computers</u>
   (2) insert a comma after <u>television</u>
   (3) change <u>has</u> to <u>have</u>
   (4) change the spelling of <u>tremendous</u> to <u>tremendus</u>
   (5) no correction is necessary

2. Sentence 2: <u>**While even though some would argue**</u> **that electronic advances have aided the education of our youth, others point out that these machines represent the growing trend of passive activity.**

   Which of the following is the best way to write the underlined portion of this sentence? If you think the original is the best way, choose option (1).

   (1) While even though some would argue
   (2) While some would argue,
   (3) While even though some would argue,
   (4) While some would argue
   (5) While, even some would argue,

3. Sentences 3 and 4: **A 1985 survey was conducted by the President's Council on Physical Fitness and Sports. It showed the results of a lack of enough active participation in exercise.**

The most effective combination of sentences 3 and 4 would include which of the following groups of words?

(1) survey, conducted by the President's Council on Physical Fitness and Sports, showed the results of a lack

(2) survey conducted by the President's Council on Physical Fitness and Sports, showed the results of a lack

(3) survey, conducted by the President's Council on Physical Fitness and Sports showed the results of a lack

(4) 1985, survey conducted by the President's Council on Physical Fitness and Sports showed the results of a lack

(5) 1985, survey conducted by the President's Council on Physical Fitness and Sports, showed the results of a lack

4. Sentence 5: **A total of 18,857 boys and girls, ages 6 though 17, were studied.**

What correction should be made to this sentence?

(1) insert a comma after <u>18,857</u>

(2) insert a comma after <u>boys</u>

(3) remove the comma after <u>girls</u>

(4) change <u>ages</u> to <u>age</u>

(5) replace <u>though</u> with <u>through</u>

5. Sentence 6: **Of <u>these, 40 percent of the boys, and</u> 70 percent of the girls could not do more than one pull-up.**

Which of the following is the best way to write the underlined portion of this sentence? If you think the original is the best way, choose option (1).

(1) these, 40 percent of the boys, and

(2) these 40 percent of the boys, and

(3) these, 40 percent, of the boys, and

(4) these, 40 percent of the boys and

(5) these, 40 percent of the boys and,

6. Sentence 7: **In addition, About 50 percent of the girls and 30 percent of the boys, ages 6-12, couldn't run a mile in less than 10 minutes.**

What correction should be made to this sentence?

(1) remove the comma after <u>addition</u>

(2) change <u>About</u> to <u>about</u>

(3) insert a comma after <u>girls</u>

(4) remove the comma after <u>boys</u>

(5) change <u>coundn't</u> to <u>could'nt</u>

7. Sentence 8: **Medically, these results illustrate a problem because poor fitness in childhood increased the likelihood of heart attacks and other health-related problems in adulthood.**

What correction should be made to this sentence?

(1) change the spelling of <u>illustrate</u> to <u>illistrate</u>

(2) insert a comma after <u>problem</u>

(3) insert a comma after <u>childhood</u>

(4) change <u>increased</u> to <u>increases</u>

(5) no correction is necessary

8. Sentence 9: **Accordingly, we need to educate <u>our children's bodies as well as his mind.</u>**

Which of the following is the best way to write the underlined portion of this sentence? If you think the original is the best way, choose option (1)

(1) our children's bodies as well as his mind.

(2) our childrens' bodies as well as his mind.

(3) our children's body as well as his mind.

(4) our children's bodies as well as their minds.

(5) no correction is necessary.

<u>Items 9 to 17</u> are based on the following passage.

(1) Many people who make the mistake of accepting the first job that is offered to them. (2) They often became frustrated and unfulfilled. (3) They find out too late that the job neither meets their needs nor uses their full potential. (4) The book *Career Planning: Skills to Build Your Future* provide a new approach to the matter of knowing when a job is right for you. (5) This approach is called P.L.A.C.E. (6) You gather information about a particular job, and you should think about these ideas. (7) First, (P) position is important, know the job description and its duties. (8) Second, (L) location should be considered for both the geographical locale, and the physical working environment. (9) Third, (A) advancement opportunities and job security should be considered. (10) Fourth, (C) conditions of employment should be made clear. (11) These include salary, hours, and benefits. (12) Fifth, (E) entry skills must be known; they include specific education and training requirements. (13) These data will help you evaluate whether or not a specific job meets you're expectations and goals.

9. Sentence 1: **Many people who make the mistake of accepting the first job that is offered to them.**

What correction should be made to this sentence?

(1) insert a comma after <u>people</u>

(2) remove the word <u>who</u>

(3) change the spelling of <u>mistake</u> to <u>misteak</u>

(4) insert a comma after <u>job</u>

(5) change <u>them</u> to <u>themselves</u>

10. Sentence 2: **They <u>often became frustrated</u> and unfulfilled.**

Which of the following is the best way to write the underlined portion of this sentence? If you think the original is the best way, choose option (1).

(1) often became frustrated
(2) , often, became frustrated
(3) often, become frustrated
(4) often become frustrated
(5) often became frustrated,

11. Sentence 3: **They find out too late that the job neither meets their needs nor uses their full potential.**

What correction should be made to this sentence?

(1) insert a comma after <u>late</u>
(2) change <u>meets</u> to <u>will</u> <u>meet</u>
(3) change <u>needs</u> to <u>need</u>
(4) insert a comma after <u>needs</u>
(5) no correction is necessary

12. Sentence 4: **The book *Career Planning: Skills to Build Your Future* <u>provide a new approach</u> to the matter of knowing when a job is right for you.**

Which of the following is the best way to write the underlined portion of this sentence? If you think the original is the best way, choose option (1).

(1) provide a new approach
(2) , provides a new approach
(3) provides a new approach
(4) provides a new approach,
(5) , provides a new approach,

13. Sentence 6: **You gather information about a particular job, and you should think about these ideas.**

If you rewrote sentence 6 beginning with

<u>As you gather information about a particular job,</u>

the next word would be

(1) thinking
(2) and
(3) because
(4) you
(5) however

14. Sentence 7: **First, (P) position is <u>important, know the job</u> description and its duties.**

Which of the following is the best way to write the underlined portion of this sentence? If you think the original is the best way, choose option (1).

(1) important, know the job
(2) important; know the job
(3) important know the job
(4) important, Know the job
(5) important? Know the job

15. Sentence 8: **Second, (L) location should be considered for both the geographical locale, and the physical working environment.**

What correction should be made to this sentence?

(1) change <u>location</u> to <u>Location</u>
(2) insert a comma after <u>considered</u>
(3) remove the comma after <u>locale</u>
(4) change the spelling of <u>environment</u> to <u>enviroment</u>
(5) no correction is necessary

16. Sentence 12: **Fifth, (E) entry skills must be known; they include specific education and training requirements.**

If you rewrote sentence 12 beginning with

Fifth, (E) entry skills that

the next word would be

(1) include
(2) they
(3) require
(4) and
(5) you

17. Sentence 13: **These data will help you evaluate whether or not a specific job meets you're expectations and goals.**

What correction should be made to this sentence?

(1) replace will help with helped
(2) insert a comma after evaluate
(3) change whether to weather
(4) change you're to your
(5) insert a comma after expectations

Items 18 to 25 are based on the following passage.

(1) Computer languages are as unique as computers themselves. (2) A computer must use a language to process data and instructions. (3) Each of the languages are unique in its purpose and has its own specialized function.(4) LOGO is used to teach programming to children. (5) It is a specialized language that uses both graphics and words. (6) On the other hand, PASCAL, named after the 17th-century Mathematician Blaise Pascal, is a high-level language used to teach the principles of computer programming. (7) Three widely used languages are actually "acronyms," which are words formed from the first letters of several words. (8) BASIC stands for Beginner's All-Purpose Symbolic Instruction Code. (9) Commonly used with smaller computers this versatile language is noted for being easy to learn and use. (10) COBOL or Common Business Oriented Language is used mainly for data processing and business applications. (11) FORTRAN is used for mathematical and scientific applications, an acronym for Formula Translator. (12) As different needs arise, different languages evolved. (13) For this reason, new computer languages are continually being developed.

18. Sentence 1: **Computer languages are as unique as computers themselves.**

What correction should be made to this sentence?

(1) change are to is
(2) remove the word as after are
(3) insert a comma after unique
(4) change themselves to theirselves
(5) no correction is necessary

19. Sentence 3: **Each of the languages are unique in its purpose and has its own specialized function.**

Which of the following is the best way to write the underlined portion of this sentence? If you think the original is the best way, choose option (1).

(1) are unique in its purpose
(2) is unique in its purpose
(3) are unique in it's purpose
(4) is unique in its purpose,
(5) are unique in its purpose,

20. Sentences 4 and 5: **LOGO is used to teach programming to children. It is a specialized language that uses both graphics and words.**

The most effective combination of sentences 4 and 5 would include which of the following groups of words?

(1) which use both graphics and words
(2) and use both graphics and words.
(3) with both graphics and words.
(4) that uses both graphics and words,
(5) in order to use graphics and words.

21. Sentence 6: **On the other hand, PASCAL, named after the 17th-century Mathematician Blaise Pascal, is a high-level language used to teach the principles of computer programming.**

What correction should be made to this sentence?

(1) remove the comma after <u>hand</u>
(2) insert a comma after <u>century</u>
(3) change <u>Mathematician</u> to <u>mathematician</u>
(4) insert a comma after <u>language</u>
(5) replace <u>principles</u> with <u>principals</u>

22. Sentence 7: **Three widely used languages are actually "acronyms," which are words formed from the first few letters of several words.**

What correction should be made to this sentence?

(1) insert a comma after <u>widely</u>
(2) change the spelling of <u>languages</u> to <u>langauges</u>
(3) change <u>which</u> to <u>who</u>
(4) change the spelling of <u>several</u> to <u>severel</u>
(5) no correction is necessary

23. Sentence 9: **Commonly used with smaller computers this versatile language is noted for being easy to learn and use.**

What correction should be made to this sentence?

(1) insert a comma after <u>used</u>
(2) insert a comma after <u>computers</u>
(3) insert a comma after <u>language</u>
(4) change <u>is</u> to <u>are</u>
(5) insert a comma after <u>noted</u>

24. Sentence 11: **FORTRAN is used for mathematical and scientific applications, an acronym for Formula Translator.**

If you rewrote sentence 11 beginning with

<u>FORTRAN, an acronym for Formula Tranlator,</u>

the next word would be

(1) are
(2) is
(3) used
(4) the
(5) and

25. Sentence 12: **As different needs arise, different languages evolved.**

What correction should be made to this sentence?

(1) change <u>needs</u> to to <u>needed</u>
(2) remove the comma after <u>arise</u>
(3) change the comma to a semicolon
(4) change <u>evolved</u> to <u>evolve</u>
(5) no correction is necessary

Items 26 to 28 are based on the following passage.

(1) A word processor is a computer that is easy to learn and easy to use. (2) A word processor produces an error-free document much more efficiently than a typewriter. (3) A word processor allows a writer to perform the following procedures: delete, insert, retrieve, change type styles, and print. (4) Like a file cabinet, it also permits you to store pages of text. (5) If you used a word processor to keep a daily journal, you could obtain a printed copy of all your entries for a week, a month, or a whole year! (6) Furthermore, you can go back to an entry and make changes at a later date.

(7) Imagine having to send the same letter to twenty different people. (8) The word processor can print a separate letter for each person you only have to insert the name and address. (9) Most word processors, in addition, has a built-in dictionary program that checks the spelling of all the words in a document.

26. Sentence 4: **Like a file cabinet, it also permits you to store pages of text.**

What correction should be made to this sentence?

(1) replace <u>file cabinet</u> with <u>File Cabinet</u>
(2) remove the comma after <u>cabinet</u>
(3) change <u>it</u> to <u>they</u>
(4) change <u>you</u> to <u>us</u>
(5) no correction is necessary

27. Sentence 8: **The word processor can print a separate letter for each person you only have to insert the name and address.**

Which of the following is the best way to write the underlined portion of this sentence? If you think the original is the best way to write the sentence, choose option (1).

(1) person you
(2) person they
(3) person. You
(4) person, however, you
(5) person and you

28. Sentence 9: **Most word processors, in addition, has a built-in dictionary program that checks the spelling of all the words in a document.**

Which of the following is the best way to write the underlined portion of this sentence? If you think the original is the best way, choose option (1).

(1) addition, has
(2) addition, have
(3) addition have
(4) addition, is having
(5) addition, had

Answers are on pages 347-348.

Part I Practice Test

Performance Analysis Chart

Directions: Circle the number of each item that you got correct on the Part I Practice Test. Count how many correct items there are in each row. Write the amount correct per row as the numerator in the fraction in the appropriate "Total Correct" box. (The denominators represent the total number of items in the row.) Write the grand total correct over the denominator, 28, at the lower right corner of the chart. (For example, if you got 20 items correct, write 20 so that the fraction reads 20/28.)

Item Type	Usage (page 24)	Sentence Structure (page 95)	Mechanics (page 140)	TOTAL CORRECT
Construction Shift		13, 16, 24	3, 20	/5
Sentence Correction	1, 7, 8, 18, 22, 25	9, 11	4, 6, 15, 17, 21, 23, 26	/15
Sentence Revision	10, 12, 19, 28	2, 14, 27	5	/8
TOTAL CORRECT	/10	/8	/10	/28

The page numbers in parentheses indicate where in this book you can find the beginning of specific instruction about the areas of grammar and about the types of questions you encountered in the Part I Practice Test.

WRITING SKILLS

Part II–Essay Writing

PART II: ESSAY WRITING

The purpose of this unit is to help you prepare for Part II of the Writing Skills Test. It is important that you work through the chapters and lessons in this unit in order.

The lessons in the first chapter offer several suggestions about ways you can help yourself become more comfortable with writing. The second chapter explains and demonstrates a process approach to essay writing. By doing all the activities in the lessons and using Chapter 3 as a review you will get plenty of practice at developing compositions on topics like those assigned in GED testing centers.

For most activities in this unit, there are no entries in the book's Answers and Explanations section. However, there are discussions, examples, and guidelines provided within the activities to assist your evaluation of your writing.

As you work through this unit, it will probably help you to have the benefit of other people's reaction to your writing. A teacher or someone else may be able to help you judge your essays and other writing better than you could working alone.

As is stressed in this unit, the best way to develop skill at writing is to write. If you use the suggestions in this unit, you will develop your skills and write essays like the one you will be expected to write when you take the GED.

Part II Progress Chart

Writing Skills, Part II: Essay Writing

Directions: Use the following chart to keep track of your work. When you complete a lesson and its activity, check the box to show you have completed that lesson.

CHAPTER 1
DAILY WRITING

Objectives

In this chapter you will be introduced to various techniques and processes for writing. The writing exercises you will work on are designed to help you

- begin personal writing

- establish a personal writing plan

- keep a daily journal

Introduction to Personal Writing

This chapter will show you how to become a more productive and effective writer. As you complete the activities in this chapter, you will find that writing become easier and more automatic.

Sometimes it can be difficult just to get started writing. A good way to break through this barrier is to practice a technique known as **fastwriting.** In fastwriting, you write as fast as possible and you do not worry about what you are writing or how correctly you are writing it. Your goal is simply to write. Fastwriting can be practiced every day, beginning with perhaps as little as five minutes and increasing the time every few days.

Lesson 1 Activity

For five minutes, use fastwriting to write about what you think the world would be like if there were no automobiles. If nothing comes to mind immediately, you may write about any other topic that occurs to you. The purpose of this activity is to practice the fastwriting method. Don't stop to correct your mistakes and don't pause to think of ways to make your writing better. Just write for five minutes. No one else will read what you have written.

Developing a Personal Writing Plan

Fastwriting can be used to help you develop the habit of daily writing. As you become used to it, increase your writing time to ten minutes daily. You can write about anything at all, but remember that topics that are more personal will probably be more enjoyable for you to write about. These topics, therefore, will be easier to write about for longer periods of time. Should you have difficulty coming up with ideas, topics are suggested in this lesson.

Use a calendar to record your progress. Each day, record the number of words you have written and how long you spent writing. If you continue to write every day and record your progress, you will soon find that you are writing more each day.

Monday	Tuesday	Wednesday	Thursday	Friday	Saturday	Sunday
1	2	3	4	5	6	7
8	9	10	11	12	13	14

Lesson 2 Activity

Do at least ten minutes of fastwriting every day. Suggested topics follow. Either choose from among these or come up with your own ideas. Write about a different topic every day, but try to choose topics that interest you. You will find it easier to write about topics that are of personal interest.

Suggested Topics

1. Describe the things in the room where you are now sitting.

2. Write about one of your favorite movies.

3. Summarize a recent newspaper article you have read or a television program you have seen.

4. Write about what you intend to do when you have passed your GED exam.

5. Write about what kind of car you would buy if you could afford any car in the world. Explain why you would select that particular car.

6. Write about how our lives would be changed if gravity on earth were only one fourth what it is now.

7. Write about a pet that has meant a lot to you.

8. Write about the job you would most like to have.

9. Write about your family traditions. Explain the way your family celebrates a particular holiday.

10. Write about how computers have changed your life. Think about how your dealings with the government and business have changed as a result of computer advancements.

Keeping a Journal

Keeping a journal can be an interesting alternative to fastwriting. Many people find that keeping a daily record of their thoughts and feelings is a relaxing and interesting activity. It helps them clear their minds of things that may be bothering them, and sometimes it even helps them solve problems. Beside benefits such as these, journal writing is definitely a good way to improve your writing skills.

Try to make a journal writing a daily habit. Set aside a time each day when you will have ten or fifteen minutes without interruptions. Remember that when you write in your journal, you are writing for no one else but yourself. You are writing a personal record of your thoughts, feelings, and experiences.

However, make sure you are using your time to write. If you are spending too much time thinking instead of writing, try fastwriting about personal topics.

Read the following examples of journal entries.

EXAMPLE 1

"...I'm especially looking forward to a summer vacation this year. It will be the first time where I might have enough money to go somewhere and do what I want to do. I still don't know where I'm going to go, but I know I will spend most of my time relaxing as much as I can. Of course, I'll still do some things other people might not consider relaxing that are relaxing to me. I plan to do some hiking and other outdoor things."

EXAMPLE 2

"...I enjoyed the movie last night. I enjoy movies that are both funny and serious. I think most really good movies have funny scenes in them as well as sad scenes. I like to both laugh and cry when I go to the movies. But my favorite movies are the ones that make me laugh."

EXAMPLE 3

"...I intend to let my brother know how much I appreciate his help over the years. When I was in school, he always gave me a little extra money to spend. He also used to take me to baseball games. Some of my friends' older brothers ignored them when they were little, but my brother never ignored me. I always felt important when he was around."

These examples are intended to show you that you can write about anything when you keep a journal. Remember that you do not have to worry about correctness because you are keeping the journal for yourself only. Journal writing will help you write faster and more easily. As with any skill, writing practice will help you perform the activity better and with less effort.

Suggestions for Keeping a Journal

- Use a special notebook or blank bound book for your journal writing.

- Try to write in the same place and at the same time each day.

- Record the date of each journal entry.

- Write in your journal every day. Don't worry about grammar, spelling, or punctuation. Write quickly without being concerned about whether your writing is perfect.

- Think of your journal writing as a time when you can enjoy thinking about yourself, other people, and the events in your life.

Lesson 3 Activity

Begin keeping a journal today. The first step is to find a comfortable place to write. Then choose a topic that interests you. The following suggestions may help you get started, but you should write about anything that is of personal interest to you.

For your first entries, try writing for at least ten minutes each time. As you become used to journal writing, increase the time, spending as much time as you need to get as many thoughts as possible on paper. Some topics that might be of interest to you are listed here.

- A law that you think isn't fair

- A conversation you had recently that bothered you

- An event that may have changed the course of your life

- The recent actions or behavior of someone in your family

- Something beautiful you have seen recently

- Your feelings about the place in which you are currently living

- A description of your dream house

- One thing in the world that you would most like to change, and why

- One thing about yourself that you would most like to change, and why

CHAPTER 2
THE WRITING PROCESS

Objectives

This chapter will take you through the development of a sample essay. Following the process will help you begin to develop your own writing skills and apply them to essay writing. In this chapter, you will also develop an essay using a six-step process to

- **understand essay topics**

- **generate ideas**

- **organize ideas for essays**

- **write essays**

- **revise essays**

- **edit essays**

Introduction to Writing as a Process

Writing can be viewed as a product or a process. Viewing it as a *product* causes the writer to focus on what the paper will look like when it is finished. This causes the writer to concentrate too heavily on correctness while writing. But viewing writing as a *process* helps the writer see the steps involved in writing. These steps are part of a simple process outlined in the following chart.

The Six Steps in the Writing Process
Step 1. Understand the topic and formulate your opinion.   ☐ Underline key words   ☐ State your opinion in one sentence.
Step 2. Generate ideas   ☐ Use brainstorming or clustering to generate ideas about your essay topic.
Step 3. Organize ideas   ☐ Select the most appropriate ideas to support your point of view or opinion.   ☐ Decide which facts, reasons, and/or examples best support your point of view.   ☐ Decide how to arrange your ideas for your audience (the reader).   ☐ Decide which facts, reasons, and/or examples to present first, second, and so on.
Step 4. Write essay   ☐ Put your ideas in sentences and paragraphs following the organization your planned.
Step 5. Revise essay   ☐ Make sure that your point of view or opinion is stated clearly in the first paragraph and that your examples support your point of view.   ☐ Add information needed for clarity.   ☐ Remove information that is not needed.
Step 6. Edit essay   ☐ Correct errors in usage, sentence structure, spelling, punctuation, and capitalization.

When you read through the chart, you may have noticed that you already use some or all of these steps when you write an essay. The activity that follows will help you determine exactly which steps you do and don't use. This will help you put the whole process together to write more effective essays.

For this activity, use the essay you wrote for the Predictor Test (see page 9). If you have not written this essay, do so now. The topic for the essay is reprinted below.

TOPIC

Credit cards are responsible for changes in the ways many Americans spend their money. Some of these changes have been for the good while others have caused problems for consumers.

Write an essay, approximately 200 words long, explaining some of the effects of the credit card. You may describe positive effects, negative effects, or both. Be specific, and use facts, reasons, and examples to support your view.

Think about the process you used when you wrote your essay. Now use the following checklist to find out how many of the steps of the writing process presented in this lesson you used. Answer the questions in the checklist by writing *yes* or *no* in the space provided.

1. Formulating your opinion.

_____ Did you focus on the key words in the essay topic?

_____ Did you state your opinion in one sentence?

2. Generating ideas.

_____ Did you spend time thinking about ideas (brainstorming) to put in your essay?

_____ Did you write down these ideas?

3. Organizing ideas.

_____ Did you take time to plan what to write first, second, third, and so on?

_____ Did you make notes about your plan?

4. Writing.

_____ Did you follow your plan when you wrote your essay?

5. Revising.

_____ After you wrote your essay, did you read it to see how effectively you presented your ideas?

_____ Did you make any changes to increase the effectiveness of your essay?

6. Editing.

_____ Did you correct all the errors you could find in your essay—errors in usage, sentence structure, spelling, punctuation, and capitalization?

Discussion

Use your answers to the questions to help you write more effective essays. Every time you answered *yes* to one of the questions, you identified a step in the writing process that you are already using. Every time you answered *no*, you identified a step you should learn to use.

Understanding Essay Topics

One of the skills involved in writing an effective essay is understanding the topic you are writing about. You will have forty-five minutes to write your 200-word GED essay. Some of that time should be spent making sure you understand the topic and its limits. This lesson will show you a method for reading topics carefully and developing a point of view about them.

When you are assigned a topic, take some time to think about it and make sure you understand it. The following steps suggest a process for understanding essay topics.

Steps for Understanding an Essay Topic

Step 1.   Underline the sentence that gives the direction you are to follow. It will often be worded as a command.

Step 2.   Underline any other key words that help you decide what you are to write about.

Step 3.   Make sure you understand all of the key points of the topic.

Step 4.   Decide on your own point of view and state it in one sentence.

TOPIC

In each of our lives there is a certain person who played a very important role in helping us understand something that will always be important to us. This person may be someone in your family who helped raise you or perhaps someone you came to know on your own. Identify a person in your life who played an important role in shaping your view of the world and explain how your life may have been changed by this person. Include facts, reasons and examples that support your explanation.

Lesson 2 Activity

1. In the topic, underline the direction sentence. Then reread the remaining sentences and underline other key words and phrases that help you know what to write about.

Discussion

The direction sentence is: *Identify a person in your life who played an important role in shaping your view of the world and explain how your life may have been changed by this person.*

Some other key words and phrases are *understand something, always be important, raise, know on your own.* These are important because your essay must be about someone who helped you **understand something** that will **always be important.** This person may have **raised** you or may be someone you came to **know on your own.**

A good way to be sure that you have underlined all of the important concepts in the topic is to use the underlined words to form a question. Use as many of the underlined words and phrases (including those from the direction sentence) as you can.

What <u>person</u> played an <u>important role</u> in helping you <u>understand something important</u> and in <u>shaping your view of the world?</u>

As you continue with this chapter, you will do all six steps in the writing process to write an essay on this topic.

2. Complete this sentence to answer the question about the topic.

"A person who played an important role in my life was..."

Discussion

Your answer to the question acts as a focus for the topic. It will become the topic of the essay you will begin planning in Lesson 3.

Generating Ideas

In this lesson you will be introduced to the second part of the writing process that will help you write an essay for the GED Writing Skills Test. This is the planning stage of the process, in which you generate ideas about your topic.

Once you have figured out your opinion or point of view on the topic, the most important step in writing a good essay is **planning** what you will write. Spend some time generating ideas *before* you begin to write. This will help you write a better organized and more effective essay. In this lesson you will learn two ways of generating ideas for your essay: brainstorming and clustering.

Brainstorming

Brainstorming is a way of gathering information for writing. When you brainstorm, you write all the words you can think of that relate to the topic you are going to write about. Even if a word or phrase doesn't seem to relate to the topic, you should write it down; you can always decide not to use it later if it does not work well in your essay. Spend anywhere from three to five minutes brainstorming to be sure you have covered all the thoughts you may have on the topic. The topic for this chapter will be used to illustrate how this strategy works.

TOPIC

In each of our lives there is a certain person who played a very important role in helping us understand something that will always be important to us. This person in your life may be someone in your family who helped raise you or perhaps someone you came to know on your own. Identify a person in your life who played an important role in shaping your view of the world and explain how your life may have been changed by this person. Include facts, reasons and examples that support your explanation.

After thinking over the topic, one writer decided to write from this point of view.

A person who played an important role in shaping my life was Uncle Ned.

This writer then began to brainstorm and wrote down all the words that came to mind about the topic. Here are the results of his brainstorming.

Topic: Uncle Ned

successful
personality
retired
had freedom
teacher
truck driver
lecturer
good to people

red convertible
friends
interesting jobs
girlfriends
pet store owner
fine clothes
travel agent
paid attention to me

traveled
money
reads
happy
knows a lot
caring

Clustering

Clustering is really another method of brainstorming and generating ideas. It helps you organize your ideas by focusing first on your point of view about the topic. When you cluster, you write your position or point of view in the center of a piece of paper and draw a circle around it. Next, you brainstorm supporting ideas and place those words on an extension off the circle.

Look at the cluster that follows. It uses the same topic and words as those in the brainstorming example.

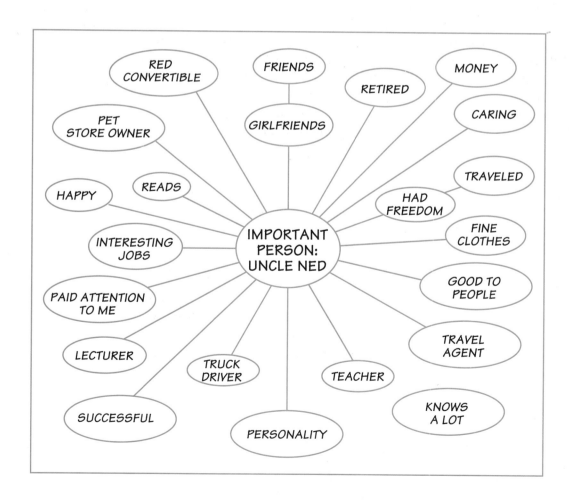

For some people, information is easier to organize when it is presented visually. As a result, clustering may help you organize your material better than brainstorming. It can be a great help when planning an essay.

Lesson 3 Activity

In this activity you will begin to plan the essay you are going to write on the "important person" topic. Read the topic again on page 238. Your essay will take this point of view.

> A person who played in important role in shaping my life was _____ .

1. Fill in the blank in the sentence and then brainstorm, keeping in mind the person you have chosen. Write at least ten words or phrases that come to mind about this person and the role he or she played in your life. (You may look at the example on page 239.)

2. Brainstorm again, keeping in mind the person you have chosen to write about. This time, however, cluster your ideas. Start by writing "Important Person" and that person's name in the middle of a piece of paper. Draw a circle around that phrase. Then write your ideas on extensions from the circle, grouping related ideas along the same extension.

(You may look at the cluster example just before the Lesson Activity.) Save this cluster to use as you work through the next lesson.

Organizing Ideas

Brainstorming and clustering help you generate ideas and, to a certain extent, organize them. However, they do not help you decide how the essay will begin, how it will end, or exactly what information to include to get your point of view across. In this lesson, you will learn a strategy called mapping that you can use to organize your information and ideas.

Mapping

Mapping is a visual way of organizing information. It helps you to actually see the organization of your essay.

To make a map, take the words you have generated in your brainstorming and clustering activities and put them in categories. To categorize words, you find those words that relate to one another.

For example, if you made a cluster, the first step in mapping would be to number or color-code the words in the cluster. All the ideas that go together would be given the same number or color, whichever works best for you.

For instance, in this cluster, any words relating to Uncle Ned's employment were marked with the number 2. At this point, the numbers or letters do not dictate a sequence. Their only purpose is to group ideas.

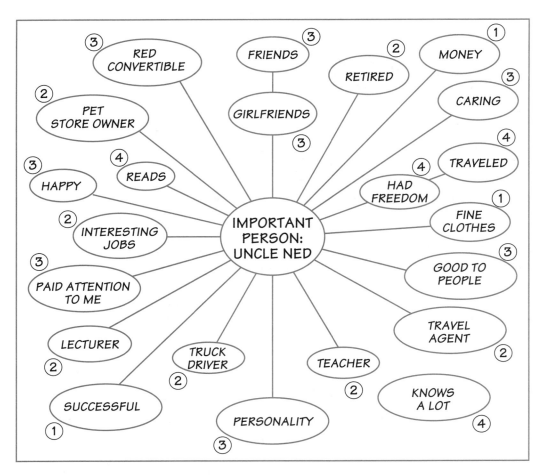

If you used brainstorming to generate a list of words, go through the list and use letters to group related words. All ideas that go together would be given the same letter.

Topic: Uncle Ned

(a) successful
(c) personality
(b) retired
(d) had freedom
(b) teacher
(b) truck driver
(b) lecturer
(c) good to people

(c) red convertible
(c) friends
(b) interesting jobs
(c) girlfriends
(b) pet store owner
(a) fine clothes
(b) travel agent
(c) paid attention to me

(d) traveled
(a) money
(d) reads
(c) happy
(d) knows a lot
(c) caring

After you have used numbers, letters, or colors to code your ideas, the next step is to create a map.

Creating a Map

Step 1.   Gather all the words from your brainstorming or clustering activities.

Step 2.   Eliminate words that have similar meanings.

Step 3.   Arrange words in categories. Give the categories titles. The titles will suggest your main ideas, and the words listed will be used as examples to support those ideas. These categories will become the paragraphs of your essay.

Step 4.   Decide which paragraph should become first and label is as the introduction. Because it is the introductory paragraph, remember to list the topics of the other paragraphs as they will be introduced by the first paragraph.

Step 5.   Decide which paragraph should be second, third, fourth, and so on. Label each one.

A map based on the cluster and brainstorming list about Uncle Ned might look like the following.

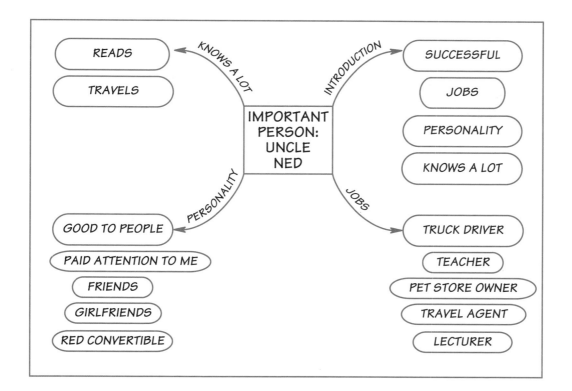

Compare the map to the cluster and brainstorming list shown earlier. All of the words do not have to be included in the map. Part of the process of organizing your essay is to weed out those ideas you do not want to include. Those words, then, will not be transferred to the map.

At the center of your map will be the point of view, in this case "Important Person: (Name.)" The different categories extend from the center. Notice that the topics of the second, third, and fourth paragraphs—*jobs, personality,* and *knows a lot*—are listed as supporting ideas in the first paragraph.

Making a map for an essay may seem difficult at this stage. As you practice doing it, you will find that you can brainstorm and cluster ideas in your head; mapping will only take a few minutes.

Lesson 4 Activity

For this activity, use the cluster you made during the Lesson 3 Activity.

1. Number or color-code the ideas in your cluster. Find ideas that go together and give them the same number or color, whichever you prefer. How many different groups do you have?

2. Use your numbered or color-coded cluster to make a map. Keep your central point in mind—an important person who shaped your life. Use the map from this lesson as an example in creating your own map.

Discussion

Look at the map. Did you identify and label which paragraph comes first, second, and so on? Did you include all of the paragraph topics in the first paragraph's supporting ideas?

Lesson 5 | Writing an Essay

Now that you have made a map for your essay, you are ready to begin writing. Following the plan you made on your map, the opening of your essay should give the reader your point of view or key idea. The next paragraphs will give the reasons that explain or describe your point of view or key idea. To explain your point of view effectively, you should use specific examples that support what you are saying. The following chart outlines the steps involved in writing an essay.

Writing an Essay

Step 1. In the opening or introductory paragraph, immediately state your point of view about the topic. Then give your reasons for your point of view.

Step 2. In the second, third, and following paragraphs, develop supporting examples to explain each of the reasons you gave in paragraph one for your point of view.

Step 3. In the final or concluding paragraph, restate and explain why you hold your point of view.

The essay that follows is based on the sample map in Lesson 4. To the left of the essay are comments that indicate how it follows the map. Following the essay is an explanation of how the essay was written according to the steps outlined in the chart on writing essays.

As you read this essay, you may notice some errors in usage, sentence structure, and mechanics. Remember that this is only a first draft and the writer is concentrating on getting the ideas on paper in an organized manner. In lessons 6 and 7, this essay will be revised and edited.

SAMPLE ESSAY

Central point of view is stated: "Uncle Ned was important person." First reason for point of view: "jobs". Second reason for point of view:"friends". Third reason for point of view: "smart".

Gives examples in support of first reason for point of view: "pet store owner, travel agent, truck driver, teacher, lecturer".

Gives example in support of second reason for point of view: "good to everybody, good to me, lots of friends, girlfriends, red convertible".

Gives examples in support of third reason for point of view: "traveled, read a lot".

Restates point of view and concludes.

One of the people who was most important in shaping my life was my Uncle Ned. He was important because he was different from my immediate family. He had many different kinds of jobs and he have many different kinds of friends and he also was very smart. I always thought his life was much more interesting than the rest of my families. I wanted to be like him to have a lot of jobs and friends and be educated from my experiences and travels and other things.

My Uncle had more jobs than anyone I ever knew. My father used to say that he had so many jobs because he couldn't keep a job, but I admired that he thought of new things to do when he got bored. He owned a pet store until he sold the store and decided to travel. When he came back after a few years he became a travel agent. Then he was a truck driver for a while. After that, he taught in a private school, and he lectured for a while for a book club in town.

He was good to everybody and he was especially good to me. He had lots of friends and he had lots of girlfriends who used to come around the house. He had a red convertible in those days and I always wanted to have a red convertible too.

Everyone thought that he was very smart. I guess he got smart from all of his travels all over the world and all over the United States too. And he read a lot of books and other kinds of things like magazines. Uncle Ned was always reading one book or another. He told me that every time he read a book he learned something he didn't know before. He once told me that because of all the characters he met in the novels he read that he never met a person in real life that he hadn't already met in a book he had read. He said that gave you an advantage when you met people.

He had lots of jobs, lots of friends and was very smart. I always wanted to be like that too. I think each of the things he had meant something to me when I was small. All the jobs meant freedom and the friends meant never being lonely. Being smart meant always being able to take care of yourself. I guess that my uncle meant the good life to me. Though I am different from my uncle, I too have tried to keep my freedom, have lots of friends, and become educated in my own way. I never got a red convertible though; it's a green one.

Discussion

Refer to the chart on the steps in writing an essay and to the essay itself. Following the guidelines in the chart, the first paragraph beings by presenting the central point of view or key idea.

One of the people who was most important in shaping my life was my Uncle Ned.

The paragraph continues with the three main reasons why Uncle Ned was important in this person's life: (1) He had so many different jobs; (2) He had many friends; and (3) He was very intelligent.

The paragraphs that follow elaborate on the points made in the first paragraph by giving specific examples of each point. The second paragraph tells of the many jobs Uncle Ned has held and gives a little information about each. The third paragraph gives details about the components of Uncle Ned's personality. The fourth paragraph gives details about why Uncle Ned was so well educated. Finally, the essay concludes with a last paragraph that restates the key idea and briefly summarizes how Uncle Ned has affected the writer's life.

Lesson 5 Activity

Write an essay approximately 200 words in length (about 4 paragraphs), using as your key idea a person who was important in shaping your life.

To develop your essay, follow the map you made in the Lesson 4 Activity. Also review the chart on Writing an Essay (page 245) before you begin. Do not worry about writing a perfect essay. For now, concentrate on getting your ideas on paper in an organized manner. Write your essay quickly. You will have a chance to change what you don't like about it later, when you revise it.

When you have finished writing this draft of your essay, keep it to make revisions when you do the Lesson 6 Activity.

Revising an Essay

Now that you have a first draft of your essay, you will want to revise it. This is an important part of the writing process for *all* writers. Even the best writers write and revise many times before they are satisfied with their work. This lesson will give you guidelines for improving your essay. It will also show you some useful techniques for making your writing clearer.

As you revise an essay, bear in mind that the essay is written for others to read. It must be well organized and clear enough for your audience to be able to follow the points you are making. Unlike a conversation, in which the other person can interrupt and ask questions, your reader must get all of the information from what you have written.

Some suggestions for things to look for when revising an essay are given in the following chart.

Chart for Revising Essays
Key Ideas
☐ Did you state the central idea of your essay in one sentence in the first paragraph?
☐ Is the central idea or point of view stated clearly enough that any reader would be able to restate it?
Content
☐ Did you use specific examples, reasons, and/or details that support your point of view?
☐ Are your examples explained clearly enough that your reader can see how they support your point of view?
☐ Does your point of view remain the same throughout your essay?
☐ Are any sentences, words, or phrases unrelated to the topic?
Organization
☐ Did you state your point of view right away?
☐ Did you present two or three important supporting ideas?
☐ Would your reader be able to restate what the important supporting ideas are?
☐ Did you use words that show how your supporting ideas relate to the central idea and to each other?
☐ Is each new paragraph indented?
Summary or Conclusion
☐ Does your summary or conclusion restate your point of view and supporting ideas so that the reader is reminded of them?
☐ Does your summary or conclusion follow logically from what you said in your essay?

Demonstration

The essay on Uncle Ned will be used to demonstrate how to use the revising chart to improve an essay. For this demonstration, the essay from Lesson 5 is printed again, paragraph by paragraph, just as it was written. It is shown with handwritten changes made during revision. The *Discussion* about each paragraph refers to the revising chart to explain why the changes were made. The sentences from the original essay are numbered to make the discussion easier to follow.

Take the time to study this demonstration. You will soon be revising your own essay about an important person who shaped your life.

PARAGRAPH 1

(1) One of the people who was most important in shaping my life was my Uncle Ned. (2) He was important because he was different from my immediate family. (3) He had many different kids of jobs and he have many different kinds of friends and he also was very smart. (4) I always thought his life was much more interesting than the rest of my families. (5) I wanted to be like him to have a lot of jobs and friends and be educated from my experiences and travels and other things.

PARAGRAPH 1 REVISED

(1) One of the people who was most important in ~~shaping~~ my life was my Uncle Ned. (2) He was important because he was different from my immediate family. (3) He had many different ~~kinds of~~ jobs ~~and he have many different kinds of friends~~ and he ~~also~~ was very smart. (4) I always thought his life was much more interesting than the rest of my families.

I wanted
(5) I wanted to be like him. to have a lot of jobs ~~and friends~~ and be educated from my experiences and travels. ~~and other things.~~

Discussion

The chart on revising an essay (page 248), suggests that the central idea should be stated immediately, in one sentence, and that it be stated clearly.

The first revision, Sentence 1, was made because the writer did not want to limit himself to ways his uncle *shaped* his life.

In Sentence 3, the writer decides to cut the reference to friends, focusing instead on his uncle's jobs and intelligence. The words *kinds of* and *also* are cut because they do not add meaning to the sentence. In Sentence 5, the last words were deleted because they did not give the reader specific information.

With these changes, Paragraph 1 clearly and immediately presents the key idea and the supporting ideas that the next three paragraphs discuss.

PARAGRAPH 2

(1) My Uncle had more jobs than anyone I ever knew. (2) My father used to say that he had so many jobs because he couldn't keep a job, but I admired that he thought of new things to do when he got bored. (3) He owned a pet store until he sold the store and decided to travel. (4) When he came back after a few years he became a travel agent. (5) Then he was a truck driver for a while. (6) After that, he taught in a private school, and he lectured for a while for a book club in town.

PARAGRAPH 2 REVISED

(1) My Uncle had more jobs than anyone In ever knew. (2) My father used to say that he had so many jobs because he couldn't keep a job, but I admired that he thought of new things to do when he got bored. (3) He owned a pet store until he sold the store and decided to travel. (4) When he came back after a few years he became a travel agent. (5) Then he was a truck driver for a while. (6) After that, he taught in a private school, and he lectured a while for a book club in town. All these different jobs made my uncle an interesting man to know.

Discussion

Sentence 2 has been deleted because it is not central to the key idea of the paragraph or the essay. The last sentence has been added to tell the reader more about why the writer thought his uncle and all his uncle's jobs were so interesting.

These changes make it clearer to the reader how the ideas in this paragraph relate to the key idea of the essay. They also show the logic of the writer's ideas, making it easier for the reader to understand the writer's point of view.

PARAGRAPH 3

(1) He was good to everybody and he was especially good to me. (2) He had lots of friends and he had lots of girlfriends who used to come around the house. (3) He had a red convertible in those days and I always wanted to have a red convertible too.

PARAGRAPH 3 REVISED

(1) He was good to everybody and he was especially good to me. ~~(2) He had lots of friends and he had lots of girlfriends who used to come around the house.~~ (3) He had a red convertible

It was just like him:
in those days. ~~and I always wanted to have a red convertible too.~~ not flashy, just nice looking and comfortable. He took me everywhere in it—movies, bowling, even a horse race. I loved that convertible.

Discussion

Paragraph 3 explains a second reason the writer feels his uncle was important in his life.

The writer decided to delete Sentence 2 because he wanted to concentrate on his relationship with his uncle, rather than talk about his uncle's friends.

The last part of Sentence 3 was deleted because it is not central to the key idea. As it stands, the paragraph is short and lacking in substance. The writer then added the last three sentences to show the reader why the red convertible was important and exactly what it had to do with Uncle Ned's personality, which is the key idea of this paragraph.

All the changes serve to make Uncle Ned's importance to the writer clearer to the reader.

PARAGRAPH 4

(1) Everyone thought that he was very smart. (2) I guess he got smart from all of his travels all over the world and all over the United States too. (3) And he read a lot of books and other kinds of things like magazines. (4) Uncle Ned was always reading one book or another. (5) He told me that every time he read a book he learned something he didn't know before. (6) He once told me that because of all the characters he met in the novels he read that he never met a person in real life that he hadn't already met in a book he had read. (7) He said that gave you an advantage when you met people.

PARAGRAPH 4 REVISED

(1) Everyone thought that he was ~~very smart.~~ *well educated.* (2) I guess ~~he~~ *from*

~~got smart from all of~~ his travels all over the world and ~~all over~~ *his reading, he became an educated man.* ~~the United States too. (3) And he read a lot of books and~~ ~~other~~ ~~kinds of things like magazines.~~ (4) Uncle Ned was always

reading *and* ~~one book or another. (5) He told me that every time~~ ~~he read a book he learned something he didn't know before.~~ ~~(6) He~~ once told me ~~that because of all the characters he met~~ ~~in the novels he read~~ that he never met a person in real life that he hadn't already met in a book he had read. (7) He said that gave you an advantage when you met people.

Discussion

Paragraph 4 presents the third reason Uncle Ned was so important in the writer's life. In Sentence 1, the writer decided to change *very smart* to *well educated* because it is truer to the meaning he is trying to convey; people can be smart but not well educated. Uncle Ned was both.

The changes in Sentences 2 and 3 were done to clean up the writing. It is not necessary to say he traveled all over the world and they say he traveled all over the United States (all over the world includes the United States). The changes in Sentences 4 through 6 also eliminate repetition and unnecessary information. Cleaning up the writing in this paragraph serves to make the supporting ideas clearer to the reader.

PARAGRAPH 5

(1) He had lots of jobs, lots of friend and was very smart. (2) I always wanted to be like that too. (3) I think each of the things he had meant something to me when I was small. (4) All the jobs meant freedom and the friends meant never being lonely. (5) Being smart meant always being able to take care of yourself. (6) I guess that my uncle meant the good life to me. (7) Though I am different from my uncle, I too have tried to keep my freedom, have lots of friends, and become educated in my own way. (8) I never got a red convertible though; it's a green one.

PARAGRAPH 5 REVISED

(1) He had lots of jobs, ~~lots of friends~~ and was very smart.

(2) I always wanted to be like that too. (3) I think *his jobs and intelligence symbolized* ~~each of the things he had meant~~ something to me when I was small. (4) All the jobs meant freedom. ~~and the friends meant never being lonely.~~ (5) Being smart meant always being able to take care of yourself.

(6) ~~I guess that my~~ *My* uncle meant the good life to me. (7) Though I am different from my uncle, I too have tried to keep my freedom, ~~have lots of friends,~~ and become educated in my own way. (8) I never got a red convertible though; it's a green one.

Discussion

The concluding paragraph sums of the ideas in the essay; it reminds the reader of the writer's point of view. It ties the whole essay together and leaves the reader with a sense of completion and understanding of what the writer has said.

The changes made in this last paragraph were made to clean up the writing. During the revision of Paragraph 3, the reference to friends was eliminated. For that reason, all references to friends in the conclusion were taken out. The other changes made the writing more specific.

There are still some error in grammar, sentence structure, and mechanics in this essay. Theres will be corrected in the next step in the writing process—editing.

Lesson 6 Activity

Now that you have seen how the revision step works, use the Chart for Revising Essays (page 248) to revise your own essay. Remember that your goal in revising is to make your ideas and point of view clear to your reader.

Ask yourself the questions on the chart and do what is necessary to improve your essay. When you believe you have made all the improvements you can, keep your revised version of the essay. You will be editing in the Lesson 7 Activity.

Editing an Essay

The last step in the writing process is to edit your essay. To edit, read over your essay, and concentrate on errors in spelling, punctuation, and grammar. Use the editing skills you learned in Part I of the Writing Skills text. At this point, you can make changes if you wish, but try to concentrate on correctness. The effect you are trying to achieve is polishing—making the paper read smoothly and flawlessly, with no errors or awkward wording that will jar the reader's attention. A polished essay is an effective essay, and the more effective your essay, the higher your score will be on the GED Writing Skills Test.

There are several ways to approach editing, all of which should be used to make sure that you have caught all your errors. The first is to read your essay aloud, or in a whisper if there are others in the room. Sometimes it is easier to spot a mistake when you actually hear it. Perhaps you will naturally pause at a place in your essay where a comma should be inserted. Hearing the pause will alert you to insert the comma. Other errors, such as overlong sentences, can also be picked up this way. First try reading your essay at a normal reading speed. See which errors you find. Then try reading it slowly, word for word. You may find it easier to catch errors at this speed. Try both speeds and see which works better for you.

Another good editing strategy is the 5-R method you learned in Part I of this book. This method gives you a systematic way of checking for errors in your writing. If you have forgotten the method, go back to pages 88-89 and review it before you begin editing your essay.

Spelling errors can be especially difficult to see. Sometimes words look right because your *expect* to see them a certain way. This becomes increasingly true when you have read the same thing many times. One way to avoid this trap is to read your essay backward, from the bottom of the page to the top. Doing this forces you to concentrate on each word. Reading backward can also help you spot words that you may have written twice in a row by mistake.

The editing chart that follows summarizes the strategies you can use.

Editing Chart

Step 1.   Read your essay aloud or in a whisper.

Step 2.   Read at the speed—normal or slow—that works best for you.

Step 3.   Use the 5-R editing method.

Step 4.   Read your essay backward while you concentrate on finding spelling errors.

Demonstration

The revised essay from Lesson 6 (pages 249-253) was edited using suggestions from the Editing Chart. Portions of the revised essay are shown below with editorial changes. Notice how these changes help polish the essay.

PARAGRAPH 1

He had many different jobs, and he was *very smart.* **well-educated**

I always thought his life was much more interesting than the

rest of my *families.* **family's**

In Paragraph 1, the first sentence shown is a compound sentence. A comma is needed at the end of the first complete idea before the coordinator *and*. The writer changed *very smart* to *well-educated* to show that his uncle was a learned man, not just an intelligent man. Another mechanical error was fixed by changing the incorrectly used plural *families* to the possessive *family's*.

PARAGRAPH 2

My ﬀncle had more jobs than anyone I ever knew.

When *came back after a few years* he became a travel agent. **returned from his travels,**

Paragraph 2 begins with an error in mechanics. The word Uncle should not be capitalized unless it si part of the person's name. A sentence was also changed to make it sound less awkward: *When he returned from his travels* sounds much better than *When he came back after a few years...* A comma was inserted after the introductory subordinate idea.

PARAGRAPH 3

My uncle
He was good to everybody, but and he was especially good to me.

Paragraph 3 originally began with the personal pronoun *He*. Who is *he*? Because the essay is about Uncle Ned, the reader assumes he is Uncle Ned, but it is better to use the specific noun here.

PARAGRAPH 4

Uncle Ned was educated through   travels all
I guess from his travels all over the world and his reading. he

He
became an educated man. Uncle Ned was always reading and once told me that he never met a person in real life that he

met in
hadn't already know from a book he had read. He said that

him   he
gave you an advantage when you met people.

In Paragraph 4, the first sentence is structurally poor and reads better changed to: *Uncle Ned was educated through his world travels and all his reading.* The last sentence in this paragraph has a pronoun shift. The two instances of the word *you* should be changed respectively to *him* and *he*.

PARAGRAPH 5

intelligent
He had lots of jobs and was very smart.

, and
All the jobs meant freedom, Being smart meant always being able to take care of yourself.

In the concluding paragraph, the writer decided to change *smart* to *intelligent*, which is a higher-level word. Also, two related sentences are joined using a comma and the coordinator *and*. Joining the sentences makes the paragraph read more smoothly.

After the editing and the last-minute revisions were completed, the essay was in its final form, as follows.

One of the people who was most important in my life was my Uncle Ned. He was important because he was different from my immediate family. He had many different jobs, and he was well-educated. I always thought his life was much more interesting than the rest of my family's. I wanted to be like him. I wanted to have a lot of jobs and be educated from my experiences and travels.

My uncle had more jobs than anyone I ever knew. He owned a pet store until he told the store and decided to travel. When he returned from his travels, he became a travel agent. Then he was a truck driver for a while. After that, he taught in a private school, and he lectured for a while for a book club in town. All these jobs made my uncle an interesting man to know.

My uncle was good to everybody, but he was especially good to me. He had a red convertible in those days. It was just like him: not flashy, just nice looking and comfortable. He took me everywhere in it—the movies, bowling, even a horse race. I loved that convertible.

Uncle Ned was educated through his world travels and all his reading. He was always reading and once told me that he never met a person in real life that he hadn't already met in a book he had read. He said that gave him an advantage when he met people.

He had lots of jobs and was very intelligent. I wanted to be like that too. I think his jobs and intelligence symbolized something to me when I was small. All the jobs meant freedom, and being smart meant always being able to take care of yourself. My uncle meant the good life to me. Though I am different from my uncle today, I too have tried to keep my freedom and become educated in my own way. I never got a red convertible though; mine is a green one.

What you have just read is an effective essay. It is the result of the six-step writing process that includes defining your opinion, clustering, mapping, writing, revising, and editing. However, saying that this essay is effective is not saying that it is perfect. There really is no such thing as a perfect essay. The essay makes its point, it is clear, and its supporting ideas are logical. There are still some mechanical and structural errors—awkward phrases, repetition of ideas, and the like.

The final, edited version of this essay is longer than 200 words. If it had been written for Part II of the GED Writing Skills Test, its score would not have been affected by its length. Since it is longer than 200 words, but not *that* much longer, it would be scored on a basis of its effectiveness. It is difficult to write an essay that is exactly 200 words long, or any particular length, for that matter. As you practice writing essays, you will become more able to judge the length of what you are writing and tailor it accordingly. Your main task, however, should be concentrating on writing effectively.

In the next chapter you will have an opportunity to practice writing essays. When you have completed this lesson's Activity, think about your completed essay. Is it better than others you have written? Are the ideas clearer? Do they flow in a more logical and organized manner?

Ideally, the answer to these questions will be *yes*. You will find that the more you write and use the techniques you have just learned, the more effective your writing will become, and the easier it will be for you to write well.

Lesson 7 Activity

Edit the essay that you revised in the Lesson 6 Activity. Follow the suggestions in the Editing Chart on page 255. When you have finished this activity, you will have developed an essay that uses every step in the writing process. You should then go to Chapter 3 to practice what you have learned by writing other essays.

CHAPTER 3
REVIEWING THE
WRITING PROCESS

Objectives

In this chapter you will

- review the steps in the writing process

- practice the writing process by developing several essays on your own

Practice the Process

If you find the process of writing to be difficult, it may seem hard to believe that, with practice, writing will become increasingly easy. You may even find at some point that you actually enjoy writing. In this lesson there are suggestions and tools that can help make writing a habit and help you prepare for the GED.

No one can *force* you to improve your writing. It is something you must want to do for yourself. One way to help yourself improve your writing is to continue writing in your journal every day. If you have stopped daily writing, start again.

Journal writing, however, is not enough for the GED. You need to practice writing essays, as that is the form of writing on which you will be judged. For the GED, you will be assigned a topic to write about. For this reason, it would be wise to practice writing on assigned topics. Furthermore, when you practice writing, use all six steps of the writing process. This will help you write an effective essay for the GED.

In Lesson 2 of this chapter, there is a summary of the activities you should do at each step in the writing process. This summary is provided as a reference for you to use as you develop more essays. For a detailed review of the writing process, you may find it helpful to refer to Chapter 2.

Lesson 1 ends with a list of topics for you to use when you practice writing essays. The following are some suggestions for using this topic list.

Ways to Use the Topic List

1. Read all the topics in the list. Choose the topics that interest you most and write about them first. Save the topics that interest you least to write about later when your skill and confidence have increased.

2. Keep the topics a secret from yourself. Write on Topic 1 first, Topic 2 next, and so on. Look at each topic only when you are ready to write an essay.

3. Have someone else assign topics from the list to you.

You might decide that you want to write on the same topic more than once, perhaps because you want to approach it from a different angle or just to see if you can improve on your first essay by starting again. Whatever your reasons, this would be a good way to measure your progress.

As you write essays and become more comfortable with the writing process, set time limits for your writing. Gradually, you should aim for completing essays in no more than 45 minutes—the time allotted for the GED essay.

The following is the list of assigned topics for this chapter.

TOPIC LIST

TOPIC 1

To help fight the war on pollution, recycling centers for glass, aluminum, and paper have sprung up in communities around the country. For such efforts to make a real difference, some people think that individuals should be fined if they don't use these centers. Others argue that such laws are hard to enforce and that using recycling centers should be voluntary.

Give your own opinion as to whether or not using recycling centers should be voluntary or mandatory. Be specific. Use reasons, facts, and examples to support your view.

TOPIC 2

In modern history, people have sealed objects from their time and place into time capsules for future generations to discover. The objects may have been wooden shoes, a souvenir from the 1939 World's Fair, or a Beatle wig. Select a typical item from your generation and write an essay to explain why you would want to include it in a time capsule. Include reasons and/or details that support your explanation.

TOPIC 3

It is almost impossible to go through a day without coming into contact with computers. You must deal with them in offices, banks, city hall, and even in the checkout line at the supermarket. How do you feel about the way computers affect your life? Write about the positive and/or negative effects of computers on modern day life. In your explanation, give two or three main ideas and support each idea with two or three details.

TOPIC 4

Some people think that being the oldest child, a middle child, or the youngest child affects them for their entire life. Do you think this makes any difference? Write an essay to express your opinion. Be specific and use examples and reasons to support your essay.

TOPIC 5

Some people in restaurants have been saved from choking to death because another diner knew just what to do. Some heart attack victims have had their lives saved because someone who was present knew what steps to take. Do you think that lifesaving techniques like these should be mandatory training? Explain your opinion and give reasons and examples for your explanation.

TOPIC 6

Many corporate leaders say that the secret of their company's success is teamwork. When employees work together as a team, they achieve success. Are you a member of a team? It may be at home, in the office, at school, or in some outside activity. In an essay, describe a team effort you are involved in. In your opinion, are the biggest strides forward made by group efforts or by individual efforts? Give supporting details and reasons for your opinion.

TOPIC 7

Recently, many school systems have been forced to cut back programs outside the regular course of study because of economics. Sports, art, and music programs have been hardest hit. Do you agree with these cutbacks? Or should schools try to find other ways to save money? In an essay, give your own position on this issue and back it up with reasons and examples.

TOPIC 8

Many cities and states prohibit landlords from advertising their apartments for adults only. On the other hand, renting to families with small children often poses problems for apartment owners. Should landlords have the right to discriminate against families with small children? Do you agree or disagree with this practice? Explain your position and back it up with reasons and examples.

TOPIC 9

Some people think that Saturday morning cartoons may be harmful to children because they are often violent. Others say that cartoons help to develop a child's imagination.

Write an essay to present your own view about the harm or benefit cartoons may bring to children. Support your opinion with specific examples and reasons.

TOPIC 10

More people are taking responsibility for their health today than ever before. Some stop smoking while others change their eating habits. Why do you think more people today are meeting the challenge of changing bad health habits? Give your own opinion and support it with specific examples and reasons.

TOPIC 11

Many men today have to buy groceries and prepare meals—whether they are single or married. They have to take responsibility for general household chores in a way their fathers and grandfathers weren't required to do. Do you think high school boys should be encouraged to enroll in a home economics class? Write an essay to express your opinion. Support your essay with reasons and examples.

TOPIC 12

Recently many cities have begun to crack down on parking ticket violators. Some drivers suddenly are forced to pay long-overdue fines of thousands of dollars. Is this fair?

State your view in an essay. Give specific reasons and details to support your position.

TOPIC 13

Powerful squirt guns, sometimes called soaker guns, have recently been introduced on the toy market. Some people insist that the guns, which can spray up to 50 feet, are good clean fun. Others counter that any kind of weapon encourages violent behavior and that these guns, in particular, may provoke violent behavior in others.

Are these toys dangerous? Do you believe they should be banned? State your view in an essay. Support your opinion with specific examples and reasons.

TOPIC 14

Americans have been encouraged to buy American-manufactured goods instead of products made in other countries. Do you agree or disagree with this? Be specific and use examples to support your opinion.

TOPIC 15

Some people find that they have a much easier time overcoming difficulties in their lives if they have the support of a group. They may face problems such as drinking, smoking, drug abuse, or losing weight. Or they may even be the victim of a violent crime. Do you think these support groups are effective? Or do you think overcoming a particular problem is solely up to the individual? In an essay, give your opinion. Use reasons and examples to support your view.

Lesson 1 Activity

1. Keep your journal on a daily basis.
2. Whenever the opportunity arises, write something that you intend for other people to read (for example, notes, letters, or reports).
3. Set a schedule that will allow you to develop essays on at least 10 of the topics listed in this lesson before you take the GED.
4. Decide how you will use the Topic List to assign yourself topics.

Before you develop any more essays, read Lesson 2 for a quick review of the writing process.

Lesson 2

The Writing Process: A Summary

Use this lesson as a guide when you develop the essays in this chapter. It summarizes all steps in the writing process that you learned in Chapter 2.

When you have become more skilled at writing essays using the writing process, you will probably find that you need to refer to the guide less and less. At this point, you will know that you are well on the way to becoming an efficient and effective writer.

The Six Steps in the Writing Process

Step 1: Understand the Topic

- **Read the topic carefully and focus on the key words.**

- **State your opinion in one sentence.**

In Step 1 of the writing process, you must be sure you understand the assigned topic. Your next task is to decide on the point of view you want to take in your essay. To understand the topic, read it a few times. Then follow the suggestions in the following chart.

Reading a Topic Carefully and Developing a Point of View
• Underline the important or key words in the topic.
• Make sure you have noticed and understood all the key ideas or concepts in the topic. It may be helpful to write a question that uses most of the words you underlined.
• Decide on your own point of view and state it in one sentence. To do this, write an answer to the question you formulated. Your answer will state the point of view you will present in your essay.

Step 2: Generate Ideas

- **Use brainstorming or clustering to generate ideas about your essay topic.**

To brainstorm, write down all the words that come to mind as you think about your point of view on the topic.

Clustering is another form of brainstorming. To cluster, follow these steps: (1) Using a few words, write your point of view on the topic in the center of a piece of paper. Circle your point of view. (2) Write the words that come to mind on extensions from the point-of-view circle. Circle each of these words or phrases.

All clusters will have a different number of circles, but in general they will look like this.

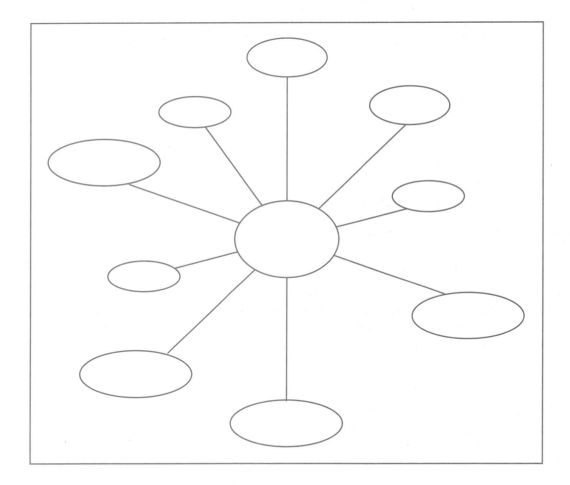

Step 3: Organize Your Ideas

- **Select the most appropriate ideas to support your point of view or opinion.**

- **Decide on how best to sequence your ideas for your audience.**

- **Decide which examples best support your point of view.**

- **Decide which examples to present first, second, and so on.**

A good method of organizing ideas is mapping. Before you begin to map, number or color-code the ideas in your cluster. Use the same number or color for all ideas that are related. The following cluster is both numbered and color-coded.

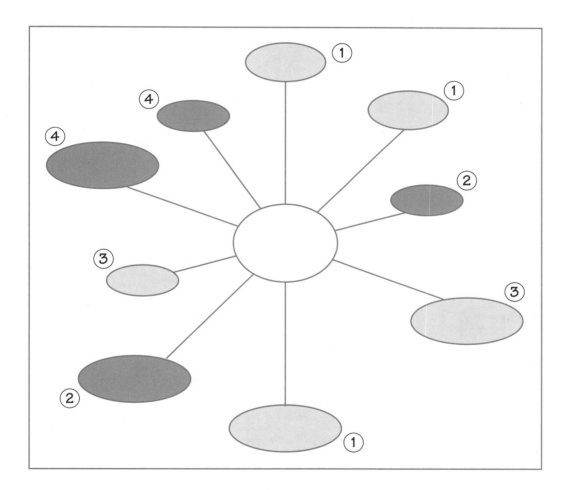

After you have grouped the ideas in your cluster, follow the steps that follow for creating a map.

Creating a Map

1. Gather all the words from your brainstorming or clustering activities.

2. Eliminate words that have similar meanings.

3. Arrange words in categories and title the categories. The titles will suggest your main ideas, and the words listed will be used as examples to support those ideas.

4. Decide which paragraph should come first and label it. Because it is the introductory paragraph, remember to list the topics of the other paragraphs as they will be introduced by the first paragraph.

5. Decide which paragraph should be second, third, fourth, and so on. Label each one.

Following is the outline of a typical map.

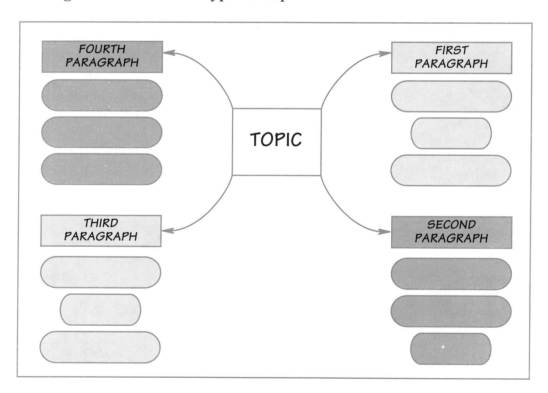

When you have finished mapping, go to the next step in the writing process.

Step 4: Write Your Essay

- **Put your ideas in sentences and paragraphs, following the organization you planned.**

Step 4 is the stage of the writing process in which you write the first draft of your essay. Since this is not the final version, at this point you should be concentrating on getting your ideas on paper in an organized fashion. Don't spend a lot of time changing what you have written. You'll have a chance to make all the changes you want in the next step.

When you write your essay, follow the instructions in this chart.

Writing Your Essay

1. In the opening paragraph, state your central point of view about the topic immediately. Then give your reasons for your point of view.

2. In the second, third, and following paragraphs, develop supporting examples, details, and reasons to support your point of view.

3. In the final or concluding paragraph, restate and explain why you hold your central point of view.

When you have finished writing, go to the next step.

Step 5: Revise Your Essay

- **Make sure that your point of view or opinion is stated clearly in the first paragraph and that your examples support your point of view.**

- **Add information needed for clarity.**

- **Remove information that is not needed.**

The revision stage is a very important step in the writing process. Always keep your audience in mind when you revise an essay. Make any changes that will make your essay clearer and easier for someone to read.

Ask yourself the questions in the following chart. If you answer *no* to any of them, make the necessary changes.

Revising Your Essay

Key Ideas

- [ ] Did you state the central idea of your essay in one sentence in the first paragraph?
- [ ] Is the central idea or point of view stated clearly enough that a reader would be able to restate it?

Content

- [ ] Did you use specific examples, reasons, and/or details that support your point of view?
- [ ] Are your examples explained clearly enough that your reader can see how they support your point of view?
- [ ] Are any sentences, words or phrases unrelated to the topic?
- [ ] Does your point of view remain the same throughout your essay?

Organization

- [ ] Did you state your point of view right away?
- [ ] Did you present two or three important supporting ideas?
- [ ] Would your reader be able to restate what the important supporting ideas are?
- [ ] Did you use words that show how your supporting ideas relate to the central idea and to each other?
- [ ] Is each new paragraph indented?

Summary or Conclusion

- [ ] Does your summary or conclusion restate your point of view and supporting ideas so that the reader is reminded of them?
- [ ] Does your summary or conclusion follow logically from what you said in your essay?

After revising, your essay is almost in its final version. To polish it, do the next and last step in the writing process.

Step 6: Edit Your Essay

- **Correct errors in usage, sentence structure, spelling, punctuation, and capitalization.**

Your essay is almost completed now. However, when you revise your essay for organization, clarity, and effectiveness, you may overlook some mechanical errors. In this step, you will correct any errors you find.

Use the following suggestions to help you polish your essay.

Editing Your Essay

- **Read your essay aloud or in a whisper.**

- **Read at the speed—normal or slow—that works best for you.**

- **Use the 5-R editing method shown on pages 88-89.**

- **Read your essay backward while you concentrate on spelling.**

When you have finished editing, your essay is in its final form.

Lesson 2 Activity

1. Continue making daily entries in your journal.
2. Without looking back at this lesson, write a brief summary of the major activities that belong in each of the six steps of the writing process. See how well you remembered by checking your summary against the summary in the lesson.
3. Before taking the Part II Test, practice writing essays. Write essays on at least 10 of the topics provided in Lesson 1 of this chapter (pages 261-264). To develop each essay, follow the writing process summary in this lesson and refer to the sample of a developed essay in Chapter 2 (page 246).
4. Also before taking the part II Test, review the GED Essay Scoring Guide on pages 12-18. Choose one of the essays you wrote for Lesson 1 of this chapter and judge its effectiveness using Holistic Scoring. Think about the strong points and weak points of your essay. Refer to the sample essays to see how you might improve your essays.

PRACTICE TEST

Directions: This is a test to see how well you can write. In this test, you are asked to write an essay in which you present your opinions about an issue. In preparing your essay, you should take the following steps.

Step 1. Read all of the information about the topic. Be sure that you understand the topic and that you write about only the assigned topic.

Step 2. Plan your essay before you write.

Step 3. Use scrap paper to make any notes.

Step 4. Write your essay on a separate sheet of paper.

Step 5. Read what you have written. Make sure that your writing is legible.

Step 6. Check your paragraphing, sentence structure, spelling, punctuation, capitalization, and usage; make any changes that will improve your essay.

TOPIC

The voting age has been lowered to eighteen. While efforts are made to recruit new voters, not everyone thinks that voting is worthwhile.

Write a composition of about 200 words in which you give your opinion on the importance of voting in national, state, or local elections. Give specific reasons and details to support your position.

When you take the GED Test, you will have 45 minutes to write about the topic you are assigned. Try to write the essay for this test within 45 minutes. Write legibly and use a ballpoint pen so that your writing will be easy to read. Any notes that you make on scrap paper will not be counted as part of your score.

After you complete this essay, you can judge its effectiveness by using the Essay Scoring Guide and Model Essays in the answer key to score your essay. Your GED essay will be judged on how clearly you make the main point of your essay, how thoroughly you support your ideas, and how clear and correct your writing is throughout the composition. You will receive no credit for writing about a question other than the one assigned.

Answers are on pages 349-351.

Perfomance Analysis Record

Directions: After you have used the guidelines in the answer key to score your essay, make a record of your evaluation here.

Write your essay's score in the box at the right.

What were some of the strong points of your essay?

What were some of the weak points of your essay?

What improvements do you plan to make when you work on your next essay?

PRACTICE

Introduction

When a person goes on a job interview, he or she often runs through practice interviews with a friend or family member. Pretending that it is an actual job interview, the interviewer asks questions that might be asked at a job interview, and the job seeker tries to answer in a way that would impress the interviewer. These mock interviews allow the job seeker to get useful interviewing practice and help him or her recognize strengths and weaknesses. If the practice interview does not go smoothly, the job seeker can practice some more to improve his or her interviewing skills. When the time for the real interview arrives, the job seeker will be as prepared as possible. The activities in the GED Practice section will serve you in the same way as the practice interview serves the job seeker. By completing the activities, you will get valuable practice at taking GED-type tests. When it comes time to take your test, you will be as prepared for the actual test as you can be.

This section is filled with GED-like test questions, or items. It provides valuable practice on the kinds of items found in the Writing Skills Test. There are two groups of items in this section, Practice Items and a Practice Test. Both groups contain 55 multiple-choice items, like those in Part I of the Writing Skills Test, and one essay topic just as in Part II of the test. Both groups of items are structured just like the GED.

By completing the Practice Items and the Practice Test, you will discover your strong points and weak points in writing skills. If you discover any weak points, you will be able to strengthen them. For the items in Part I of each section, the answer key provides correct answers to each practice question and explains why each answer is correct. There are model essays to help you evaluate the essay you write for Part II of the practices. The Performance Analysis Chart following each practice will direct you to parts of the book where you can review the skills that give you trouble.

You can use the Practice Items and the Practice Test in different ways. The introductions that precede the practices will provide you with choices for using them to best advantage. You may also wish to talk with your teacher to get suggestions about how best to make use of the Practice Items and Practice Test.

PRACTICE ITEMS

These Practice Items are similar to a real Writing Skills Test in many ways. The whole group of Practice Items is the same length as an actual GED Test. The test items are as challenging as the real test items. Your results on the Practice Items will help you determine which skills you have mastered and which you should study further.

Using the Practice Items to Best Advantage

You can use the Practice Items in the following ways:

- After you finish Unit 3 in Part I, you can test your skill by completing Part I of the Practice Items. Or, you can save the Practice Items until you've completed Part II of this book.

- You may wish to do the Part I Practice Items one group at a time and then review the chapters for the areas in which you have difficulty. After your review, when you do another group of Part I items, your performance may improve.

- You can use the Practice Items as a practice test. To do this, complete the Practice Items in one sitting. Since the actual test allows you 120 minutes, you may want to time yourself. It is suggested that you begin with Part I of the Practice Items. If 75 minutes elapse and you have not yet finished Part I, you should proceed to Part II. If you finish Part II before 120 minutes elapse and you have not finished, note how far you have gotten and then continue. This way, you can find out whether you should work at the same or a different pace. You also get a good reading on how well you will do if you work quickly enough to finish the GED Test.

Keep an accurate record of your performance. Write your answers to Part I neatly on a sheet of paper or use an answer sheet provided by your teacher. Plan and write your essay on fresh sheets of paper.

Using the Answers and Explanations

The Answers and Explanations can be a very helpful study tool. Compare your answers for Part I to those beginning on page 352, and check each item you answered correctly. Whether you answer a multiple-choice item correctly or not, you should read through the solutions given. Doing this will reinforce your writing skills and develop your test-taking skills. For Part II, follow the directions that tell you how to score your essay. You might like to have a teacher or someone else score your essay as well.

How to Use Your Score

Regardless of how you use these Practice Items, you will gain valuable experience with GED-type items. After scoring your Part I work with the answer key, fill in the Performance Analysis Chart on page 291. The chart will help you determine which grammar and editing skills and item types you are strongest in and direct you to parts of the book where you can review areas in which you need additional work. After you evaluate your Part II essay, you should record your evaluation on the Performance Analysis Chart. Refer back to the Part II lessons that cover the writing skills that you may have been weak in.

PRACTICE ITEMS

Part I

Directions: The items in Part I of this test are based on paragraphs that contain numbered sentences. Some of the sentences may contain errors in sentence structure, usage, or mechanics. **A few sentences, however, may be correct as written.** Read each paragraph and then answer the items that follow it. For each item, choose the answer that would result in the most effective writing of the sentence or sentences. The best answer must be consistent with the meaning and tone of the rest of the paragraph.

FOR EXAMPLE:

Sentence 1: **Although it may take only two hours to watch the average motion picture takes almost a year to make.**

What correction should be made to this sentence?

(1) replace <u>it</u> with <u>they</u>
(2) change <u>take</u> to <u>have taken</u>
(3) insert a comma after <u>watch</u>
(4) change <u>almost</u> to <u>all most</u>
(5) no change is necessary

The correct answer is **(3)**. In this example, a comma is needed after the introductory words <u>Although it may take only two hours to watch</u>.

Items 1 to 9 are based on the following paragraphs.

(1) Sports often have fascinating histories. (2) Volleyball, for example, was first developed for older men. (3) In 1895, William Morgan is a YMCA director in Holyoke, Massachusetts. (4) He seen that many games were too tiring for his classes of older males. (5) He set down the rules for the team sport we know as volleyball today. (6) Someone serves the ball by striking it over the net, and members of the other team try to hit the ball. (7) If they fail to get it back over the net the serving team scores a point.

(8) During World Wars I and II, American military personnel introduced the game abroad, they introduced the game to foreign countries. (9) Men's volleyball was played in the Olympics during the 1960s it wasn't until over ten years later that women's volleyball became part of the Olympic Games. (10) The women's team from china won the gold medal in the exciting final match that year. (11) William Morgan would recognize the basic rules of Olympic volleyball but he might be surprised by how strenuous the games can be.

1. Sentence 1: **Sports often have fascinating histories.**

If you rewrote sentence 1 beginning with

The history of sports

the next word should be

   (1) fascinating
   (2) have
   (3) has
   (4) is
   (5) are

2. Sentence 3: **In 1895, William Morgan is a YMCA director in Holyoke, Massachusetts.**

Which of the following is the best way to write the underlined portion of this sentence? If you think the original is the best way, choose option (1).

   (1) Morgan is a YMCA director in
   (2) Morgan been a YMCA director in
   (3) Morgan was a YMCA director in
   (4) Morgan is a YMCA director, in
   (5) Morgan is a YMCA director; in

3. Sentence 4: **He seen that many games were too tiring for his classes of older males.**

What correction should be made to this sentence?

   (1) change seen to saw
   (2) change were to was
   (3) change too with to
   (4) insert a comma after tiring
   (5) replace males with male's

4. Sentence 6: **Someone serves the ball by striking it over the net, and members of the other team try to hit the ball.**

What correction should be made to this sentence?

   (1) change serves to serve
   (2) change the spelling of striking to strikeing
   (3) remove the comma after net
   (4) change team to Team
   (5) no correction is necessary

5. Sentence 7: **If they fail to get it back over the net the serving team scores a point.**

Which of the following is the best way to write the underlined portion of this sentence? If you think the original is the best way, choose option (1).

(1) the net the serving team scores a
(2) the net the serving team, scores a
(3) the net the serving team scores, a
(4) the net, the serving team scores a
(5) the net; the serving team scores a

6. Sentence 8: **During World Wars I and II, American military personnel introduced the game abroad, they introduced the game to foreign countries.**

What correction should be made to this sentence?

(1) change <u>American</u> to <u>american</u>
(2) change the spelling of <u>personnel</u> to <u>personal</u>
(3) remove the comma after <u>abroad</u>
(4) remove <u>the game abroad, they introduced</u>
(5) change <u>foreign</u> to <u>Foreign</u>

7. Sentence 9: **Men's volleyball was played in the Olympics during the 1960s it wasn't until over ten years later that women's volleyball became part of the Olympic Games.**

What correction should be made to this sentence?

(1) replace <u>Men's</u> with <u>Mens'</u>
(2) change <u>Olympics</u> to <u>olympics</u>
(3) insert a comma after <u>1960s</u>
(4) replace <u>1960s it</u> with <u>1960s. It</u>
(5) no correction is necessary

8. Sentence 10: **The women's team from china won the gold medal in the exciting final match that year.**

What correction should be made to this sentence?

(1) change <u>women's</u> to <u>womens'</u>
(2) change <u>china</u> to <u>China</u>
(3) replace <u>won</u> with <u>were the winners of</u>
(4) insert a comma after <u>medal</u>
(5) no correction is necessary

9. Sentence 11: **William Morgan would recognize the basic rules of Olympic volleyball but he might be surprised by how strenuous the games can be.**

Which of the following is the best way to write the underlined portion of this sentence? If you think the original is the best way, choose option (1).

(1) volleyball but he might be surprised
(2) volleyball but, he might be surprised
(3) volleyball. But he might be surprised
(4) volleyball, but he might be surprised
(5) volleyball; but he might be surprised

Items 10 to 19 are based on the following paragraph.

(1) Television plays a strong role in deciding who wins an election. (2) The fastest way for politicians to get most of the American population's attention was to go on television. (3) We see the faces of candidates frequently on TV as November of any election year approaches. (4) People running for office appear in the news, in campaign advertisements, and to debate. (5) Those men and women which do not come across well on television often do not get the votes they need. (6) Those who are attractive and have good stage presence tends to be the ones who win an election. (7) Unfortunately, the people who give the most positive impression on TV is not always the best candidates. (8) There were excellent leaders among past American presidents. (9) Some of them probably would have seemed awkward and plain on television. (10) On the other hand, people with good television personalities not necessarily making the best leaders. (11) Watching television, it is easy to forget that what politicians actually do is more important than how they look.

10. Sentence 1: **Television plays a strong role in deciding who wins an election.**

What correction should be made to this sentence?

(1) change <u>plays</u> to <u>playing</u>
(2) change the spelling of <u>role</u> to <u>roll</u>
(3) insert a comma after <u>role</u>
(4) replace <u>who</u> with <u>whom</u>
(5) no correction is necessary

11. Sentence 2: **The fastest way for politicians to get most of the American population's attention was to go on television.**

What correction should be made to this sentence?

(1) insert <u>most</u> after <u>The</u>
(2) change <u>American</u> to <u>american</u>
(3) change the spelling of <u>population's</u> to <u>populatian's</u>
(4) change <u>was</u> to <u>is</u>
(5) no correction is necessary

12. Sentence 3: **We see the faces of candidates frequently on TV as November of any election year approaches.**

If you rewrote sentence 3 beginning with

<u>As November of any election year</u>

the next word should be

(1) approaches,
(2) approaches;
(3) approaching,
(4) candidates,
(5) candidates;

13. Sentence 4: **People running for office appear in the news, in campaign advertisements, and to debate.**

What correction should be made to this sentence?

(1) change <u>appear</u> to <u>appears</u>
(2) change <u>news</u> to <u>News</u>
(3) change the spelling of <u>campaign</u> to <u>campain</u>
(4) remove the comma after <u>advertisements</u>
(5) replace <u>to debate</u> with <u>in debates</u>

14. Sentence 5: **Those men and women which do not come across well on television often do not get the votes they need.**

Which of the following is the best way to write the underlined portion of this sentence? If you think the original is the best way, choose option (1).

(1) Those men and women which do not

(2) Those men and women, which do not

(3) Those men and women who do not

(4) Those men and women who does not

(5) Those men, and women who do not

15. Sentence 6: **Those who are attractive and have good stage presence tends to be the ones who win an election.**

What correction should be made to this sentence?

(1) change are to is
(2) change the spelling of presence to presents
(3) insert a comma after presence
(4) change tends to tend
(5) replace who with which

16. Sentence 7: **Unfortunately, the people who give the most positive impression on TV is not always the best candidates.**

Which of the following is the best way to write the underlined portion of this sentence? If you think the original is the best way, choose option (1).

(1) on TV is not always the best candidates.

(2) on TV, is not always the best candidates.

(3) on TV is not the best candidates, always.

(4) on TV is not always the best canidates.

(5) on TV are not always the best candidates.

17. Sentences 8 & 9: **There were excellent leaders among past American presidents. Some of them probably would have seemed awkward and plain on television.**

The most effective combination of sentences 8 and 9 would include which of the following groups of words?

(1) There were some who were excellent

(2) American presidents in the past were

(3) In the past there were some who were

(4) who probably would have seemed awkward.

(5) who probably would have seemed excellent

18. Sentence 10: **On the other hand, people with good television personalities not necessarily making the best leaders.**

What correction should be made to this sentence?

(1) insert <u>are</u> after <u>personalities</u>

(2) replace <u>not necessarily making</u> with <u>do not necessarily make</u>

(3) replace <u>necessarily making the</u> with <u>making the necessarily</u>

(4) change the spelling of <u>necessarily</u> to <u>necessaryly</u>

(5) insert <u>most</u> after <u>making the</u>

19. Sentence 11: <u>**Watching television, it is easy to**</u> **forget that what politicians actually do is more important than how they look.**

Which of the following is the best way to write the underlined portion of this sentence? If you think the original is the best way, choose option (1).

(1) Watching television, it is easy to

(2) Watching television, one easily

(3) Watching television, we may easily

(4) When you watch television, one may easily

(5) When one watches television, you may easily

Items 20 to 28 are based on the following paragraph.

(1) Scientists know that some illnesses are caused by tiny viruses. (2) Why would a doctor take a virus and injecting it into a patient? (3) Though when you may think the patient would then get the disease, the opposite is true. (4) In the late 1800s a doctor discovered something. (5) He found that patients given shots of cowpox virus were protected from smallpox. (6) Today we can often prevent patients from getting a disease by giving him a specific shot, called a vaccination. (7) Unfortunately, some vaccinations can have serious side effects. (8) There have been a few deaths associated with the whooping cough vaccine, for example. (9) Most doctors beleive that the dangers of this disease are worse than the risks posed by the vaccine. (10) The whooping cough vaccination, like many others, are only given with a parent's approval. (11) Many Doctors give parents literature about a particular vaccine before asking if the parents want the shot for their child. (12) Since more vaccines, are being developed each year, doctors will be asking parents this question more often.

20. Sentence 2: **Why would a doctor take a virus and injecting it into a patient?**

What correction should be made to this sentence?

(1) change <u>doctor</u> to <u>Doctor</u>
(2) change <u>take</u> to <u>took</u>
(3) insert a comma after <u>virus</u>
(4) replace <u>virus and</u> with <u>virus. An</u>
(5) replace <u>injecting</u> with <u>inject</u>

21. Sentence 3: <u>**Though when you may think the patient**</u> **would then get the disease, the opposite is true.**

Which of the following is the best way to write the underlined portion of this sentence? If you think the original is the best way, choose option (1).

(1) Though when you may think the patient
(2) Though you may think the patient
(3) Though when you may have thought the patient
(4) Though when you may think he
(5) Because you may think the patient

22. Sentences 4 & 5: **In the late 1800s a doctor discovered something. He found that patients given shots of cowpox virus were protected from smallpox.**

The most effective combination of sentences 4 and 5 would include which of the following groups of words?

(1) In the late 1800s he discovered
(2) He found in the late 1800s
(3) and he found that patients
(4) a doctor discovered that patients
(5) and they were protected in the late 1800s

23. Sentence 6: **Today we can often prevent patients from getting a disease <u>by giving him a specific shot, called</u> a vaccination.**

Which of the following is the best way to write the underlined portion of this sentence? If you think the original is the best way, choose option (1).

(1) by giving him a specific shot, called
(2) by given him a specific shot, called
(3) by giving him a spesific shot, called
(4) by giving them a specific shot, called
(5) by giving anyone a specific shot, called

24. Sentence 8: **There have been a few deaths associated with the whooping cough vaccine, for example.**

What correction should be made to this sentence?

(1) replace <u>There</u> with <u>Their</u>
(2) change <u>have</u> to <u>has</u>
(3) change the spelling of <u>associated</u> to <u>assosiated</u>
(4) remove the comma after <u>vaccine</u>
(5) no correction is necessary

25. Sentence 9: **Most doctors beleive that the dangers of this disease are worse than the risks posed by the vaccine.**

What correction should be made to this sentence?

(1) change the spelling of <u>beleive</u> to <u>believe</u>
(2) change <u>are</u> to <u>is</u>
(3) insert a comma after <u>disease</u>
(4) insert <u>more</u> after <u>are</u>
(5) replace <u>than</u> with <u>then</u>

26. Sentence 10: **The whooping cough vaccination, <u>like many others, are only given</u> with a parent's approval.**

Which of the following is the best way to write the underlined portion of this sentence? If you think the original is the best way, choose option (1).

(1) like many others, are only given
(2) like many other's, are only given
(3) like many others are only given
(4) like many others, is only given
(5) like many others is only given

27. Sentence 11: **Many Doctors give parents literature about a particular vaccine before asking if the parents want the shot for their child.**

What correction should be made to this sentence?

(1) change <u>Doctors</u> to <u>doctors</u>
(2) change <u>give</u> to <u>gave</u>
(3) change the spelling of <u>literature</u> to <u>litterature</u>
(4) insert a comma after <u>vaccine</u>
(5) change the spelling of <u>their</u> to <u>they're</u>

28. Sentence 12: **Since more <u>vaccines, are being developed each year, doctors</u> will be asking parents this question more often.**

Which of the following is the best way to write the underlined portion of this sentence? If you think the original is the best way, choose option (1).

(1) vaccines, are being developed each year, doctors
(2) vaccines are being developed each year, doctors
(3) vaccines is being developed each year, doctors
(4) vaccines, are being develloped each year, doctors
(5) vaccines, are being developed each year, doctor's

Items 29 to 37 are based on the follow-ing paragraphs.

(1) Adults often ask how they can help a child learn to read. (2) Reading to you're child is one of the best ways to teach about reading. (3) Listening while you read your child learns that reading is enjoyable. (4) There have even been cases of children learning to read without any instruction because they listened as a brother sister, parent, or someone else read to them. (5) While reading, you may want to stop at times and talking with a child about letters, words, or the meaning of the story.

(6) Many children do not like to read on their own. (7) If you offer to take turns reading some of the paragraphs, the same children are often willing to read for quite a while. (8) The child enjoys spending time with you while you read; consequent-ly, beginning to find reading a good experience.

(9) Either your library or the bookstores nearby is sure to contain a book you and a child you know would both enjoy. (10) Somewhere on the bookshelves are the first half of a gift you might want to give a child. (11) When you sit down and read the book with the child on his or her birthday, New Year's Day, or any other day, you are giving him or her the rest of the gift.

29. Sentence 2: **Reading to you're child is one of the best ways to teach about reading.**

What correction should be made to this sentence?

(1) change you're to your
(2) insert a comma after child
(3) change is to are
(4) insert a comma after ways
(5) change reading to Reading

30. Sentence 3: **Listening while you read your child learns that reading is enjoyable.**

Which of the following is the best way to write the underlined portion of this sentence? If you think the original is the best way, choose option (1).

(1) while you read your child learns
(2) while you read. Your child learns
(3) while you read, your child learns
(4) while you read; your child learns
(5) while you read your child, learns

31. Sentence 4: **There have even been cases of children learning to read without any instruction because they listened as a brother sister, parent, or someone else read to them.**

What correction should be made to this sentence?

(1) change have to has
(2) replace even been with been even
(3) replace they with he
(4) insert a comma after brother
(5) change read to reads

32. Sentence 5: **While reading, you may want to stop at times and talking with a child about letters, words, or the meaning of the story.**

Which of the following is the best way to write the underlined portion of this sentence? If you think the original is the best way, choose option (1).

(1) times and talking with a child about letters,
(2) times, and talking with a child about letters,
(3) times and talk with a child about letters,
(4) times and will talk with a child about letters,
(5) times and talking with a child about letters

33. Sentences 6 & 7: **Many children do not like to read on their own. If you offer to take turns reading some of the paragraphs, the same children are often willing to read for quite a while.**

The most effective combination of sentences 6 and 7 would include which of the following groups of words?

(1) who do not like to read on their own

(2) which refuse to read much on their own

(3) offer to take turns for quite a while

(4) is often willing to read

(5) were often willing to read

34. Sentence 8: **The child enjoys spending time with you while <u>you read; consequently, beginning to find</u> reading a good experience.**

Which of the following is the best way to write the underlined portion of this sentence? If you think the original is the best way, choose option (1).

(1) you read; consequently, beginning to find

(2) one reads; consequently, beginning to find

(3) you read, consequently, beginning to find

(4) you read; consequently, he or she begins to find

(5) you read; consequently, he or she began to find

35. Sentence 9: **Either your <u>library or the bookstores nearby is</u> sure to contain a book you and a child you know would both enjoy.**

Which of the following is the best way to write the underlined portion of this sentence? If you think the original is the best way, choose option (1).

(1) library or the bookstores nearby is

(2) Library or the bookstores nearby is

(3) library, or the bookstores nearby is

(4) library or the bookstores nearby, is

(5) library or the bookstores nearby are

36. Sentence 10: **Somewhere on the bookshelves are the first half of a gift you might want to give a child.**

What correction should be made to this sentence?

(1) insert a comma after <u>bookshelves</u>

(2) change <u>are</u> to <u>is</u>

(3) change the spelling of <u>half</u> to <u>haft</u>

(4) replace <u>you</u> with <u>they</u>

(5) no correction is necessary

37. Sentence 11: **When you sit down and read the book with the child on his or her birthday, New Year's Day, or any other day, you are giving him or her the rest of the gift.**

What correction should be made to this sentence?

(1) insert a comma after <u>down</u>

(2) change <u>New Year's Day</u> to <u>new year's day</u>

(3) remove the comma after <u>other day</u>

(4) change <u>are giving</u> to <u>gave</u>

(5) no correction is necessary

Items 38 to 47 are based on the following paragraph.

(1) As anyone who has growed up in a military family can tell you, military children face some special challenges. (2) For one thing, many military families make frequent moves. (3) Having to change schools especially in the middle of the year, can be difficult. (4) Take the case of a child who is learning to do long division. (5) Just as he is being taught this, his Father is transferred from Germany to California. (6) The child's new class in San Diego may be in the middle of fractions, the child may get confused. (7) On the other hand, he will probably know more than his classmates about European geography and the german language. (8) Neither this child nor his parents enjoy leaving old friends, but they may learn to make friends faster than other people. (9) Another problem for some military children is the absense of a parent for long periods of time. (10) This separation is more common if the parent, usually the father, is in the Navy or Marine Corps, Army and Air Force personnel are sent away on duty less often. (11) Each branch of the military has set up family service centers. (12) It offers assistance with a variety of problems.

38. Sentence 1: **As anyone <u>who has growed up in a military family</u> can tell you, military children face some special challenges.**

Which of the following is the best way to write the underlined portion of this sentence? If you think the original is the best way, choose option (1).

(1) who has growed up in a military family
(2) which has growed up in a military family
(3) who have growed up in a military family
(4) who has grown up in a military family
(5) who has growed up, in a military family

39. Sentence 2: **For one thing, many military families make frequent moves.**

What correction should be made to this sentence?

(1) change <u>make</u> to <u>made</u>
(2) change the spelling of <u>frequent</u> to <u>freequint</u>
(3) change <u>families</u> to <u>family</u>
(4) change <u>make</u> to <u>makes</u>
(5) no correction is necessary

40. Sentence 3: **Having to change <u>schools especially in the middle</u> of the year, can be difficult.**

Which of the following is the best way to write the underlined portion of this sentence? If you think the original is the best way, choose option (1).

(1) schools especially in the middle
(2) schools; especially in the middle
(3) schools and especially in the middle
(4) schools but especially in the middle
(5) schools, especially in the middle

41. Sentence 5: **Just as he is being taught this, his Father is transferred from Germany to California.**

What correction should be made to this sentence?

(1) remove the comma after <u>this</u>
(2) change <u>Father</u> to <u>father</u>
(3) replace <u>is transferred</u> with <u>was transferred</u>
(4) change <u>Germany</u> to <u>germany</u>
(5) change <u>California</u> to <u>california</u>

42. Sentence 6: **The child's new class in San Diego may be in the middle of fractions, the child may get confused.**

What correction should be made to this sentence?

(1) replace <u>in San Diego</u> with <u>at San Diego</u>
(2) change <u>San Diego</u> to <u>san diego</u>
(3) remove the comma after <u>fractions</u>
(4) insert <u>and</u> after <u>fractions,</u>
(5) change <u>may get</u> to <u>may have gotten</u>

43. Sentence 7: **On the other hand, he will probably know more than his classmates about European geography and the german language.**

What correction should be made to this sentence?

(1) replace <u>know</u> with <u>no</u>
(2) replace <u>more than</u> with <u>more as</u>
(3) change <u>European</u> to <u>european</u>
(4) change <u>german</u> to <u>German</u>
(5) no correction is necessary

44. Sentence 8: **Neither this child nor his parents enjoy leaving old friends, but they may learn to make friends faster than other people.**

What correction should be made to this sentence?

(1) change <u>enjoy</u> to <u>enjoys</u>
(2) change the spelling of <u>friends</u> to <u>freinds</u>
(3) remove the comma after <u>friends</u>
(4) replace <u>they</u> with <u>families who move a lot</u>
(5) insert <u>more</u> after <u>friends</u>

45. Sentence 9: **Another problem for some military children is the absense of a parent for long periods of time.**

What correction should be made to this sentence?

(1) insert a comma after <u>children</u>
(2) change <u>is</u> to <u>are</u>
(3) change the spelling of <u>absense</u> to <u>absence</u>
(4) insert a comma after <u>parent</u>
(5) no correction is necessary

46. Sentence 10: **This separation is more common if the parent, usually the father, is in the <u>Navy or Marine Corps, Army and Air Force</u> personnel are sent away on duty less often.**

Which of the following is the best way to write the underlined portion of this sentence? If you think the original is the best way, choose option (1).

(1) Navy or Marine Corps, Army and Air Force
(2) Navy, or Marine Corps, Army and Air Force
(3) Navy or Marine Corps; Army and Air Force
(4) Navy or Marine Corps, Army, and Air Force
(5) Navy or Marine Corps and Army and Air Force

47. Sentences 11 & 12: **Each branch of the military has set up family service centers. It offers assistance with a variety of problems.**

The most effective combination of sentences 11 and 12 would include which of the followint groups of words?

(1) in order to serve the purpose of
(2) and it offers assistance with
(3) to offer its assistance with a
(4) to assist with a variety
(5) with a variety of different

Items 48 to 55 are based on the following paragraph.

(1) When computers were first invented, many people are really frightened of them. (2) One fear was that everyone's job would be took by computers. (3) In addition, the thought of working with more computers and fewer people, made many workers anxious. (4) The first worry turned out to be needless, in most cases; the use of computers has actually increased the total number of jobs. (5) There is some basis for the second concern. (6) Employees in the automobile industry in detroit, for example, often work with computers. (7) Robots who are controlled by computers now do many of the repetitive tasks in factories. (8) These tasks used to be done by employees working side by side in an assembly line. (9) One good side of this whole thing is that because of them the workplace is safer. (10) In an accident that might have injured a worker in the passed, there might only be damage to a robot today.

48. Sentence 1: **When computers were first invented, many people are really frightened of them.**

Which of the following is the best way to write the underlined portion of this sentence? If you think the original is the best way, choose option (1).

(1) invented, many people are really frightened

(2) invented many people are really frightened

(3) invented; many people are really frightened

(4) invented, many people were really frightened

(5) invented, many people are real frightened

49. Sentence 2: **One fear was that everyone's job would be took by computers.**

Which of the following is the best way to write the underlined portion of this sentence? If you think the original is the best way, choose option (1).

(1) job would be took by computers.

(2) job, would be took by computers.

(3) job were took by computers.

(4) job will be took by computers.

(5) job would be taken by computers.

50. Sentence 3: **In addition, the thought of working with more computers and fewer people, made many workers anxious.**

What correction should be made to this sentence?

(1) insert a comma after thought

(2) replace fewer with less

(3) remove the comma after people

(4) replace made with making

(5) change the spelling of anxious to angshous

51. Sentence 4: **The first worry turned out to be needless, in most cases; the use of computers has actually increased the total number of jobs.**

What correction should be made to this sentence?

(1) change the spelling of first to furst

(2) replace cases; the with cases, unless the

(3) insert a comma after computers

(4) change has to have

(5) no correction is necessary

52. Sentence 6: **Employees in the automobile industry in detroit, for example, often work with computers.**

What correction should be made to this sentence?

(1) change the spelling of automobile to autamobile

(2) change detroit to Detroit

(3) remove the comma after example

(4) insert to after often

(5) change work to works

53. Sentence 7: **Robots who are controlled by computers now do many of the repetitive tasks in factories.**

What correction should be made to this sentence?

(1) replace who with that

(2) change the spelling of controlled to controled

(3) replace controlled by with under the control

(4) insert a comma after tasks

(5) no correction is necessary

54. Sentence 9: **One good side of this whole thing is that because of robots the workplace is safer.**

If you rewrote sentence 9 beginning with

Fortunately, the workplace has been made safer

The next word should be

(1) by

(2) from

(3) that

(4) however

(5) and

55. Sentence 10: **In an accident that might have injured a worker in the passed, there might only be damage to a robot today.**

Which of the following is the best way to write the underlined portion of this sentence? If you think the original is the best way, choose option (1).

(1) in the passed, there might

(2) in the passed there might

(3) in the past, there might

(4) in the passed, their might

(5) in the passed, they're might

Answers are on pages 352-354.

PRACTICE ITEMS

Part II

Directions: This is a test to see how well you can write. In this test, you are asked to write an essay in which you present your opinions about an issue. In preparing your essay, you should take the following steps.

Step 1. Read all of the information about the topic. Be sure that you understand the topic and that you write about only the assigned topic.

Step 2. Plan your essay before you write.

Step 3. Use scrap paper to make any notes.

Step 4. Write your essay on a separate sheet of paper.

Step 5. Read what you have written. Make sure that your writing is legible.

Step 6. Check your paragraphing, sentence structure, spelling, punctuation, capitalization, and usage; make any changes that will improve your essay.

TOPIC

Hobbies may help develop an outside interest or just allow enjoyable time away from normal routine. Many people feel that having a hobby enriches their lives.

Write an essay, approximately 200 words long, in which you give your opinion on the importance of a hobby. Be specific and use examples to support your opinion.

When you take the GED Test, you will have 45 minutes to write about the topic you are assigned. Try to write the essay for this test within 45 minutes. Write legibly and use a ballpoint pen so that your writing will be easy to read. Any notes that you make on scrap paper will not be counted as part of your score.

After you complete this essay, you can judge its effectiveness by using the Essay Scoring Guide and Model Essays in the answer key to score your essay. Your GED essay will be judged on how clearly you make the main point of your essay, how thoroughly you support your ideas, and how clear and correct your writing is throughout the composition. You will receive no credit for writing about a topic other than the one assigned.

Answers are on pages 355-357.

Performance Analysis Chart

Part I

Directions: Circle the number of each item that you got correct on the Practice Items. Count how many items you got correct in each row; count how many items you got correct in each column. Write the amount correct per row and column as the numerator in the fraction in the appropriate "Total Correct" box. (The denominators represent the total number of items in the row or column.) Write the grand total correct over the denominator, 53, at the lower right corner of the chart. (For example, if you got 48 items correct, write 48 so that the fraction reads 48/53.)

Item Type	Usage (page 24)	Sentence Structure (page 95)	Mechanics (page 140)	TOTAL CORRECT
Construction Shift	1	12, 17, 22, 33, 47, 54		/7
Sentence Correction	3, 11, 15, 24, 36, 39, 44, 53	6, 7, 13 18, 20, 42, 51	4, 8, 10, 25, 27, 29, 31, 37, 41, 43, 45,	/26
Sentence Revision	2, 14, 16, 23, 26, 35, 38, 48, 49	19, 21, 32, 34, 46	5, 9, 28, 30, 40, 55	/20
TOTAL CORRECT	/18	/18	/19	/53

The page numbers in parentheses indicate where in this book you can find the beginning of specific instruction about the areas of grammar and about the types of questions you encountered in the Practice Items.

Part II

Write your essay's score in the box at the right.

What were some of the strong points of your essay?

What were some of the weak points of your essay?

What improvements do you plan to make when you work on your next essay?

PRACTICE TEST

This Practice Test is like the actual test. There are 55 items in Part I and one essay topic in Part II. By taking the Practice Test, you can gain valuable test-taking experience and you will know what to expect when you sit down to take the actual Writing Skills Test.

Using the Practice Test to Best Advantage

You can use the Practice Test in the following ways:

- To get hands-on, test-taking experience, you may wish to take the Practice Test under conditions similar to those of the actual test. To do this, do the Practice Test in one sitting and try to complete it within the 120-minute time limit. Although you can complete the test in any order you choose, it is to your advantage to begin with Part I. If 75 minutes elapse and you have not yet finished Part I, you should proceed to Part II. If you finish Part II before 120 minutes have elapsed, you can go back to the items in Part I. If 120 minutes elapse and you have not finished, note how far you have gotten and continue. You will learn whether you need to change your pace to complete the test. You will also learn about how well you will do if you complete the Writing Skills Test.

- If you want, you can take the Practice Test in sections. One way to do this is to do Parts I and II at different times. You can also break Part I of the test into smaller sections. For example, you can complete one set of Part I items at a time. Then you can write your Part II essay in one sitting. While this does not simulate the actual testing situation, your results still will give you a pretty good idea of how well you would do on the real test.

When you take the Practice Test, write your answers for Part I neatly on a sheet of paper or use an answer sheet provided by your teacher. If you don't know how to answer a question, skip it and come back to it after you have answered the other questions. Plan and write your Part II essay on fresh sheets of paper. Express your thoughts as clearly as possible. Remember that this is not the actual test, just some helpful practice. If you relax, you may discover that you actually perform better!

Using the Answers and Explanations

Compare your answers for Part I to those in the Answer Key on page 358, and check each item you answered correctly. Whether you answer a multiple-choice item correctly or not, you should read through the explanations. Doing this will reinforce your writing skills and develop your test-taking skills. For Part II, follow the directions that tell you how to score your essay. You might like to have a teacher or someone else score your essay as well.

How to Use Your Score

Regardless of how you use the items in the Practice Test, your final score will point out your strengths and weaknesses in writing and editing. After scoring your Part I work with the answer key, fill in the Performance Analysis Chart on page 307. This chart will help you determine which grammar and editing skills and item types you are strongest in and direct you to parts of the book where you can review areas in which you need additional work. Record your evaluation of your essay on the Performance Analysis Chart. If you discover weaknesses while evaluating your Part II essay, you should refer back to the Part II lessons that cover the composition skills you had difficulty with.

PRACTICE TEST

Part I

Directions: The items in Part I of this test are based on paragraphs that contain numbered sentences. Some of the sentences may contain errors in sentence structure, usage, or mechanics. **A few sentences, however, may be correct as written.** Read each paragraph and then answer the items that follow it. For each item, choose the answer that would result in the most effective writing of the sentence or sentences. The best answer must be consistent with the meaning and tone of the rest of the paragraph.

FOR EXAMPLE:

Sentence 1: **Although it may take only two hours to watch the average motion picture takes almost a year to make.**

What correction should be made to this sentence?

(1) replace <u>it</u> with <u>they</u>
(2) change <u>take</u> to <u>have taken</u>
(3) insert a comma after <u>watch</u>
(4) change <u>almost</u> to <u>all most</u>
(5) no change is necessary

The correct answer is **(3)**. In this example, a comma is needed after the introductory words <u>Although it may take only two hours to watch</u>.

Items 1 to 9 are based on the following paragraph.

(1) Thinking of an appropriate gift for a graduation or birthday celebration are often difficult. (2) Calculators can make good presence on such occasions; these devices help make decisions about spending easier. (3) Suppose the members of a family decides to go to a restaurant for Sunday dinner. (4) Using a calculator, the tip can easily be figured out. (5) Perhaps a husband and wife are going to buy living room furniture. (6) Before they decide whether to pay all at once, they used a calculator to find the total cost of paying in installments. (7) Maybe they are going to spend some money on painting their kitchen. (8) If they have a calculator, they will have no problem determining how much paint they need to buy. (9) Imagine that the couple plans to go to the grand canyon for a vacation. (10) A calculator will prove handy in figuring out the cost of driving staying in a motel, and taking a tour. (11) Of course, paper and pencil can be used to do all this math; but however, using a calculator is a lot more convenient.

1. Sentence 1: **Thinking of an appropriate gift for a graduation or birthday celebration are often difficult.**

   What correction should be made to this sentence?

   (1) change the spelling of <u>appropriate</u> to <u>apropriate</u>
   (2) change <u>birthday</u> to <u>Birthday</u>
   (3) change <u>celebration</u> to <u>celebrations</u>
   (4) change <u>are</u> to <u>is</u>
   (5) no correction is necessary

2. Sentence 2: **Calculators can make good presence on such occasions; these devices help make decisions about spending easier.**

   What correction should be made to this sentence?

   (1) change the spelling of <u>presence</u> to <u>presents</u>
   (2) insert <u>because</u> after <u>occasions;</u>
   (3) change the spelling of <u>devices</u> to <u>devises</u>
   (4) change <u>help</u> to <u>helping</u>
   (5) replace <u>easier</u> with <u>easily</u>

3. Sentence 3: **Suppose the members of a family decides to go to a restaurant for Sunday dinner.**

   What correction should be made to this sentence?

   (1) replace <u>Suppose</u> with <u>If</u>
   (2) change <u>decides</u> to <u>decide</u>
   (3) change the spelling of <u>restaurant</u> to <u>restaraunt</u>
   (4) insert a comma after <u>restaurant</u>
   (5) change <u>Sunday</u> to <u>sunday</u>

4. Sentence 4: **Using a calculator, the tip can easily be figured out.**

   If you rewrote sentence 4 beginning with

   <u>With a calculator,</u>

   the next word(s) should be

   (1) tip
   (2) figure out
   (3) can be
   (4) they
   (5) using

5. Sentence 6: **Before they decide whether to pay all at <u>once, they used</u> a calculator to find the total cost of paying in installments.**

Which of the following is the best way to write the underlined portion of this sentence? If you think the original is the best way, choose option (1).

(1) once, they used
(2) once; they used
(3) once, they can use
(4) once they used
(5) once, one used

6. Sentence 8: **If they have a calculator, they will have no problem determining how much paint they need to buy.**

If you rewrote sentence 7 beginning with

Determining how much paint

the next word should be

(1) if
(2) you
(3) will
(4) to
(5) so

7. Sentence 9: **Imagine that the couple plans to go to the grand canyon for a vacation.**

What correction should be made to this sentence?

(1) change <u>plans</u> to <u>planned</u>
(2) change <u>plans</u> to <u>plan's</u>
(3) insert a comma after <u>plans</u>
(4) change <u>grand canyon</u> to <u>Grand Canyon</u>
(5) no correction is necessary

8. Sentence 10: **A calculator will prove handy in figuring out the cost of <u>driving staying in a motel,</u> and taking a tour.**

Which of the following is the best way to write the underlined portion of this sentence? If you think the original is the best way, choose option (1).

(1) driving staying in a motel
(2) to drive, staying in a motel
(3) driving or staying in a motel
(4) driving and staying in a motel
(5) driving, staying in a motel,

9. Sentence 11: **Of course, paper and pencil can be used to do all <u>this math; but however,</u> using a calculator is a lot more convenient.**

Which of the following is the best way to write the underlined portion of this sentence? If you think the original is the best way, choose option (1).

(1) this math; but however,
(2) this math; but although,
(3) this math. But however,
(4) this math; however,
(5) this math, however,

Items 10 to 19 are based on the following paragraph.

(1) Are you trying to learn about careers, your public library is a good place to start. (2) Try to find the *Occupational Outlook Handbook*, published by the U.S. Department of Labor. (3) They will give you helpful descriptions of many different jobs. (4) If in case you want more information about specific jobs, look in the card catalog. (5) Arranged in alphabetical order by subject is cards that tell you where to look for the books you want. (6) There may even be magazines or journels about the career in which you are interested. (7) Find out if the library had filmstrips, tapes, or computerized information about jobs. (8) Always ask yourself who wrote the information and why. (9) An example of the reason why is that employers sometimes pay writers to write pamphlets about a company. (10) The pamphlets may exaggerate job benefits. (11) They may fail to mention problems with the job. (12) Its better to find out the drawbacks of a job now than to discover them later.

10. Sentence 1: **Are you trying to learn about <u>careers, your public</u> library is a good place to start.**

    Which of the following is the best way to write the underlined portion of this sentence? If you think the original is the best way, choose option (1).

    (1) careers, Your public
    (2) careers? Your public
    (3) careers. Your public
    (4) careers, then your public
    (5) careers, and your public

11. Sentence 3: **<u>They will give you</u> helpful descriptions of many different jobs.**

    Which of the following is the best way to write the underlined portion of this sentence? If you think the original is the best way, choose option (1).

    (1) They will give you
    (2) They gives you
    (3) They gave you
    (4) It will give you
    (5) They will give people

12. Sentence 4: **If in case you want more information about specific jobs, look in the card catalog.**

    What correction should be made to this sentence?

    (1) remove <u>in case</u>
    (2) change <u>want</u> to <u>wanted</u>
    (3) insert a comma after <u>information</u>
    (4) change <u>look</u> to <u>looking</u>
    (5) replace <u>jobs, look</u> with <u>jobs; look</u>

13. Sentence 5: **Arranged in alphabetical order by subject is cards that tell you where to look for the books you want.**

    What correction should be made to this sentence?

    (1) Change the spelling of <u>Arranged</u> to <u>Aranged</u>
    (2) change <u>is</u> to <u>are</u>
    (3) insert a comma after <u>cards</u>
    (4) replace <u>that</u> with <u>who</u>
    (5) replace <u>you want</u> with <u>one wants</u>

14. Sentence 6: **There may even be magazines or journels about the career in which you are interested.**

What correction should be made to this sentence?

(1) insert a comma after <u>magazines</u>

(2) change the spelling of <u>journels</u> to <u>journals</u>

(3) replace <u>in which</u> with <u>that</u>

(4) change <u>you are</u> to <u>one is</u>

(5) no correction is necessary

15. Sentence 7: **Find out if the library had filmstrips, tapes, or computerized information about jobs.**

What correction should be made to this sentence?

(1) change <u>library</u> to <u>Library</u>

(2) change <u>had</u> to <u>has</u>

(3) remove the comma after <u>filmstrips</u>

(4) change <u>jobs</u> to <u>job's</u>

(5) no correction is necessary

16. Sentence 8: <u>**Always ask yourself who wrote**</u> **the information and why.**

Which of the following is the best way to write the underlined portion of this sentence? If you think the original is the best way, choose option (1).

(1) Always ask yourself who wrote

(2) Ask yourself who always wrote

(3) Always ask oneself who wrote

(4) Always ask yourself whom wrote

(5) Always ask yourself who had written

17. Sentence 9: **An example of the reason why is that employers sometimes pay writers to write pamphlets about a company.**

If you rewrote sentence 9 beginning with

<u>Sometimes, for example,</u>

the next word should be

(1) the

(2) that

(3) employers

(4) payment

(5) putting

18. Sentences 10 & 11: **The pamphlets may exaggerate job benefits. They may fail to mention problems with the job.**

The most effective combination of sentences 10 and 11 would include which of the following groups of words?

(1) There may be a benefits exaggeration

(2) An exaggeration of job benefits and a failure

(3) and there also may be a failure

(4) as well as there being a failure

(5) may exaggerate job benefits and fail

19. Sentence 12: **Its better to find out the drawbacks of a job now than to discover them later.**

What correction should be made to this sentence?

(1) change <u>Its</u> to <u>It's</u>

(2) change <u>Its</u> to <u>Its'</u>

(3) insert a comma after <u>now</u>

(4) insert a semicolon after <u>now</u>

(5) change <u>them</u> to <u>it</u>

Items 20 to 28 are based on the following paragraph.

(1) To make sure that high school graduates have basic computer skills, computer literacy is a requirement in many schools. (2) Such skills as English and math have always been important; now knowlege of computers is needed for more and more jobs. (3) Even if computers are not needed for a particular job at present, in the future they probably are. (4) You can probably picture computers being used by people who work in such places as banks or business offices. (5) You might think that truckers, artists, and, musicians would not use computers, but many of them do. (6) Students learn about computers in special computer classes. (7) They also learn about cmputers in regular classes. (8) When schools order textbooks in the spring or summer they often buy accompanying computer programs. (9) Students taking french, for example, may learn some of the vocabulary and grammar from a computer. (10) There is computer programs, known as software, that deal with everything from applying for a bank loan to taking a driving test. (11) The workplace is only one of many areas computers have entered; their use in a variety of areas is becoming more widespread every day.

20. Sentence 1: **To make sure that high school graduates have basic computer skills, computer literacy is a requirement in many schools.**

Which of the following is the best way to write the underlined portion of this sentence? If you think the original is the best way, choose option (1).

(1) computer literacy is a requirement in many schools.
(2) computer literacy being a requirement in many schools.
(3) computer literacy is a requirement, in many schools.
(4) many school officials have made computer literacy a requirement.
(5) many are requiring computer literacy.

21. Sentence 2: **Such skills as English and math have always been important; now knowlege of computers is needed for more and more jobs.**

What correction should be made to this sentence?

(1) change math to Math
(2) change have to has
(3) replace important; now with important, now
(4) change the spelling of knowlege to knowledge
(5) change is to being

22. Sentence 3: **Even if computers are not needed for a particular job at present, in the future they probably are.**

Which of the following is the best way to write the underlined portion of this sentence? If you think the original is the best way, choose option (1).

(1) they probably are.
(2) computers probably are.
(3) they are probably.
(4) they probably will be.
(5) their need is probable.

23. Sentence 5: **You might think that truckers, artists, and, musicians would not use computers, but many of them do.**

What correction should be made to this sentence?

(1) insert a comma after <u>think</u>
(2) insert a comma after <u>that</u>
(3) remove the comma after <u>and</u>
(4) replace <u>but</u> with <u>however</u>
(5) replace <u>do</u> with <u>have</u>

24. Sentences 6 & 7: **Students learn about computers in special computer classes. They also learn about computers in regular classes.**

The most effective combination of sentences 6 and 7 would include which of the following groups of words?

(1) Students learn about them
(2) Learning about computers,
(3) in both special computer classes and
(4) in special computer classes both
(5) and they also learn about computers

25. Sentence 8: **When schools order textbooks in the spring or summer they often buy accompanying computer programs.**

What correction should be made to this sentence?

(1) change <u>spring or summer</u> to <u>Spring or Summer</u>
(2) insert a comma after <u>summer</u>
(3) replace <u>they often buy</u> with <u>one often buys</u>
(4) change the spelling of <u>accompanying</u> to <u>acompanying</u>
(5) no correction is necessary

26. Sentence 9: **Students taking french, for example, may learn some of the vocabulary and grammar from a computer.**

What correction should be made to this sentence?

(1) change <u>french</u> to <u>French</u>
(2) remove the comma after <u>example</u>
(3) change <u>learn</u> to <u>have learned</u>
(4) insert a comma after <u>vocabulary</u>
(5) change the spelling of <u>grammar</u> to <u>grammer</u>

27. Sentence 10: <u>**There is computer programs, known**</u> **as software, that deal with everything from applying for a bank loan to taking a driving test.**

Which of the following is the best way to write the underlined portion of this sentence? If you think the original is the best way, choose option (1).

(1) There is computer programs, known
(2) There are computer programs, known
(3) There are computer programs known
(4) Computer programs are known
(5) Computer programs is known

28. Sentence 11: **The workplace is only one of many areas computers have entered; their use in a variety of areas is becoming more widespread every day.**

What correction should be made to this sentence?

(1) replace <u>The</u> with <u>Because the</u>
(2) change <u>their use</u> to <u>they're use</u>
(3) change <u>is becoming</u> to <u>are becoming</u>
(4) insert a comma after <u>widespread</u>
(5) no correction is necessary

Items 29 to 37 are based on the following paragraph.

(1) Most of us have received at least one notice in the mail announcing that you've won a valuable prize. (2) The news usually comes in a letter, on a post card, or a computer form arrives. (3) When someone from a television audience wins a prize, they sometimes shrieks or faints. (4) Unlike the ecstatic winner on television, you may have your doubts about what you've won, you should. (5) The note of congratulations you've been sent, is most likely from someone who is trying to sell you something. (6) In bold letters at the top of the page often describing a vacation that can be yours. (7) You are offered the opportunity to travel to Florida, the Gulf of Mexico, Ulster County, or the Pocono Mountains, for example. (8) In fine print at the bottom or on the back is the catch. (9) First you have to listen to a sales pitch about buying land or vacation property may be for rent. (10) Absent altogether is any mention of the fact that you are responsible for air fare, meals, and other expenses. (11) Some unfortunate people have their time and money wasted on these scams; don't be one of them. (12) Before throwing away your notice, make a complaint to the Better Business Bureau.

29. Sentence 1: **Most of us have received at least one notice in the mail announcing that you've won a valuable prize.**

Which of the following is the best way to write the underlined portion of this sentence? If you think the original is the best way, choose option (1).

(1) Most of us have received
(2) Most of us has received
(3) Most all of us have received
(4) Most of you have received
(5) Probably having received

30. Sentence 2: **The news usually comes in a letter, on a post card, or a computer form arrives.**

What correction should be made to this sentence?

(1) change the spelling of usually to usuelly
(2) change comes to come
(3) remove on
(4) remove the comma after card
(5) replace a computer form arrives with on a computer form

31. Sentence 3: **When someone from a television audience wins a prize, they sometimes shrieks or faints.**

What correction should be made to this sentence?

(1) remove the comma after prize
(2) replace they with the person
(3) change the spelling of shrieks to shreiks
(4) replace shrieks or faints with shriek or faint
(5) no correction is necessary

32. Sentence 4: **Unlike the ecstatic winner on television, you may have your doubts about what you've won, you should.**

What correction should be made to this sentence?

(1) insert a comma after winner
(2) replace you with one
(3) change your to you're
(4) replace won, you with won. You
(5) insert have one's doubts after should

33. Sentence 5: **The note of congratulations you've been sent, is most likely from someone who is trying to sell you something.**

What correction should be made to this sentence?

(1) replace <u>been sent</u> with <u>sent</u>
(2) remove the comma after <u>sent</u>
(3) replace <u>is</u> with <u>are</u>
(4) insert a comma after <u>someone</u>
(5) replace <u>to sell</u> with <u>and sell</u>

34. Sentence 6: **In bold letters at the top of the <u>page often describing a vacation</u> that can be yours.**

Which of the following is the best way to write the underlined portion of this sentence? If you think the original is the best way, choose option (1).

(1) page often describing a vacation
(2) page, often describing a vacation
(3) page; often describing a vacation
(4) page are often a description of a vacation
(5) page is often a description of a vacation

35. Sentence 7: **You are offererd the opportunity to travel to Florida, the Gulf of Mexico, Ulster County, or the Pocono Mountains, for example.**

What correction should be made to this sentence?

(1) change the spelling of <u>offered</u> to <u>oferred</u>
(2) insert a comma after <u>opportunity</u>
(3) change <u>County</u> to <u>county</u>
(4) change <u>Mountains</u> to <u>mountains</u>
(5) no correction is necessary

36. Sentence 9: **First you have to listen to a sales pitch about <u>buying land or vacation property may be for rent.</u>**

Which of the following is the best way to write the underlined portion of this sentence? If you think the original is the best way, choose option (1).

(1) buying land or vacation property may be for rent.
(2) buying land; or vacation property may be for rent.
(3) buying land or renting vacation property.
(4) buying land or rented vacation property.
(5) buying land, or vacation property that is rented.

37. Sentence 11: **Some unfortunate people have their time and money wasted on these scams; don't be one of them.**

If you rewrote sentence 11 beginning with

<u>Don't be one of those unfortunate people</u>

the next word should be

(1) which
(2) who
(3) having
(4) these
(5) and

Items 38 to 47 are based on the following paragraph.

(1) An increasing number of employers are hiring temporary employees. (2) The jobs these workers are given anywhere from one day to several weeks. (3) Temporaries are hired to fill in for absint file clerks, typists, bookkeepers, and truck loaders, among other workers. (4) Agencies that handle temporary jobs are advertised in the telephone book. (5) They are also advertised in the classified section of your newspaper. (6) When you call the Agency, someone there will set up an appointment for you to come in and take a test. (7) An agency that handles clerical jobs, for example, probably tested your spelling, grammar, and typing speed. (8) Weigh the pros and cons before deciding whether or not one wants to work for a temporary agency. (9) One advantage was that you will probably be paid within a week or two of the week you work. (10) On the other hand, paychecks are fairly small because as a result the agency takes a large percentage of your earnings. (11) You may become more versatile as you train for many different jobs but you may not enjoy making frequent job changes. (12) Having decided that the benefits of working for a temporary agency would outweigh the drawbacks, it might be worth a try.

38. Sentence 2: **The jobs these workers are given anywhere from one day to several weeks.**

Which of the following is the best way to write the underlined portion of this sentence? If you think the original is the best way, choose option (1).

(1) The jobs these workers are given anywhere

(2) The jobs who these workers are given anywhere

(3) The jobs, these workers are given, anywhere

(4) The jobs given these workers anywhere

(5) The jobs these workers are given last anywhere

39. Sentence 3: **Temporaries are hired to fill in for absint file clerks, typists, bookkeepers, and truck loaders, among other workers.**

What correction should be made to this sentence?

(1) replace are hired to with which are hired

(2) change the spelling of absint to absent

(3) insert and after typists

(4) remove the comma after bookkeepers

(5) no correction is necessary

40. Sentences 4 & 5: **Agencies that handle temporary jobs are advertised in the telephone book. They are also advertised in the classified section of your newspaper.**

The most effective combination of sentences 4 and 5 would include which of the following groups of words?

(1) They are advertised in the telephone book

(2) Agencies also advertise in the classified

(3) Temporary agencies who are advertised

(4) or they also are found

(5) and in the classified section

41. Sentence 6: **When you call the Agency, someone there will set up an appointment for you to come in and take a test.**

What correction should be made to this sentence?

(1) replace you call with you called

(2) change Agency to agency

(3) replace there with their

(4) insert a comma after in

(5) no correction is necessary

42. Sentence 7: **An agency that handles clerical jobs, for example, probably tested your spelling, grammar, and typing speed.**

What correction should be made to this sentence?

(1) replace <u>that</u> with <u>who</u>
(2) change <u>jobs</u> to <u>jobs'</u>
(3) remove the comma after <u>example</u>
(4) replace <u>probably tested</u> with <u>will probably test</u>
(5) remove the comma after <u>grammar</u>

43. Sentence 8: **Weigh the pros and cons before deciding whether or not <u>one wants to work</u> for a temporary agency.**

Which of the following is the best way to write the underlined portion of this sentence? If you think the original is the best way, choose option (1).

(1) one wants to work
(2) one will be wanting
(3) a person wants to work
(4) you want working
(5) you want to work

44. Sentence 9: **One advantage was that you will probably be paid within a week or two of the week you work.**

What correction should be made to this sentence?

(1) change <u>was</u> to <u>is</u>
(2) change <u>that</u> to <u>which</u>
(3) insert a comma after <u>paid</u>
(4) change <u>two</u> to <u>to</u>
(5) no correction is necessary

45. Sentence 10: **On the other hand, paychecks are fairly small because as a result the agency takes a large percentage of your earnings.**

What correction should be made to this sentence?

(1) remove the comma after <u>hand</u>
(2) remove <u>because</u>
(3) remove <u>as a result</u>
(4) replace <u>agency takes</u> with <u>agency's taking</u>
(5) replace <u>your</u> with <u>one's</u>

46. Sentence 11: **You may become more versatile as you train for many different <u>jobs but you may not enjoy</u> making frequent job changes.**

Which of the following is the best way to write the underlined portion of this sentence? If you think the original is the best way, choose option (1).

(1) jobs but you may not enjoy
(2) jobs; but you may not enjoy
(3) jobs, but you may not enjoy
(4) jobs but not enjoying
(5) jobs and you may not enjoy

47. Sentence 12: **<u>Having decided that the benefits of working</u> for a temporary agency would outweigh the drawbacks, it might be worth a try.**

Which of the following is the best way to write the underlined portion of this sentence? If you think the original is the best way, choose option (1).

(1) Having decided that the benefits of working
(2) Having decided that, the benefits of working
(3) Having decided that the benefits, of working
(4) If you decide that the benefits of working
(5) If one decides that the benefits of working

Items 48 to 55 are based on the following paragraph.

(1) Pets make popular Easter gifts, but you should think carefully before we give an animal as a present. (2) Your little niece might love getting a chick for Easter, but how would her mother feel about it? (3) Besides, after the chick grows to full size, it won't be happy staying in a small pen. (4) Your elderly aunt lives alone. (5) You might think that she needs a guard dog. (6) Before giving her a lively Great Dane for christmas, consider whether she will be able to handle such a large dog. (7) The turtle might seem like the perfect gift for your brother that crawled into your yard. (8) Did you realize that wild turtles often carry disease? (9) You may be certain that your sister would enjoy owning a Siamese kitten. (10) Have you think about whether she may be allergic to cat hairs or how the cat will bet along with her pet mice? (11) Once the cat is hers, will your sister mind the expense of food vaccinations, and emergency trips to the veterinarian? (12) Before you decide to give an animal as a present your best bet is to check first with the potential owner.

48. Sentence 1: **Pets make popular Easter gifts, but you should think carefully before we give an animal as a present.**

What correction should be made to this sentence?

(1) change the spelling of popular to populer
(2) change Easter to easter
(3) remove the comma after gifts
(4) replace we with you
(5) no correction is necessary

49. Sentence 3: **Besides, after the chick grows to full size, it won't be happy staying in a small pen.**

Which of the following is the best way to write the underlined portion of this sentence? If you think the original is the best way, choose option (1).

(1) grows to full size, it won't be
(2) grow to full size, it won't be
(3) grows to full size it won't be
(4) grows to full size it wo'nt be
(5) grows to full size, it won't being

50. Sentences 4 & 5: **Your elderly aunt lives alone. You might think that she needs a guard dog.**

The most effective combination of sentences 4 and 5 would include which of the following groups of words?

(1) Your elderly aunt might think
(2) Your aunt is elderly and lives
(3) You might think that she
(4) which lives alone is in need
(5) who lives alone needs

51. Sentence 6: **Before giving her a lively Great Dane for christmas, consider whether she will be able to handle such a large dog.**

What correction should be made to this sentence?

(1) change whether to weather
(2) change christmas to Christmas
(3) insert a comma after she
(4) replace consider with considering
(5) change will be to was

52. Sentence 7: **The turtle <u>might seem like the perfect gift for your brother that crawled into your yard.</u>**

Which of the following is the best way to write the underlined portion of this sentence? If you think the original is the best way, choose option (1).

(1) might seem like the perfect gift for your brother that crawled into your yard.

(2) might seem like the perfect gift for your brother, that crawled into your yard.

(3) might seem like the perfect gift for your brother who crawled into your yard.

(4) that crawled into your yard might seem like the perfect gift for your brother.

(5) who crawled into your yard might seem like the perfect gift for your brother.

53. Sentence 10: **<u>Have you think about whether she</u> may be allergic to cat hairs or how the cat will get along with her pet mice?**

Which of the following is the best way to write the underlined portion of this sentence? If you think the original is the best way, choose option (1).

(1) Have you think about whether she

(2) Have we think about whether she

(3) Have you thinking about whether she

(4) Have you think about whether her

(5) Have you thought about whether she

54. Sentence 11: **Once the cat is hers, will your sister mind the expense of food vaccinations, and emergency trips to the veterinarian?**

What correction should be made to this sentence?

(1) replace <u>hers</u> with <u>her's</u>

(2) insert a comma after <u>food</u>

(3) insert a comma after <u>trips</u>

(4) change the spelling of <u>emergency</u> to <u>emergancy</u>

(5) change <u>veterinarian</u> to <u>Veterinarian</u>

55. Sentence 12: **Before you decide to give an animal as a present your best bet is to check first with the potential owner.**

What correction should be made to this sentence?

(1) replace <u>Before</u> with <u>To help</u>

(2) insert a comma after <u>present</u>

(3) replace <u>present your</u> with <u>present. Your</u>

(4) replace <u>your</u> with <u>you're</u>

(5) no correction is necessary

Answers are on pages 358-360.

PRACTICE TEST

Part II

Directions: This is a test to see how well you can write. In this test, you are asked to write an essay in which you present your opinions about an issue. In preparing your essay, you should take the following steps.

Step 1. Read all of the information about the topic. Be sure that you understand the topic and that you will write about only the assigned topic.

Step 2. Plan your essay before you write

Step 3. Use scrap paper to make any notes.

Step 4. Write your essay on a separate sheet of paper.

Step 5. Read what you have written. Make sure that your writing is legible.

Step 6. Check your paragraphing, sentence structure, spelling, punctuation, capitalization, and usage; make any changes that will improve your essay.

TOPIC

Nearly one-third of all television and radio airtime is taken up with commercials. Magazines and newspapers contain numerous advertisements.

Do you ever purchase one particular brand of an item over another because of the advertisements you have seen and heard? What effect does advertising have on your decisions? Write an essay approximately 200 words long, in which you give your opinion on the influence advertising has on consumer purchases. Be specific and use examples to support your opinion.

When you take the GED Test, you will have 45 minutes to write about the topic you are assigned. Try to write the essay for this test within 45 minutes. Write legibly and use a ballpoint pen so that your writing will be easy to read. Any notes that you make on scrap paper will not be counted as part of your score.

After you complete this essay, you can judge its effectiveness by using the Essay Scoring Guide and Model Essays in the answer key to score your essay. Your GED essay will be judged on how clearly you make the main point of your essay, how thoroughly you support your ideas, and how clear and correct your writing is throughout the composition. You will receive no credit for writing about a topic other than the one assigned.

Answers are on pages 361-363.

Performance Analysis Chart

Part I

Directions: Circle the number of each item that you got correct on the Practice Test. Count how many items you got correct in each row; count how many items you got correct in each column. Write the amount correct per row and column as the numerator in the fraction in the appropriate "Total Correct" box. (The denominators represent the total number of items in the row or column.) Write the grand total correct over the denominator, 55, at the lower right corner of the chart. (For example, if you got 48 items correct, write 48 so that the fraction reads 48/55.)

Item Type	Usage (page 24)	Sentence Structure (page 95)	Mechanics (page 140)	TOTAL CORRECT
Construction Shift	37, 50	4, 6, 17, 18, 24, 40		/8
Sentence Correction	1, 3, 13, 15, 28, 31, 42, 44, 48	12, 30, 32, 45	2, 7, 14, 19, 21, 23, 25, 26, 33, 35, 39, 41, 51, 54, 55	/28
Sentence Revision	5, 11, 16, 22, 27, 29, 43, 53	9, 10, 20, 34, 36, 38, 47, 49, 52	8, 46	/19
TOTAL CORRECT	/19	/19	/17	/55

The page numbers in parentheses indicate where in this book you can find the beginning of specific instruction about the areas of grammar and about the types of questions you encountered in the Practice Test.

Part II

Write your essay's score in the box at the right.

What were some of the strong points of your essay?

What were some of the weak points of your essay?

What improvements do you plan to make when you work on your next essay?

Introduction

Using the Simulated Test to Best Advantage

There is only one way you should take the Simulated Test. You should take the test under the same conditions as the real test.

- When you take the GED, you will have 120 minutes to complete both parts of the test.

- Do not talk to anyone or consult any books as you take the test. If you have a question on how to take the test, ask your instructor.

- If you have trouble answering a question, eliminate the choices that you know are wrong. Then mark the best remaining choice. On the real GED, you are not penalized more for wrong answers than for not answering. Guessing a correct answer will better your score.

- Although you can complete the test in any order you choose, it is to your advantage to begin with Part I. If 75 minutes elapse and you have not yet finished Part I, you should proceed to Part II. If you finish Part II before 120 minutes have elapsed, you can go back to the items in Part I.

As you take the Simulated Test, write your answers for Part I neatly on a sheet of paper or use an answer sheet provided by your teacher. Write your Part II essay as neatly as you can on a fresh sheet of paper.

Using the Answers and Explanations

Use the Answer Key (page 364) to check your answers. Mark each item in Part I that you answered correctly. Regardless of whether you correctly answer an item or not, you should look over each item explanation given. This will reinforce your testing skills and your understanding of the material. For Part II, follow the directions that tell you how to score your essay. You might like to have a teacher or someone else score your essay as well.

How to Use your Score

Your score on the Writing Skills Test will be made up of a combination of your scores on both parts of the test.

If you get 44 items or more in Part I correct, you will have done 80 percent or better. This shows that you are most likely working at a level that would allow you to do well in Part I of the actual Writing Skills Test. If you get a few less than 44 items correct, then you should spend time reviewing the lessons that will strengthen the areas in which you are weak. The Performance Analysis Chart at the end of the test will help you identify these areas.

If your essay merits a score of 4 or higher, you most likely will be able to write an essay on the actual test that will contribute to a passing score. If your essay earns a score of below 4, you should refer back to the Part II lessons that cover the writing skills you had difficulty with and practice by writing essays about other appropriate topics.

SIMULATED TEST

Part I

TIME: 75 minutes

Directions: The items in Part I of this test are based on paragraphs that contain numbered sentences. Some of the sentences may contain errors in sentence structure, usage, or mechanics. **A few sentences, however, may be correct as written.** Read the paragraph and then answer the items that follow it. For each item, choose the answer that would result in the most effective writing of the sentence or sentences. The best answer must be consistent with the meaning and tone of the rest of the paragraph.

FOR EXAMPLE:

Sentence 1: **Although it may take only two hours to watch the average motion picture takes almost a year to make.**

What correction should be made to this sentence?

(1) replace <u>it</u> with <u>they</u>
(2) change <u>take</u> to <u>have taken</u>
(3) insert a comma after <u>watch</u>
(4) change <u>almost</u> to <u>all most</u>
(5) no change is necessary

The correct answer is (3). In this example, a comma is needed after the introductory words <u>Although it may take only two hours to watch.</u>

Items 1 to 9 are based on the following paragraph.

(1) Millions of people are finding that it is often cheaper and more nutritious to pack a lunch than to buy them. (2) Packing a lunch used to mean putting a sandwich and a piece of fruit in a brown paper bag. (3) Lunch bags and lunch boxes now come in every shape, size, and color, that you can imagine. (4) The range of possibilities for filling them is enormous, nevertheless, the rule of thumb for packing a healthful lunch hasn't changed. (5) Choose something from each food group. (6) There is protein contained in meat, fish, chicken, nuts, and beans. (7) In the grain group are such items as whole-wheat bread, crackers, and pita bread, a flat bread from the middle east. (8) It's a good idea to include one vegetable and one fruit, slices of carrot or green pepper are good sources of vitamin A. (9) An orange for dessert would meet your daily vitamin C requirement. (10) Either milk or a milk product such as cheese provide the calcium needed for strong bones. (11) Calcium, like all of the nutrients mentioned in the preceeding section, is needed by adults as well as children. (12) Whether the lunch is put in a plain paper bag or a lunch box, its what's inside that counts.

1. Sentence 1: **Millions of people are finding that it is often cheaper and more nutritious to pack a lunch than to buy them.**

   What correction should be made to this sentence?

   (1) change the spelling of Millions to Milions
   (2) change are to is
   (3) insert more after often
   (4) replace to pack a lunch with packing a lunch
   (5) replace them with one

2. Sentence 3: **Lunch bags and lunch boxes now come in every shape, size, and color, that you can imagine.**

   Which of the following is the best way to write the underlined portion of this sentence? If you think the original is the best way, choose option (1).

   (1) shape, size, and color, that you
   (2) shape, size, and color that you
   (3) shape, size and color, you
   (4) shape, size, and color, which you
   (5) shape, size, and all the colors, you

3. Sentence 4: **The range of possibilities for filling them is enormous, nevertheless, the rule of thumb for packing a healthful lunch hasn't changed.**

   What correction should be made to this sentence?

   (1) change the spelling of enormous to enoarmous
   (2) replace enormous, with enormous;
   (3) remove the comma after nevertheless
   (4) replace healthful with healthy
   (5) no correction is necessary

4. Sentence 6: **There is protein contained in meat, fish, chicken, nuts, and beans.**

   If you rewrote sentence 6 beginning with

   Meat, fish, chicken, nuts, and beans

   the next word should be

   (1) contain
   (2) contained
   (3) contains
   (4) are
   (5) is

5. Sentence 7: **In the grain group are such items as whole-wheat bread, crackers, and pita bread, a flat bread from the middle east.**

What correction should be made to this sentence?

(1) change <u>are</u> to <u>is</u>
(2) replace <u>as</u> with <u>like</u>
(3) remove the comma after <u>pita bread</u>
(4) change <u>middle east</u> to <u>Middle East</u>
(5) no correction is necessary

6. Sentence 8: **It's a good idea to include one vegetable and one <u>fruit, slices</u> of carrot or green pepper are good sources of vitamin A.**

Which of the following is the best way to write the underlined portion of this sentence? If you think the original is the best way, choose option (1).

(1) fruit, slices
(2) fruit. Slices
(3) fruit slices
(4) fruit and slices
(5) fruit because slices

7. Sentence 10: **Either milk or a milk <u>product such as cheese provide</u> the calcium needed for strong bones.**

Which of the following is the best way to write the underlined portion of this sentence? If you think the original is the best way, choose option (1).

(1) product such as cheese provide
(2) product, such as cheese provide
(3) product such as cheese provides
(4) product such as cheese provided
(5) product such as cheese providing

8. Sentence 11: **Calcium, like all of the nutrients mentioned in the preceeding section, is needed by adults as well as children.**

What correction should be made to this sentence?

(1) replace <u>mentioned</u> with <u>mentioning</u>
(2) change the spelling of <u>preceeding</u> to <u>preceding</u>
(3) remove the comma after <u>section</u>
(4) change <u>is</u> to <u>was</u>
(5) replace <u>children</u> with <u>a child</u>

9. Sentence 12: **Whether the lunch is put in a plain paper bag or a lunch box, its what's inside that counts.**

What correction should be made to this sentence?

(1) change <u>is</u> to <u>was</u>
(2) replace <u>plain</u> with <u>plane</u>
(3) insert a comma after <u>bag</u>
(4) change <u>lunch box</u> to <u>lunch boxes</u>
(5) replace <u>its</u> with <u>it's</u>

Items 10 to 19 are based on the following paragraph.

(1) The Presidency is an office that has changed substantially over the years. (2) Today's American President has not only more responsibilities than President George Washington ever had and more complex problems to handle. (3) Studies have shown that recent Democratic and Republican presidents have spent most of his time on foreign affairs. (4) Those financial matters concerning goods and services are called economic issues, and these issues have gotten less attention. (5) Domestic issues, questions concerning the quality of life in this country, the least presidential attention. (6) Of course, many issues belong to two to three areas. (7) This country's drug problem, for example, was not only a domestic problem but also a foreign policy issue. (8) By working with Mexico and other countries, drugs are kept from being imported here. (9) Some critics say that Presidents should divide there time more equally. (10) Other people feel there are some areas who will always deserve more of the President's attention than others. (11) In their judgement, for example, keeping peace in the Middle East should come first; whether or not to raise our minimum wage a few cents should come second. (12) According to many people, Presidents are expected to do too much, but they disagree about how to change the situation.

10. Sentence 2: **Today's American President has not only more responsibilities than President George Washington ever had and more complex problems to handle.**

What correction should be made to this sentence?

(1) change <u>and</u> to <u>or</u>
(2) change <u>and</u> to <u>nor</u>
(3) change <u>and</u> to <u>but also</u>
(4) change <u>and</u> to <u>yet</u>
(5) no correction is necessary

11. Sentence 3: **Studies have shown that recent Democratic and Republican presidents <u>have spent most of his time</u> on foreign affairs.**

Which of the following is the best way to write the underlined portion of this sentence? If you think the original is the best way, choose option (1).

(1) have spent most of his time
(2) has spent most of his time
(3) had spent most of his time
(4) will have spent most of his time
(5) have spent most of their time

12. Sentence 4: **Those financial matters concerning goods and services are called economic issues, and these issues have gotten less attention.**

If you rewrote sentence 4 beginning with

<u>Economic</u>

the next words should be

(1) issues, those financial matters
(2) issues; those financial matters
(3) attention, about financial matters
(4) attention; about financial matters
(5) goods, and services

13. Sentence 5: **Domestic issues, questions concerning the quality of life in this country, the least presidential attention.**

What correction should be made to this sentence?

(1) remove the comma after <u>issues</u>
(2) insert <u>are</u> after <u>issues,</u>
(3) insert <u>and</u> after <u>country,</u>
(4) insert <u>receive</u> after <u>country,</u>
(5) replace <u>least</u> with <u>most least</u>

14. Sentence 7: **This country's drug <u>problem, for example, was not only</u> a domestic problem but also a foreign policy issue.**

Which of the following is the best way to write the underlined portion of this sentence? If you think the original is the best way, choose option (1).

(1) problem, for example, was not only
(2) problem for example, was not only
(3) problem, for example was not only
(4) problem, for example, is not only
(5) problem for example is not only

15. Sentence 8: <u>**By working with Mexico and other countries, drugs are kept**</u> **from being imported here.**

Which of the following is the best way to write the underlined portion of this sentence? If you think the original is the best way, choose option (1).

(1) By working with Mexico and other countries, drugs are kept
(2) By working with Mexico and other countries drugs are kept
(3) Having worked with Mexico and other countries, drugs are kept
(4) By working with Mexico and other countries, to keep drugs
(5) The U.S. has worked with Mexico and other countries to keep drugs

16. Sentence 9: **Some critics say that Presidents should divide there time more equally.**

What correction should be made to this sentence?

(1) change <u>say</u> to <u>says</u>
(2) insert a comma after <u>that</u>
(3) replace <u>there</u> with <u>their</u>
(4) replace <u>equally</u> with <u>equal</u>
(5) no correction is necessary

17. Sentence 10: **Other people feel there are some areas who will always deserve more of the President's attention than others.**

What correction should be made to this sentence?

(1) change <u>feel</u> to <u>felt</u>
(2) replace <u>there</u> with <u>they're</u>
(3) change <u>are</u> to <u>is</u>
(4) change <u>who</u> to <u>that</u>
(5) no correction is necessary

18. Sentence 11: **In their judgment, for example, keeping peace in the Middle East should come first; whether or not to raise our minimum wage a few cents should come second.**

If you rewrote sentence 11 beginning with

<u>For example, they feel that keeping peace in the Middle East should</u>

the next words should be

(1) take priority
(2) be one
(3) raise our
(4) not be considered
(5) earn more

19. Sentence 12: **According to many people, Presidents are expected to do too much, but they disagree about how to change the situation.**

What correction should be made to this sentence?

(1) replace <u>to many</u> with <u>too many</u>
(2) remove the comma after <u>people</u>
(3) remove the comma after <u>much</u>
(4) replace <u>they</u> with <u>everyone</u>
(5) replace <u>they disagree</u> with <u>there is disagreement</u>

Items 20 to 28 are based on the following paragraph.

(1) Experts in child psychology feel that many children watch too much television there is a lot of upsetting violence on television. (2) After watching actors yell and fight children may act this way. (3) Advertisements appear throughout most television programs. (4) If you discuss with children the reason behind advertising, they wont be as likely to be swayed by ads. (5) Studies show that many children watch a lot of television and do poorly on reading tests. (6) Other children watch less television and do better on reading tests. (7) Television, rather than reading and homework, is occupying the time of frequent watchers. (8) Too many hours spent in front of saturday morning cartoons or weeknight movies can cause physical problems. (9) Children who sit or lie on the floor looking up at the television developing neck and back problems. (10) Eyestrain and fatigue can result from watching television, expecially in a darkened room. (11) If you have children in the family, one should ask them to sit in a chair so that their eyes are level with the set. (12) Parents controlling their children's television viewing—what they watch, how much, and under what conditions.

20. Sentence 1: **Experts in child psychology feel that many children watch too much television there is a lot of upsetting violence on television.**

    What correction should be made to this sentence?

    (1) change the spelling of psychology to phsycology
    (2) change feel to feels
    (3) insert a comma after that
    (4) replace too with to
    (5) replace television there with television. There

21. Sentence 2: **After watching actors yell and fight children may act this way.**

    What correction should be made to this sentence?

    (1) insert a comma after yell
    (2) replace fight with fighting
    (3) insert a comma after fight
    (4) replace children may with you may see children
    (5) no correction is necessary

22. Sentence 4: **If you discuss with children the reason behind advertising, they wont be as likely to be swayed by ads.**

    What correction should be made to this sentence?

    (1) change discuss to discussed
    (2) remove the comma after advertising
    (3) replace they with he
    (4) replace wont with won't
    (5) replace ads with them

23. Sentences 5 & 6: **Studies show that many children watch a lot of television and do poorly on reading tests. Other children watch less television and do better on reading tests.**

    The most effective combination of sentences 5 and 6 would include which of the following groups of words?

    (1) that the more television children watch,
    (2) that the more television they watch,
    (3) a lot of television, and others watch less
    (4) the less they watch, the worse
    (5) some do poorly, and others do better

24. Sentence 7: **Television, rather than reading and homework, is occupying the time of frequent watchers.**

What correction should be made to this sentence?

(1) remove the comma after <u>Television</u>
(2) insert a comma after <u>reading</u>
(3) change <u>is</u> to <u>are</u>
(4) change the spelling of <u>frequent</u> to <u>frequant</u>
(5) no correction is necessary

25. Sentence 8: **Too many hours spent in front of saturday morning cartoons or weeknight movies can cause physical problems.**

What correction should be made to this sentence?

(1) replace <u>Too</u> with <u>Two</u>
(2) change <u>saturday</u> to <u>Saturday</u>
(3) insert a comma after <u>cartoons</u>
(4) insert a comma after <u>movies</u>
(5) replace <u>can cause</u> with <u>causing</u>

26. Sentence 9: **Children who sit or lie on the floor looking up at the <u>television developing neck</u> and back problems.**

Which of the following is the best way to write the underlined portion of this sentence? If you think the original is the best way, choose option (1).

(1) television developing neck
(2) television can develop neck
(3) television, developing neck
(4) television will developing neck
(5) television have developing neck

27. Sentence 11: **If you have children in the family, <u>one should ask them to sit</u> in a chair so that their eyes are level with the set.**

Which of the following is the best way to write the underlined portion of this sentence? If you think the original is the best way, choose option (1).

(1) one should ask them to sit
(2) you should ask them to sit
(3) one should ask them, to sit
(4) one should ask they to sit
(5) you should ask him to sit

28. Sentence 12: **Parents <u>controlling their children's</u> television viewing – what they watch, how much, and under what conditions.**

Which of the following is the best way to write the underlined portion of this sentence? If you think the original is the best way, choose option (1).

(1) controlling their children's
(2) controlled their children's
(3) should control their children's
(4) controlling their childrens'
(5) controlling there children's

Items 29 to 37 are based on the following paragraph.

(1) Chances are that you will never have to help someone who's choking; yet you should know what to do, just in case. (2) Suppose someone is choking on something. (3) Before doing anything for the person, wait a moment to see if he coughs it up himself. (4) Show a small child how to raise both arms straight up over his head. (5) If the person can't breath, however, you should try the Heimlich maneuver. (6) There are several ways to do this procedure, developed by Dr. Henry J. Heimlich. (7) One of the most common ways to start are by standing behind the person. (8) Wrap both your arms around him that your hands meet right below his ribs. (9) Clench one hand against his stomach so that beneath his bottom ribs are the thumb of your fist. (10) Cup your other hand over the fist, give a hard upward pull. (11) If the object does not come out of the person's throat, repeat the maneuver. (12) Fortunately, the Heimlich maneuver is extremely effective brain damage begins about four minutes after breathing stops.

29. Sentence 1: **Chances are that you will never have to help someone who's choking; yet you should know what to do, just in case.**

    What correction should be made to this sentence?

    (1) change <u>are</u> to <u>is</u>
    (2) replace <u>who's</u> with <u>whose</u>
    (3) replace <u>choking;</u> with <u>choking,</u>
    (4) insert a comma after <u>yet</u>
    (5) replace <u>you should</u> with <u>one should</u>

30. Sentences 2 & 3: **Suppose someone is choking on something. Before doing anything for the person, wait a moment to see if he coughs it up himself.**

    The most effective combination of sentences 2 and 3 would include which of the following groups of words?

    (1) Suppose someone who is choking
    (2) Before a person chokes on something
    (3) Before you do anything for someone who is choking,
    (4) A person who is choking on something
    (5) While you wait a moment,

31. Sentence 5: **If the person can't breath, however, you should try the Heimlich maneuver.**

    What correction should be made to this sentence?

    (1) change <u>can't</u> to <u>ca'nt</u>
    (2) change the spelling of <u>breath</u> to <u>breathe</u>
    (3) remove the comma after <u>however</u>
    (4) change <u>Heimlich</u> to <u>heimlich</u>
    (5) change the spelling of <u>maneuver</u> to <u>manuver</u>

32. Sentence 6: **There are several ways to do this procedure, developed by Dr. Henry J. Heimlich.**

    What correction should be made to this sentence?

    (1) replace <u>There</u> with <u>They're</u>
    (2) change <u>procedure</u> to <u>Procedure</u>
    (3) change the spelling of <u>procedure</u> to <u>proceedure</u>
    (4) change <u>Dr.</u> to <u>dr.</u>
    (5) no correction is necessary

33. Sentence 7: **One of the most common ways to start are by standing behind the person.**

Which of the following is the best way to write the underlined portion of this sentence? If you think the original is the best way, choose option (1).

(1) ways to start are by standing
(2) ways to start, are by standing
(3) ways to start are to stand
(4) ways to start is by standing
(5) ways to start is having stood

34. Sentence 8: **Wrap both your arms around him that your hands meet right below his ribs.**

Which of the following is the best way to write the underlined portion of this sentence? If you think the original is the best way, choose option (1).

(1) him that your hands meet
(2) him, that you hands meet
(3) him that one's hands meet
(4) him so that your hands meet
(5) him so that your hands met

35. Sentence 9: **Clench one hand against his stomach so that beneath his bottom ribs are the thumb of your fist.**

What correction should be made to this sentence?

(1) replace one hand with one's hand
(2) insert a comma after that
(3) change the spelling of stomach to stomack
(4) change are to is
(5) no correction is necessary

36. Sentence 10: **Cup your other hand over the fist, give a hard upward pull.**

Which of the following is the best way to write the underlined portion of this sentence? If you think the original is the best way, choose option (1).

(1) Cup your other hand over the fist, give
(2) Cup your other hand over the first give
(3) With your other hand cupped over the fist, give
(4) With your other hand cupped over the fist give
(5) With your other hand cupped over the fist, giving

37. Sentence 12: **Fortunately, the Heimlich maneuver is extremely effective brain damage begins about four minutes after breathing stops.**

Which of the following is the best way to write the underlined portion of this sentence? If you think the original is the best way, choose option (1).

(1) effective brain damage
(2) effective, brain damage
(3) effective and brain damage
(4) effective; brain damage
(5) effective; because brain damage

Items 38 to 47 are based on the following paragraph.

(1) Holidays such as Thanksgiving, Christmas, and Hanukkah are traditionally times for families to gather. (2) When television families have these reunions, everyone usually has a wonderful time. (3) In real life, however, many people felt wretched after spending holidays with relatives. (4) Any arguing done by TV relatives usually taking the form of lighthearted kidding. (5) At real family gatherings, disagreements are not always in such an affectionate vein. (6) Anger may be suppressed for months or even years, and then it erupts when family members see each other again. (7) Fatigue and irritability goes hand in hand; thus, all the tiring traveling, cooking, and shopping that accompany holidays might make you irritable. (8) If you're a parent who's just flown from the West Coast to Newark, you probably are exhausted and need a brake from your children. (9) Even if you've only driven from one part of Long island to another, the traffic has probably gotten you pretty tense. (10) Standing in line waiting to buy six pumpkin pies doesn't lead to feeling very relaxed, and baking six of them doesn't, either. (11) After spending more than you can afford on a Father's Day present your not sure your father will like, you may feel somewhat anxious. (12) On the other hand, the way TV families act on holidays is not wholly unrealistic because keeping a sense of humor when tensions arise often does help.

38. Sentence 2: **When television families have these reunions, everyone usually has a wonderful time.**

Which of the following is the best way to write the underlined portion of this sentence? If you think the original is the best way, choose option (1).

(1) reunions, everyone usually has a
(2) reunions everyone usually has a
(3) reunions, everyone usually had a
(4) reunions, everyone usually have a
(5) reunions, everyone has a usually

39. Sentence 3: **In real life, however, many people felt wretched after spending holidays with relatives.**

What correction should be made to this sentence?

(1) remove the comma after <u>however</u>
(2) change <u>felt</u> to <u>feel</u>
(3) change the spelling of <u>wretched</u> to <u>retched</u>
(4) replace <u>spending holidays</u> with <u>holidays spended</u>
(5) change <u>holidays</u> to <u>Holidays</u>

40. Sentence 4: **Any arguing done by TV <u>relatives usually taking</u> the form of lighthearted kidding.**

Which of the following is the best way to write the underlined portion of this sentence? If you think the original is the best way, choose option (1).

(1) relatives usually taking
(2) relatives usually takes
(3) relatives usually take
(4) relatives usualy taking
(5) relatives, usually taking

41. Sentence 6: **Anger may be suppressed for months or even years, and then it erupts when family members see each other again.**

If you rewrote sentence 6 beginning with

<u>Anger that has been suppressed for months or even years may</u>

the next word should be

(1) be
(2) again
(3) erupt
(4) when
(5) erupted

42. Sentence 7: **Fatigue and irritability goes hand in hand; thus, all the tiring traveling, cooking, and shopping that accompany holidays might make you irritable.**

What correction should be made to this sentence?

(1) change the spelling of <u>Fatigue</u> to <u>Fatige</u>
(2) change <u>goes</u> to <u>go</u>
(3) replace <u>hand; thus,</u> with <u>hand, thus,</u>
(4) remove the comma after <u>cooking</u>
(5) change <u>accompany</u> to <u>accompanies</u>

43. Sentence 8: **If you're a parent who's just flown from the West Coast to Newark, you probably are exhausted and need a brake from your children.**

What correction should be made to this sentence?

(1) replace <u>who's</u> with <u>whose</u>
(2) change <u>flown</u> to <u>new</u>
(3) change the spelling of <u>exhausted</u> to <u>exausted</u>
(4) change the spelling of <u>brake</u> to <u>break</u>
(5) no correction is necessary

44. Sentence 9: **Even if you've only driven from one part of Long island to another, the traffic has probably gotten you pretty tense.**

What correction should be made to this sentence?

(1) replace <u>if</u> with <u>whenever</u>
(2) replace <u>driven</u> with <u>drove</u>
(3) change <u>island</u> to <u>Island</u>
(4) change <u>gotten you</u> to <u>gotten one</u>
(5) no correction is necessary

45. Sentence 10: **Standing in line waiting to buy six pumpkin pies doesn't lead to feeling very relaxed, and baking six of them doesn't, either.**

If you rewrote sentence 10 beginning with

<u>Neither waiting in line to buy six pumpkin pies nor baking six of them</u>

the next word should be

(1) lead
(2) leads
(3) feel
(4) feels
(5) relax

46. Sentence 11: **After spending more than you can afford on a <u>Father's Day present your not sure</u> your father will like, you may feel somewhat anxious.**

Which of the following is the best way to write the underlined portion of this sentence? If you think the original is the best way, choose option (1).

(1) Father's Day present your not sure
(2) Father's day present your not sure
(3) Father's Day present you're not sure
(4) Father's Day Present your not sure
(5) Father's Day present your aren't sure

47. Sentence 12: **On the other hand, the way TV families act on holidays is not wholly unrealistic because keeping a sense of humor when tensions arise often does help.**

What correction should be made to this sentence?

(1) insert a semicolon after <u>unrealistic</u>
(2) insert a comma after <u>unrealistic</u>
(3) replace <u>unrealistic because</u> with <u>unrealistic. Because</u>
(4) replace <u>unrealistic because</u> with <u>unrealistic; because,</u>
(5) no correction is necessary

Items 48 to 55 are based on the following paragraph.

(1) Dentists' offices have changed in appearance over the years, but the dentist's role is basically unchanged. (2) There are many new pieces of equipment as well as new prodedures, thanks to modern technology. (3) Some dentists ask their patients to sit in a chair that goes around in circles while x-rays of the jaw were taken. (4) Many dentists now have a device that used very high-pitched sound to clean your teeth. (5) To prevent cavities in a child's teeth, a dentist often paints her teeth with flouride, which helps prevent tooth decay. (6) One new and controversial proceedure involves attaching a computer chip to a child's tooth so that she could be identified if kidnapped or lost. (7) Still, the dentist's main goal is to help keep your teeth healthy, and the advice dentists give is pretty much what it has always been. (8) At least once a day, brush your teeth thoroughly and dental floss should be used. (9) If when you have a choice between fruit and a sticky dessert, you are better off taking the fruit. (10) Avoid cigarettes and brush once a week with baking soda to keep your teeth white. (11) Finally, the American Dental association recommends that you make an appointment to see your dentist every six months.

48. Sentence 1: **Dentists' offices have changed in appearance over the years, but the dentist's role is basically unchanged.**

If you rewrote sentence 1 beginning with

Although dentists' offices have changed in appearance over the years,

the next word should be

   (1) but
   (2) still
   (3) the
   (4) his
   (5) roles

49. Sentence 3: **Some dentists ask their patients to sit in a chair that goes around in circles while x-rays of the jaw were taken.**

What correction should be made to this sentence?

   (1) change ask to asking
   (2) change the spelling of patients to patience
   (3) change were to are
   (4) change taken to took
   (5) no correction is necessary

50. Sentence 4: **Many dentists now have a device that used very high-pitched sound to clean your teeth.**

Which of the following is the best way to write the underlined portion of this sentence? If you think the original is the best way, choose option (1).

   (1) that used very high-pitched
   (2) who used very high-pitched
   (3) that use very high-pitched
   (4) that has used very high-pitched
   (5) that uses very high-pitched

51. Sentence 5: **To prevent cavities in a child's teeth, a dentist often paints her teeth with flouride, which helps prevent tooth decay.**

Which of the following is the best way to write the underlined portion of this sentence? If you think the original is the best way, choose option (1).

   (1) a dentist often paints her teeth
   (2) a dentist often paints their teeth
   (3) a dentist often paints the child's teeth
   (4) a dentist often paints our teeth
   (5) dentists often paint their teeth

52. Sentence 6: **One new and controversial proceedure involves attaching a computer chip to a child's tooth so that she could be identified if kidnapped or lost.**

What correction should be made to this sentence?

(1) change the spelling of <u>new</u> to <u>knew</u>

(2) change <u>child's</u> to <u>childs</u>

(3) change the spelling of <u>proceedure</u> to <u>procedure</u>

(4) replace <u>tooth so that she</u> with <u>tooth, she</u>

(5) no correction is necessary

53. Sentence 8: **At least once a day, brush your teeth <u>thoroughly and dental floss should be used.</u>**

Which of the following is the best way to write the underlined portion of this sentence? If you think the original is the best way, choose option (1).

(1) thoroughly and dental floss should be used.

(2) thoroghly and dental flos should be used.

(3) thoroughly and use dental floss.

(4) thoroughly and using dental floss.

(5) thoroughly, use dental floss.

54. Sentence 9: **If when you have a choice between fruit and a sticky dessert, you are better off taking the fruit.**

What correction should be made to this sentence?

(1) remove the word <u>when</u>

(2) change the spelling of <u>dessert</u> to <u>desert</u>

(3) remove the comma after <u>dessert</u>

(4) insert <u>more</u> after <u>are</u>

(5) change <u>taking</u> to <u>taken</u>

55. Sentence 11: **Finally, the American Dental association recommends that you make an appointment to see your dentist every six months.**

What correction should be made to this sentence?

(1) change <u>association</u> to <u>Association</u>

(2) change the spelling of <u>recommends</u> to <u>reccomends</u>

(3) replace <u>you</u> with <u>we</u>

(4) change <u>make</u> to <u>made</u>

(5) insert a comma after <u>appointment</u>

Answers are on pages 364-366.

SIMULATED TEST

Part II

TIME: 45 minutes

Directions: This is a test to see how well you can write. In this test, you are asked to write an essay in which you present your opinions about an issue. In preparing your essay, you should take the following steps.

Step 1. Read all of the information about the topic. Be sure that you understand the topic and that you write about only the assigned topic.

Step 2. Plan your essay before you write.

Step 3. Use scrap paper to make any notes.

Step 4. Write your essay on a separate sheet of paper.

Step 5. Read what you have written. Make sure that your writing is legible.

Step 6. Check your paragraphing, sentence structure, spelling, punctuation, capitalization, and usage; make any changes that will improve your essay.

TOPIC

Traditionally, pioneers, war heroes, politicians, and movie stars have been models for young people to look up to because they have successfully achieved their goals. How important are role models to our culture today?

Write an essay, approximately 200 words long, in which you give your opinion on the importance of role models today. Be specific, and use examples and reasons to support your opinion.

When you take the GED Test, you will have 45 minutes to write about the topic you are assigned. Try to write the essay for this test within 45 minutes. Write legibly and use a ballpoint pen so that your writing will be easy to read. Any notes that you make on scrap paper will not be counted as part of your score.

After you complete this essay, you can judge its effectiveness by using the Essay Scoring Guide and Model Essays in the answer key to score your essay.

Answers are on pages 367-369.

Performance Analysis Chart
Part I

Directions: Circle the number of each item that you got correct on the Simulated Test. Count how many items you got correct in each row; count how many items you got correct in each column. Write the amount correct per row and column as the numerator in the fraction in the appropriate "Total Correct" box. (The denominators represent the total number of items in the row or column.) Write the grand total correct over the denominator, 55, at the lower right corner of the chart. (For example, if you got 48 items correct, write 48 so that the fraction reads 48/55.)

Item Type	Usage (page 24)	Sentence Structure (page 95)	Mechanics (page 140)	TOTAL CORRECT
Construction Shift	4, 45	8, 23, 30, 41, 48	12	/8
Sentence Correction	1, 17, 19, 24, 35, 39, 42, 49	3, 10, 13, 20, 47, 54	5, 8, 9, 16, 21, 22, 25, 29, 31, 32, 43, 44, 52, 55	/28
Sentence Revision	7, 11, 14, 27, 33, 38, 40, 50, 51	6, 15, 26, 28, 34, 36, 37, 53	2, 46	/19
TOTAL CORRECT	/19	/19	/17	/55

The page numbers in parentheses indicate where in this book you can find the beginning of specific instruction about the areas of grammar and about the types of questions you encountered in the Simulated Test.

Part II

Write your essay's score in the box at the right.

What were some of the strong points of your essay?

What were some of the weak points of your essay?

What improvements do you plan to make when you work on your next essay?

Unit 1 Usage

Chapter 1 Preview

1. There **are** two national anthems played at every All-Star baseball game. The subject of this sentence is *anthems;* a plural verb, therefore, is required.

2. The most popular street name in the United States **is** Park Street. The subject and verb have been separated by an interrupting phrase. The singular subject, *name,* requires a singular verb.

3. Into the crowded parking garage **drive** the employees. This sentence is an example of inverted structure. The subject, *employees,* requires a plural verb.

4. Correct. Since both parts of the compound subject are singular, the verb must be singular.

5. Ms. Wilson **spends** about two hours each day answering her mail. The singular subject, *Ms. Wilson,* requires a singular verb.

Lesson 1 Exercise

1. <u>Henry</u> <u>bought</u> a newspaper at the drugstore this morning.

2. <u>He</u> always <u>reads</u> the newspaper on the bus.

3. The <u>newspaper</u> on weekdays <u>has</u> five sections.

4. The <u>section</u> with the national news <u>is</u> the longest one.

5. <u>Advertisements</u> for movies <u>start</u> on page 6 of the last section.

Lesson 2 Exercise

Part 1.

1. S <u>Someone</u> holds the winning ticket.

2. P Five <u>boxes</u> on the last truck were empty.

3. S <u>That</u> is not a good idea.

4. S A <u>salesperson</u> will help you immediately.

5. P <u>We</u> are leaving for Miami in the afternoon.

6. P The <u>supervisors</u> left the office at 4 P.M.

7. S <u>She</u> wants to hire an employee with good typing skills.

8. P The <u>students</u> asked the teacher for extra practice.

9. S <u>It</u> is not in the glove compartment.

10. S My <u>brother</u> works at the university.

Part 2.

1. Because of budget problems, many **cities** (change the *y* to *i* and add *es*) are raising **taxes** (add *es* to a noun ending in *x*).

2. Neither of his **wishes** (add *es* to a noun ending in *sh*) came true.

3. The **secretaries** (change the *y* to *i* and add *es*) *work at different* **branches** (add *es* to a noun ending in *ch*) *of the same company.*

4. Each of the frames is 3 **feet** by 2 feet (change the spelling to form the plural), 6 **inches** (add *es* to a noun ending in *ch*).

5. Our **lives** (change the spelling to form the plural) *changed dramatically after we won the lottery.*

Lesson 3 Exercise.

1. The team **has** lost four games. *Team* is considered one unit and takes a singular verb.

2. Correct. *Measles* is a singular noun.

3. The pair of jeans **was** in the dryer. Use a singular verb with the word *pair.*

4. Correct. *No one* is a singular indefinite pronoun.

5. Tea leaves **need** to be stored in a tight container. *Leaves* is plural and takes a plural verb.

6. A correctly written résumé **lists** your most recent job first. *Résumé* is singular and takes a singular verb.

7. Many experts **disagree** with that answer. The subject *experts* is plural and takes a plural verb.

8. Both **show** the same talent in music. *Both* is a plural noun.

9. *Several senators* **were** *touring the flood-damaged area. Several refers to more than one person and therefore takes a plural verb.*

10. *They* **realize** *the importance of a healthy diet. They is a plural pronoun.*

Lesson 4 Exercise.

1. Correct. The subject of the sentence, *broiling,* is singular, agreeing with the singular verb, *is.*

2. *Requirements for a driver's license* **vary** *from state to state. Requirements is plural and takes a plural verb.*

3. *Successful dieting, according to nutritionists,* **demands** *patience and determination. Dieting is singular and takes a singular verb.*

4. *One of the best salt substitutes* **is** *lemon juice. One is singular and takes a singular verb.*

5. *Foods with a high moisture content, such as lettuce,* **do** *not freeze well. Foods is plural and takes a plural verb.*

Lesson 5 Exercise

1. *At the bottom of the contract was the space for their signatures.* Invert the sentence to read, *The space for their signatures was at the bottom of the contract.* The singular subject is *space;* a singular verb is needed.

2. Correct. The plural subject *bills* agrees with the plural verb *increase.*

3. **Are** *the doctors at the hospital this afternoon?* Change the question to a statement to find the subject: *The doctors are at the hospital this afternoon.* Change *is* to *are* to agree with the plural subject *doctors.*

4. *In the shuttle sit the astronauts.* Invert the sentence to read, <u>The astronauts sit in the shuttle.</u> Change *sits* to *sit* to agree with the plural subject *astronauts.*

5. **Does** *the customer in Line 5 have a receipt?* Change the question to a sentence and cross out the interrupting phrase: *The customer in Line 5 does have a receipt.* The verb <u>do</u> must be changed to *does* to agree with the singular subject *customer.*

Lesson 6 Exercise

1. Correct. The plural subject is *people* and the plural verb *are* is needed.

2. *Here* **is** *the map of the Hawaiian islands.* The subject *map* is singular and requires the singular verb *is.*

3. *There* **are** *many ancient myths that explain forces in nature.* The subject *myths* is plural and requires the plural verb *are.*

4. *Here* **comes** *the winner of the Boston Marathon.* The subject *winner* is singular and requires the singular verb *comes.*

5. *There* **are** *11 players on each team in field hockey.* The subject *players* is plural and requires the plural verb *are.*

Lesson 7 Exercise.

1. Correct. The plural subject *diamonds* is closer to the verb; therefore, the verb must be plural.

2. *Either gravel or crushed rock* **combines** *with cement to form concrete.* The singular subject *crushed rock* is closer to the verb; therefore, the verb must be singular.

3. *The Rocky Mountains and the Andes* **are** *part of the same mountain chain.* Plural subjects joined by *and* take a plural verb.

4. *Both a blanket and warm clothing* **are** *recommended when traveling in the winter. Blanket* and *clothing* form a plural subject, requiring a plural verb.

5. *Neither creams nor lotions* **are** *effective in the prevention of wrinkles.* Because both subjects are plural, a plural verb is required.

Chapter 1 Review

1. *Everyone* **needs** *a passport to travel in a foreign country. Everyone is singular and takes a singular verb.*

2. *Neither Jesse nor Barbara* **is** *able to attend the class.* Singular subjects joined by *neither...nor* take a singular verb.

3. *There* **are** *14 offices on the West Coast.* The subject *offices* is plural and takes a plural verb.

4. *One of the most common diseases in the world* **is** *malaria.* The subject *One* is singular and takes a singular verb.

5. *Both Robert De Niro and Dustin Hoffman* **have** *won Academy Awards.* Subjects joined by *both...and* take a plural verb.

6. **Are** *Donna and Gordon planning to take a vacation this summer?* The compound subject *Donna and Gordon* is plural and takes a plural verb.

7. *On 6th Street and Broadway* **is** *a new camera repair shop.* The subject *shop* is singular and takes a singular verb.

8. *That typewriter, the larger of the two,* **costs** *less than $500.* The subject *typewriter* is singular and takes a singular verb.

9. Correct. The subject *Risa* is singular and takes a singular verb.

10. *Ms. Novoa, a member of the PTA for three years,* **has** *strong opinions on the subject.* The subject *Ms. Novoa* is singular and takes a singular subject.

11. *In large cities, the schools* **are** *often overcrowded.* The subject *schools* is plural and takes a plural verb.

12. *Here* **is** *the list of phone numbers.* The subject *list* is singular and takes a singular verb.

13. *Everyone* **wants** *job security and adequate benefits.* The subject *Everyone* is a singular pronoun and always takes a singular verb.

14. Correct. The subject *members* is plural and takes a plural verb.

15. *Either Jim or Claudia* **plans** *to drive Mr. Phillips to the airport.* Singular subjects joined by *either...or* take a singular verb.

GED Review 1

1. **(4)** *Usage/Plurals/Sentence Correction.* When a noun ends in *y*, it is made plural by changing the *y* to *i* and ending *es*.

2. **(1)** *Usage/Subject-Verb Agreement /Sentence Correction.* Invert the question: The people in your house **do** have what they need to survive. The plural subject *people* takes the plural verb *do*.

3. **(3)** *Usage/Subject-Verb Agreement /Sentence Correction.* The subject of the sentence is the singular pronoun *One* which takes the singular verb *is*.

4. **(3)** *Usage/Subject-Verb Agreement /Sentence Correction.* The subject of the sentence is the singular pronoun *everybody* which takes the singular verb *needs*.

5. **(5)** *Usage/Subject-Verb Agreement /Sentence Correction.* When two singular subjects are joined by *or* the subject is singular and takes a singular verb.

6. **(4)** *Usage/Subject-Verb Agreement /Sentence Correction.* When any subjects are joined by *both...and* the result is plural and the subject requires a plural verb. In this case, the verb *are* is correct.

7. **(5)** *Usage/Subject-Verb Agreement /Sentence Correction.* The subject of the sentence is the singular pronoun *It* which takes the singular verb *is*.

8. **(3)** *Usage/Subject-Verb Agreement /Sentence Correction.* The subject of the sentence is the singular noun *Food* which takes a singular verb. Do not consider the long interrupting phrase between the subject and the verb.

9. **(2)** *Usage/Plurals/Sentence Correction.* The plural of the noun *woman* is irregular. The spelling changes to form the plural. The word *woman* changes to *women*.

10. **(4)** *Usage/Plurals/Sentence Correction.* The plural of the noun *knife* is irregular. The spelling changes to form the plural. The word *knife* changes to *knives*.

Chapter 2 Preview

1. *The Julian calendar **was developed** in 46 B.C. by Julius Caesar.* The sentence refers to a historical event; the verb, therefore, must be in the past tense.

2. *The diameter of the moon is about 2,160 miles, and its surface area **is** 14,650,000 square miles.* Because the sentence describes a current state, both verbs should be in the present tense.

3. Correct. The past tense verb *spent* is correct because the sentence concerns a historical event.

4. *Beethoven **had written** nine symphonies before his death in 1827.* The past participle of *write* is *written*.

5. *Tomorrow we **will learn** about Sir John A. Macdonald, the first Prime Minister of Canada.* The word *Tomorrow* provides a clue that the action should be expressed in the future tense.

Lesson 1 Exercise

The correct form of the verb is boldfaced.

1. The Supreme Court **begins** each term on the first Monday in October.

2. Chester Gould **drew** the popular cartoon "Dick Tracy" for may years.

3. A bird **builds** its nest using many different materials.

4. In years past, most tornadoes **happened** in the central section of the country.

5. Scientists have **done** many experiments to determine the mineral composition of the moon.

6. Germany **broke** its treaty with the Soviet Union in 1941.

7. The president of the company had **said** that the hiring freeze was temporary.

8. Native Americans **taught** the early colonists how to grow corn.

9. Many people have **written** to their representatives about the proposed law.

10. Currently, Anita **swims** ten laps each day as part of her fitness program.

Lesson 2 Exercise

1. *Ms. Jemison **will call** the office next Monday.* The phrase *next Monday* tells you that future tense is needed.

2. *Risa **gave** Margo the message yesterday.* The word *yesterday* indicates that past tense is needed.

3. *Mary **will be working** from 9 A.M. until 1:30 P.M. for the next week.* A continuing tense is needed because the work will take place over time. Future tense is indicated by the phrase *for the next week.*

4. Correct. Use present tense for actions that are performed regularly.

5. *The election results **were announced** an hour ago.* The phrase *an hour ago* indicates that past tense is needed. Because the verb is passive, the helping verb *were* is added to the past participle *announced.*

Lesson 3 Exercise

1. *Cynthia **has worked** for MarketCom Inc. since 1985.* Use present perfect when something started in the past and continues into the present.

2. *Mrs. Garcia **will have completed** the project by the end of the day tomorrow.* The phrase *by the end of the day tomorrow* indicates a specific time in the future; therefore, future perfect tense is needed.

3. Correct. Use present perfect tense when something happened in the past and is likely to continue happening.

4. *Before last Friday, Bob **had made** only 8 sales.* The phrase *Before last Friday* indicates a specific time in the past; therefore, past perfect tense is needed.

5. *By the time Ms. Anderson arrives in Nashville next week, Jim **will have finished** the plans.* The phrases *By the time* and *next week* indicate that the first event, *Ms. Anderson's arrival*, will take place at a specific time in the future; therefore, future perfect tense is needed.

Lesson 4 Exercise

1. *The first depression in the United States **happened** at the end of the Revolutionary War.* The *Revolutionary War* is a clue that the action has already taken place.

2. *Right now, we **import** more goods than we **export**.* The words *Right now* are a clue to use the present tense.

3. *During the next decade, new kinds of heart surgery **will be developed**.* The phrase *During the next decade* is a clue to use the future tense.

4. Correct. Both verbs are correctly written in the past tense.

5. *The last survivor of the Mayflower **was** John Alden.* Use the past tense; the sentence refers to a historical event.

Lesson 5 Exercise

1. *The light from a laser is very powerful and* **travels** *in one direction.* The second verb in the sentence, *travels*, must be in the present tense to be consistent with the present tense form of *to be* in the first part of the sentence.

2. *The hospital receptionist paged the doctor while the patient's father* **completed** *the forms.* The second verb in the sentence, *completed*, must be in the past tense to be consistent with the past tense verb, *paged*, in the first part of the sentence.

3. *Mr. Gonzalez is scheduled to work 40 hours next week, whereas Ms. Morgan* **is** *scheduled to work only 30 hours.* The present tense form, *is*, should be the same in both parts of the sentence.

4. *The company profits were higher last January than they* **were** *in July of the previous year.* Company profits from two different times are being compared. Since both times are in the past, past tense should be used in both parts of the sentence.

5. *The person who said "If you can't stand the heat, get out of the kitchen"* **was** *Harry Truman.* Because the sentence is about an event in the past, both of the verbs, *said* and *was* are past tense forms.

Lesson 6 Exercise

Joseph Priestley, an eighteenth-century chemist, made several discoveries through his mistakes. For example, he **invented** seltzer quite by accident. While he **was** performing an experiment, he added gas to water. Priestley was amazed at the new taste that **resulted** from the combination. During another experiment, he studied a certain type of tree sap. Some of the substance **fell** onto a piece of paper. He noticed the sap **made** pencil marks on the paper disappear. This **led** to the development of what we now call the *eraser*.

Chapter 2 Review

1. *The new version of the software* **will be** *available in March of next year.* The phrase *next year* indicates that future tense is needed.

2. *In 1804, Lewis and Clark* **began** *their expedition to the Northwest.* The date provides a clue that past tense should be used.

3. *Tomorrow the president* **will discuss** *the new tax bill with several of his advisors.* The word *Tomorrow* indicates that future tense is needed.

4. *The deepest lake in the world is Lake Baikal in Siberia which* **measures** *almost a mile deep in some places.* Both parts of the sentence should be in present tense because these facts are true now.

5. Correct. Use present perfect tense when something started in the past and has just been completed.

6. *Charles F. Carlson invented the photocopy machine, although he* **had** *difficulty finding financial support.* Use past tense for both parts of the sentence.

7. *The words "Mankind must be put an end to war or war will put an end to mankind"* **were spoken** *by John Kennedy.* This verb is written in a passive form. Use the past tense helping verb with the part participle of the verb *speak*.

8. *Millions of years ago, glaciers* **covered** *parts of North America.* Simple past tense should be used because the action of the sentence took place in the past. Past perfect is not needed because the two times in the past are not compared.

9. *Ms. Carter* **had seen** *the results before Mr. Langley made the announcement.* The past perfect tense is correct because two events in the past are compared. The past perfect tense should be formed by combining the helping verb *had* with the past participle of the verb *see*.

10. *The Puritans* **thought** *soap and water were bad for one's health.* The verb *think* should be changed to the past tense because the sentence is about a historical belief.

11. *Lochner v. New York was a Supreme Court case that* **gave** *employees and employers the right to decide hours and wages without government interference.* Because the sentence is about a historical occurrence, the verb *give* should be changed to the past tense.

12. Correct. Future perfect is used because one future event will have taken place before the other future event.

13. *In 1930, Sinclair Lewis became the first American author who* **won** *the Nobel prize for literature.* Both verbs should be in the past tense because the sentence is about a historical event.

14. *The Larsen project **was begun** two years ago.* This sentence uses a passive verb. The helping verb *was* should be combined with the past participle of the verb *begin*.

15. *The first American to fly in space **was** Alan Shepard, and he **flew** for a total of 15 minutes.* Both verbs in the sentence should be changed to the past.

GED Review 2

1. **(3)** *Usage/Verb Tense/Sentence Correction.* The phrase *next Friday* indicates that future tense is needed.

2. **(1)** *Usage/Verb Tense/Sentence Revision.* The phrase *last month* indicates that past tense is needed. The past tense of the verb *teach* is *taught*.

3. **(1)** *Usage/Subject-Verb Agreement /Sentence Correction.* The verb *have* agrees with the subject *you*. Present tense is correct for this sentence, since the action is taking place now.

4. **(2)** *Usage/Verb Tense/Sentence Correction.* The verb *to sell* is an irregular verb. The correct past tense form is *sold*.

5. **(4)** *Usage/Verb Tense/Sentence Revision.* The phrase *last year* indicates that the action took place in the past. Past perfect is not needed because the action did not occur before another specific time in the past. Simple past tense is correct.

6. **(2)** *Usage/Subject-Verb Agreement /Sentence Revision.* The tense is correct because the action is taking place in the present; however, the plural subject *we* does not agree with the singular verb *is*. The plural form *are* is needed.

7. **(3)** *Usage/Verb Tense/Sentence Correction.* From the previous sentence, *On another note, we are having problems in the parking lot again,* you know the problems are taking place in the present. Sentence 7 tells one of those problems. Change <u>were</u> to <u>are</u> to change to present tense.

8. **(5)** *Usage/Subject-Verb Agreement /Sentence Correction.* Structure. The subject of the last part of the sentence, *there is a problem,* is the singular noun *problem*. The singular form <u>is</u> agrees with the singular subject.

9. **(3)** *Usage/Verb Tense/Construction Shift.* By the beginning of next month, every car will need an identification sticker. The phrase *By the beginning of next month* indicates the future tense form *will need* is required.

10. **(2)** *Usage/Verb Tense/Sentence Correction.* The phrase *Next month* indicates that future tense is needed. Past perfect tense is used when a past event occurs before another specific time in the past.

Chapter 3 Preview

1. Correct. When *either...or* is used to connect two antecedents, the pronoun should agree with the nearest antecedent. Since *pepper* is singular, the singular pronoun *it* is correct.

2. *Joseph will ride home with Samantha and **me** after the game.* The subject of the sentence is Joseph. Since the pronoun in question does not show possession, you know an object pronoun is needed.

3. *We benefit from studying history because it helps **us** learn from past mistakes.* Change *you* to *us* to eliminate the pronoun shift.

4. *Plants and flowers, **which** (or **that**) are often given to people in the hospital, may have a healing effect on chronically ill patients.* Change *who* to *which* or *that*. *Who* is used to refer only to people or animals, whereas *that* or *which* are used for people, animals, or things.

5. *Michelle did not see Diane again after **Michelle** changed jobs.* OR *Michelle did not see Diane again after **Diane** changed jobs.* Repeat the noun because it is impossible to tell whether the pronoun *she* refers to *Michelle* or *Diane*.

Lesson 1 Exercise

1. *Ms. Warnick ordered four tickets for **them.*** The subject of the sentence is Ms. Warnick. Since the pronoun is not a subject and does not show possession, the object form is needed.

2. *We gave Mr. Franco and **her** the opportunity to express their opinions.* The subject is the subject pronoun *We*. The possessive pronoun *their* is used correctly before the noun *opinions*. Since the pronoun following *and* is not a subject and does not show possession, the object form is needed.

3. *Bill and **she** will be going to the job fair in Sacramento.* The pronoun is part of a compound subject; a subject pronoun is needed.

4. *Julie recommended **her** friend for the job.* Before the noun *friend*, a pronoun from the first set of possessives is needed.

5. Correct. Both of these possessive pronouns refer to *Dennis and I*, a compound subject. *His* refers only to *Dennis,* so it is singular. *Our* refers to *Dennis and I,* two people, so it is plural.

Lesson 2 Exercise

1. *Each person has to learn **his or her** lessons the hard way.* The antecedent *person* is singular and needs a singular pronoun. OR *People have to learn their lessons the hard way.*

2. *A new cosmetic or drug must be tested before **it** can be sold to the public.* When two antecedents are joined by *or*, the pronoun should agree with the nearest antecedent. The antecedent *drug* is singular, so a singular pronoun is needed.

3. Correct. When two antecedents are joined by *neither...nor*, the pronoun should agree with the nearest antecedent. The antecedent *salespeople* is plural, so a plural pronoun is needed.

4. *Both Mr. Gordon and Mr. Sjue park **their** cars in the lot on the corner.* When two antecedents are joined by *and*, the result is plural and a plural pronoun is needed.

5. *Harry Truman became President of the United States, but **he** did not attend college.* The singular antecedent *Harry Truman* requires a singular pronoun.

Lesson 3 Exercise

The rule that governs all of these sentences is that pronoun shifts in person should be avoided.

1. *I exercise daily because physical exercise helps **me** maintain good health.*

2. Correct. The second-person pronoun *you* is used appropriately and consistently.

3. *When we are nervous, **our** pulse may quicken.* OR *When **you** are nervous, your pulse may quicken.*

4. *It is important for **you** to understand the new tax law before filing your tax returns.*

5. *People are more likely to be injured while they are at home than while **they** are riding in a car.*

Lesson 4 Exercise

1. *Only drivers **who** are licensed may drive in the United States.* Use *who* or *that* to refer to people.

2. Correct. The relative pronoun *that* is correct when referring to animals.

3. *Ants and humans are the only two animal species **that** wage war on their own kind.* The use of *what* as a relative pronoun is always incorrect. Because species is the antecedent, the pronoun *that* or *which* may be used.

4. *The state **that** uses the phrase "Land of Lincoln" on its license plates is Illinois. That* or *which* may be used to refer to things.

5. *The first American astronaut **who** orbited Earth was John Glenn. Who* is correct, because it may be replaced by *he.*

Lesson 5 Exercise

The rewording of these sentences may vary.

1. *The machinist violated the company's policy by not wearing safety goggles.* Reword the sentence to eliminate *which*, which has no clear antecedent.

2. *On last night's weather forecast, **the weather forecaster** said there was an 80 percent chance of rain.* Substitute a noun for the pronoun *they.*

3. *Helium causes the pitch of the voice to rise by contracting the vocal cords.* Reword the sentence to eliminate *which*, which has no clear antecedent.

4. ***My science textbook** says that ten inches of snow equals once inch of rain.* Substitute a noun for the pronoun *it.*

5. ***Real estate developers** predict that during the next decade the price of housing will triple.* Substitute a noun for the pronoun *They.*

Lesson 6 Exercise

1. *Because the discussion leader and the secretary were responsible for the minutes of the meeting, **the discussion leader** (or **the secretary**) was told to take accurate notes.* In the original sentence, it is not clear whether *he* refers to the discussion leader or the secretary.

2. *When **the supervisor** returned from vacation, she gave the employee additional responsibilities.*

OR

*When **the employee** returned from vacation, the supervisor gave her additional responsibilities.* In the original sentence, it is not clear whether *she* refers to the supervisor or the employee.

3. *The student asked the teacher if she, **the student**, could change the assignment.*

OR

*The student asked **the teacher** if she, the teacher, could change the assignment.* In the original sentence, it is not clear whether *she* refers to the student or the teacher.

4. *If a child has an allergic reaction to a certain food, throw **the food** away. It* should be replaced with a noun to avoid an ambiguous pronoun reference.

5. *Mike told Randy that he, **Mike**, was the starting pitcher for tomorrow's game.*

OR

*Mike told Randy that he, **Randy**, was the starting pitcher for tomorrow's game.* In the original sentence, it is not clear whether *he* refers to Mike or Randy.

Chapter 3 Review

1. *A mosquito cannot beat **its** wings in temperatures below 60 degrees.* The singular antecedent *mosquito* needs a singular pronoun.

2. *Vince and **I** are looking for someone to join our carpool group.* Change *me* to **I** because the pronoun in question is a subject of the sentence.

3. *A man **who** is at rest breathes about 16 times per minute.* Do not use *which* as a relative pronoun when referring to people.

4. *Neither potato chips nor candy bars give us the nutrition **we** need to stay healthy.*

OR

*Neither potato chips nor candy bars give **you** the nutrition you need to stay healthy.* Eliminate the pronoun shift.

5. *The advisor told the president to cancel tomorrow's press conference.*

OR

The president told the advisor to cancel tomorrow's press conference. Eliminate the ambiguous pronoun, *she*, by rewording the sentence.

6. *Nancy gave Ms. Prow and **him** two copies of her résumé.* Change *he* to the object pronoun *him* because the pronoun is not part of the subject.

7. Correct. *That* or *who* may be used to refer to people.

8. *Mr. Garrett told Phil that **Mr. Garrett** would be getting a promotion.*

OR

*Mr. Garrett told Phil that **Phil** would be getting a promotion.* Repeat the noun because it is impossible to tell to which antecedent the pronoun refers.

9. *Whales use **their** tails to make slapping sounds on the surface of the ocean.* The plural antecedent *Whales* requires a plural pronoun.

10. *Frank Lloyd Wright was an architect **who** designed houses with low, horizontal shapes.* The subject pronoun *who* is needed because it functions as the subject for the verb *designed*. Think: *He designed houses.*

11. *Animals living in cold climates have smaller ears than **their** cousins in warmer climates.* The plural antecedent *Animals* requires a plural pronoun.

12. *Rick, **whom** we wanted for the job, is no longer available.* The subject that goes with the verb *wanted* is the pronoun *we*. So the object pronoun *whom* is needed. Think: *We wanted him for the job.*

13. *The legends **that** are told about King Arthur may be based on historical facts.* *What* is not a relative pronoun; either *that* or *which* may be used.

14. *The letter was addressed to **them.*** Change *they* to *them*. The subject of the sentence is the noun *letter*. Since the pronoun in question is not a subject, use the object pronoun *them*.

15. *After World War II, the housing supply could not keep up with the demand because **the demand** grew so rapidly.* Eliminate the ambiguous use of the pronoun *it*.

GED Review 3

1. **(3)** *Usage/Pronoun-Antecedent Agreement/Sentence Correction.* The plural antecedent *candidates* requires a plural pronoun.

2. **(2)** *Usage/Subject and Object Pronouns /Sentence Correction.* The pronoun *who* is the subject of the verb *ran*. Think: *She ran for the only vacant seat on the city council.* Since the subject pronoun <u>she</u> is correct, you know that *who* is the correct choice.

3. **(5)** *Usage/Pronoun Reference/Sentence Correction.* All the pronouns in this sentence are used correctly.

4. **(2)** *Usage/Person Shift/Sentence Correction.* The sentence shifts from third person *(anyone)* to second person *(you)*. To correct the shift, change the second part of the sentence to third person.

5. **(3)** *Usage/Ambiguous Pronoun Reference /Sentence Correction.* It is impossible to tell to whom the pronoun *they* refers. Replace **they** with a more specific subject.

6. **(3)** *Usage/Relative Pronouns/Sentence Revision.* Use *who* to refer to people or animals only. Use *that* or *which* to refer to things.

7. **(3)** *Usage/Pronoun-Antecedent Agreement /Sentence Correction.* The antecedent *employee* is singular; therefore, a singular pronoun is needed. Use *his or her* since the gender of the employee may be male or female.

8. **(4)** *Usage/Person Shift/Construction Shift.* *If you need a textbook, you can buy your books from one of the teachers, either Mike Goldhamer or Stephanie Utley.* Use the second-person pronoun *you* in both parts of the sentence.

9. **(1)** *Usage/Subject and Object Pronouns /Sentence Correction.* Mike and *she* is the compound subject of the sentence so the object pronoun *she* is needed.

10. **(5)** *Usage/Subject and Object Pronouns /Sentence Correction.* The words *Stephanie and I* are not a subject for any verb in this sentence. Therefore, an object pronoun is needed. Read the sentence without the words *Stephanie and: The employees who finish the class will get a certificate signed by* **me.**

Strategy 1 Exercises

1. **(3)** *Usage/Verb Tense/Sentence Correction.* Use present perfect tense when something happened in the past and is likely to continue happening. The present perfect tense is formed by adding *has* or *have* to the past participle of the verb. The subject *use* requires the singular verb *has*.

2. **(2)** *Usage/Relative Pronouns/Sentence Correction.* Use *that* or *which* to refer to things. The pronoun *who* refers only to people or animals.

3. **(2)** *Usage/Pronoun-Antecedent Agreement/Construction-Shift.* The antecedent for the pronoun in question is the possessive noun *food's* in Sentence 6. Since *food* is singular and third person, the correct choice is *its*.

4. **(1)** *Usage/Subject-Verb Agreement /Sentence Correction.* The subject of the sentence is the singular noun *motion* which requires the singular verb *produces*.

5. **(4)** *Usage/Verb Tense/Sentence Revision.* Present tense is needed because this face is presented as true at the present time. The subject *containers* requires the plural verb *are*.

Unit 1 Review

1. **(3)** *Usage/Subject-Verb Agreement /Sentence Revision.* The plural subject *women* requires the plural verb *are*.

2. **(3)** *Usage/Relative Pronouns/Sentence Correction.* Use the relative pronouns *who* or *that* when referring to people. In this case, the antecedent for the relative pronoun is *husbands*.

3. **(5)** *Usage/Pronoun-Antecedent Agreement/Sentence Correction.* The antecedent *families* requires the plural pronoun *their*.

4. **(2)** *Usage/Verb Shift/Sentence Revision.* The verbs *continues* and *insist* indicate present tense. Use the present tense *give* to eliminate the shift in tense.

5. **(3)** *Usage/Verb Tense/Sentence Correction.* The first sentence in the paragraph indicates that Rick Barry was a basketball player in the past. To be consistent, this sentence should also be in past tense. The singular subject *ability* requires the singular verb *was*.

6. **(2)** *Usage/Principal Parts of a Verb /Sentence Revision.* The verb is in passive form which requires a helping verb (a form of *to be*) and the past participle of the verb. The correct past participle for the irregular verb *choose* is *chosen*.

7. **(3)** *Usage/Object Pronouns/Construction Shift.* The antecedent for the pronoun in question is the noun *Rick*. Since the pronoun is not the subject of the verb *named*, you can tell that a singular object pronoun is needed.

8. **(3)** *Usage/Verb Tense/Sentence Correction.* From Sentence 4, you can know that the phrase *next year* refers to 1966, a date in the past. Use past tense to be consistent.

9. **(2)** *Usage/Subject-Verb Agreement /Construction Shift.* The singular subject *food* requires the singular verb *contains*.

10. **(4)** *Usage/Pronoun-Antecedent Agreement/Person Shift/Sentence Correction.* The sentence shifts from first person *(us)* to second person *(your)*. Change *us* to *you* to eliminate the shift.

11. **(1)** *Usage/Subject-Verb Agreement /Sentence Correction.* The subject of the sentence is the singular pronoun *one* which requires the singular verb *has*.

12. **(4)** *Usage/Relative Pronouns/Sentence Revision.* Use wither *who* or *that* to refer to people. The plural verb *have* agrees with the plural subject *Patients* and should not be changed.

ANSWER KEY
UNIT 2

Unit 2 Sentence Structure

Chapter 1 Preview

There may be more than one correct way to edit some sentences.

1. *There are 206 bones in the human body; the thigh bone is the longest.* This is a run-on sentence. Add a semicolon or a period after *body.*

2. *The movie was not successful, but the book on which it was based was a bestseller for six months.* This is a comma splice. Add a coordinating conjunction that shows contrast. You may also use a semicolon after *successful* and use another coordinator that shows contrast, such as *however.* Use a comma after *however.*

3. *The total shown on the receipt is incorrect.* This is a sentence fragment. Add a verb and any other words needed to complete the meaning.

4. Correct. The first idea in this sentence is a subordinate, or incomplete, idea. The second idea is the main idea.

5. *William Henry Harrison was president of the United States for only 31 days, for he died of pneumonia in 1841.* Substitute the coordinator *for* for *as a result* to show the correct relationship between ideas. Use a comma instead of a semicolon. There are many possible ways to correct sentences.' Make sure you have shown the correct relationship between the two ideas.

Lesson 1 Exercise

There may be more than one correct way to edit some sentences.

1. Correct. This sentence has a subject, *cash registers*, and a verb, *are*, and expresses a complete thought.

2. *Even though I missed my usual train, I got to work on time.* Add words to complete the meaning.

3. *We stood and cheered the home team's victory.* Add a subject.

4. *The treasurer of the Hikers' Club resigned.* Add a verb.

5. *Tomatoes that are grown on hothouses have very little flavor.* Add a verb and words to complete the meaning.

Lesson 2 Exercise

Each run-on sentence or comma splice can be correct by writing each complete thought as a separate sentence.

1. *Woodrow Wilson was our 28th president. He was the only president who had a Ph.D. degree.*

2. *The Nineteenth Amendment to the Constitution gave women the right to vote. It was adopted in 1920.*

3. *Congress established the first U.S. mint. It was located in Philadelphia.*

4. Correct. This sentence includes a compound verb but expresses only one complete thought.

5. *The state flag of Alaska was chosen in a competition. The winner was only 13 years old.*

Lesson 3 Exercise

There may be more than one correct way to edit some sentences. If a semicolon is used after the first complete thought, a connecting word may also be used. If a comma is used after the first complete thought, a connecting words must be used.

1. *Egyptians made candy over 4,000 years ago; they used dates and honey.*

2. *England and France fought the longest war, for it lasted from 1337 to 1453 and was called the Hundred Years' War.*

3. *The first African-American to become a Supreme Court justice was Thurgood Marshall, and he was appointed in 1967 by President Lyndon Johnson.*

4. Correct. This is not a compound sentence.

5. *This apartment needs some repairs; however, the rent is reasonable.* With *however* a semicolon must be used.

6. *The United States is the world's largest producer of cheese; France is second.*

7. Correct. The connecting word *nor* can be used with comma.

8. *The first government employee strike was the Boston police strike; in fact, it happened in 1919.*

9. *Pluto takes 248 years to complete one orbit around the sun. Many comets orbit beyond Pluto.* Use separate sentences because the ideas are not closely related.

10. *Pretzels were invited by a French monk, and he shaped the dough to represent arms folded in prayer.*

11. *Irving Berlin wrote "White Christmas," the most popular song ever recorded; in fact, over 100 million copies have been sold.* Use a coordinator that gives a reason or an example.

12. *The Great Wall of China is 1,684 miles long; in fact, it is the longest wall in the world.* Use a coordinator that gives emphasis.

13. *O'Hare Airport in Chicago is the busiest in the world, and delays in landing there are common.* Change the second idea to one that is related to the first or write them as two separate sentences.

14. Correct. The coordinator *in fact*, which shows a reason, may be used with a semicolon.

15. *John Fitch designed the first steamboat; it looked like a canoe but had steam-driven paddles. He also built a boat that had paddle wheels on the side. However, he had difficulty finding people to back him financially, so his designs failed to be successful.* The original sentence has too many ideas. Divide the sentence into smaller units of information. This is one of several correct ways of doing so.

Lesson 4 Exercise

1. Correct. This subordinate idea is correctly followed by a comma.

2. *Even though some mushrooms are poisonous, others can be eaten safely.* Do not use a coordinator (*but*) along with a subordinator (*even though*).

3. *After the stock market crashed in 1929, many people refused to put their money in banks.* Use only one subordinator.

4. *When Shakespeare wrote his historical plays, he sometimes altered the truth to fit his story lines.* Use a comma after a subordinate idea that comes first in the sentence.

5. *Pollution will continue to be a major problem in many of our cities unless people show more concern for their environment.* Do not combine unrelated ideas.

Lesson 5 Exercise

1. *Seneca Lake and Cayuga Lake are in western New York State.* Use the plural verb *are* when compound subjects are joined by *and*.

2. *Mr. Wittenberg and Mr. Bush did not enjoy the concert.*

    OR

    Neither Mr. Wittenberg nor Mr. Bush enjoyed the concert. When using the paired coordinators *neither...nor*, do not also use *not*.

3. *You can buy that book in a hardcover edition or in paperback. Or* is a reasonable coordinator to use because a person would probably buy a book in only one form, hardcover or paperback.

4. *Roberta is making a skirt and a blazer. Roberta* is making one thing and another thing.

5. *Eliot fixed the faucet with a wrench and a screwdriver. Eliot* used one tool *and* another tool.

Chapter 1 Review

1. *The most common hand injury is a smashed fingertip; a painful bruise often appears beneath the fingernail within hours.* Or use a period, a semicolon and a connecting word, or a comma and a connecting word.

2. *Redness or swelling in a child's hand could be serious and should be seen by a doctor.* Do not use a comma between compound verbs.

3. *A severe sprain may require a cast.* Add words to the sentence fragment to make the idea complete.

4. *Wilt Chamberlain holds the record for scoring the most points in a basketball game; he scored 100 points in a game against the New York Knicks.* Or use a period, a semicolon and a connecting word, or a comma and a connecting word.

5. *The coach called three timeouts during the last 10 minutes.* Add words to the sentence fragment to make the idea complete.

6. *In the first three quarters on Saturday, the Jazz played near perfect basketball; however, the team quickly lost momentum in the final quarter.* Use a semicolon with the coordinator *however.* Use a comma after a connecting word that is used with a semicolon.

7. *That was the wildest game I have ever seen.* Add words to the sentence fragment to complete the thought.

8. *Morale among employees is affected greatly by the mood of their employers; for example, an argument between two bosses reduces the productivity of the employees in the office.* The second idea gives an example of the first idea. Use a connecting word that shows the correct relationship.

9. *Whenever a new contract is being negotiated, tension among employees increases.* When using a subordinator *(whenever)*, do not also use a coordinator *(and).*

10. *Some company owners reward their employees for ideas that save the company money, I plan to own my own business.* Use separate sentences for unrelated ideas, or change the second idea to one that relates to the first.

11. *One concern that companies and families share is the high cost of utilities; for instance, energy costs are rising with each passing year.* Use a coordinator that connects the second idea with the first. The second idea is not a result of the first.

12. *In the public schools, children are taught the importance of recycling; however, many adults resist the extra work involved in sorting the trash.* Use a semicolon with the connector *however.*

13. *When they are washing dishes or brushing their teeth, many people waste water without realizing it.* Use a comma after a subordinate idea when it begins the sentence.

14. Correct. A comma correctly follows the subordinate idea that begins the sentence.

15. *Microwave ovens are very popular; in fact, estimates show that at least three-quarters of American households now own one of these ovens. Accordingly, food manufacturers are developing new lines of frozen microwave products for people who want quick, easy meals. For example, single-serving kid's meals are a new item that is selling well.* The original sentence has too many ideas. Divide it into shorter sentences. This is one of several correct ways of doing so.

GED Review 4

1. **(3)** *Sentence Structure/Sentence Fragment/Sentence Revision.* An idea that begins with a subordinator cannot be a complete thought alone. This is a sentence fragment. Either remove the subordinator or add a second complete thought.

2. **(4)** *Sentence/Structure/Combining Sentences/Construction Shift. A hundred years ago, rickets was the most common serious disease of children in Europe and America.* The two ideas are the same except for the locations *Europe* and *America.* Joining them with a coordinate conjunction eliminates the repetition of the second idea.

3. **(2)** *Sentence Structure/Subordinators /Sentence Revision.* Always place a comma after a subordinate idea that begins a sentence.

4. **(4)** *Usage/Verb Tense/Sentence Correction.* Sentences 1 through 6 refer to a time in the past. Change *blocks* to *blocked* to eliminate the shift in verb tense.

5. **(3)** *Sentence Structure/Coordinators /Construction Shift.* The second idea is a result of the first idea, and the only coordinator among the choices that shows a result is the word *hence.*

6. **(3)** *Sentence Structure/Coordinators /Sentence Correction.* When a coordinate conjunction is used to join two complete ideas, a comma is needed at the end of the first complete thought.

7. **(5)** *Sentence Structure/Coordinators /Sentence Revision.* Do not join two unrelated thoughts. Correct the run-on my making two separate sentences.

8. **(2)** *Sentence Structure/Coordinators /Sentence Revision.* The words after the conjunction *and* are not a complete thought. Do not use a comma unless there are two complete thoughts joined by a coordinate conjunction.

9. **(4)** *Sentence Structure/Combining Sentences/Construction Shift. The center is energy efficient since three giant solar panels provide most of the center's hot water and lighting.* The second sentence repeats much of the information from the first sentence. By joining *lighting* to *hot water* using the conjunction *and*, you avoid the repetition.

10. **(3)** *Sentence Structure/Sentence Fragments/Sentence Correction.* As written, the subject *Astronauts* needs a verb. By eliminating the relative pronoun *who* the idea becomes a complete sentence.

11. **(5)** *Sentence Structure/Coordinators /Construction Shift. There is very little air in space to replenish the oxygen supply to a fire; however a fire in space does not go out immediately.* From the passage, you learned that a fire needs oxygen. Because there is little air in space, you assume that a fire would not be able to get the oxygen it needs and would go out. The second idea shows a contrasting thought; the fire does not go out. The only coordinator that shows contrast among the choices is the word *however.*

12. **(3)** *Sentence Structure/Coordinators /Sentence Revision.* The words after the conjunction *and* are not a complete thought. Do not use a comma unless there are two complete thoughts joined by a coordinate conjunction.

Chapter 2 Preview

1. *At last we had all the boxes packed and sealed.* Avoid wordiness; the phrase *at last* and *finally* have the same meaning.

2. Correct. The related ideas *enjoy* and *learn* are written in parallel form.

3. *Ms. Fischer gladly accepted the promotion.* Avoid wordiness. The phrase *with happiness* and *gladly* have the same meaning.

4. *Flown from sunrise to sunset, the U.S. flag is displayed at the White House every day.* Move the words being modified closer to the modifier.

5. *The dog waited patiently to go for a walk while his owner read the newspaper.* Add words that will make clear who is logically reading the newspaper.

Lesson 1 Exercise

There may be more than one way to correct a sentence.

1. *Mr. Marshall believes he hurt his back because he lifted heavy boxes.* Avoid wordiness by simplifying the ideas in the sentence.

2. *Her supervisors plan to combine all the ideas from the meeting.* The phrase *combine together* is repetitious. Avoid wordiness.

3. *I warned Diane to be on time for the job interview.* Avoid unnecessary words. State ideas simply whenever possible.

4. *We spent last summer in Florida.* Avoid wordiness. The phrases *last summer* and *last year* are repetitious. *Last summer* is the better choice because it is more specific.

5. *The driver shouted furiously.* Avoid wordiness. The words and phrases *in a rage, furious,* and *angrily* all express similar ideas.

Lesson 2 Exercise

There may be more than one way to correct a sentence.

1. *Running into the end zone, the linebacker scored the winning touchdown.* Introduce a word than can be modified by *Running.*

2. Correct. *Wishing* modifies *Ernest.*

3. *A rainbow can be seem from an airplane as a complete circle.* Move *from an airplane* to a position where it clearly modifies *can be seen.*

4. *While lying on his back, Michelangelo painted the ceiling of the Sistine Chapel.* Introduce words to make the meaning of *on his back* clearer, and move the modifier closer to the word it modifies, *Michelangelo.*

5. *Wearing a disguise, the detective watched the suspect's house.* Move *wearing* closer to the word it modifies, *detective.*

Lesson 3 Exercise

1. *A U.S. senator must be at least 30 years old, be a U.S. citizen for a minimum of 9 years, and live in the state in which he or she seeks election.* Drop the word *to* to obtain parallel structure.

2. *Activities that strengthen the heart muscle include swimming, jogging, and bicycling.* Change *to ride a bike* to *bicycling* for parallel structure.

3. *I enjoy sports that are challenging, fast-paced, and inexpensive.* Change *don't cost much money* to *inexpensive* for parallel structure.

4. *Is the birthstone of those born in July a ruby, sapphire, or diamond?* Drop *is it the* for parallel structure.

5. Correct. The related ideas *to be treated* and *to be given* are written in parallel form.

Chapter 2 Review

There may be more than one way to correct a sentence.

1. *The museum will be closed for remodeling during July.* Avoid wordiness. The words *for all days and nights during the month of* adds no new information.

2. *Many people use computers in their jobs.* Avoid wordiness.

3. *Please sign the form and return it in the enclosed envelope.* Avoid wordiness. Get to the point in as few words as possible.

4. *While taking a shower, I heard the telephone ring.* Add a subject that could logically be modified by *While taking a shower.*

5. *Margaret enjoyed singing and dancing more than acting.* Change *to act* to *acting* for parallel structure.

6. *After Greg proofread the letter, he retyped it.*

OR

After Greg checked the letter carefully for errors, he retyped it. Avoid unnecessary words. The meaning of the word *scrutinized* may be unclear to the reader. Express the same idea clearly in as few words as possible.

7. *The doctor explained the patient's symptoms, diagnosis, and treatment.* Change *what treatment would be used* to *treatment* for parallel structure.

8. Correct. The modifying phrase is next to the word it modifies.

9. *Excited and anxious, she quickly unwrapped her birthday gifts.* Add a subject that could logically be modified by *Excited and anxious.*

10. *The stories of Edgar Allen Poe are unusual, exciting, and suspenseful.* Change *they have suspense* to *suspenseful* for parallel structure.

GED Review 5

1. **(2)** *Sentence Structure/Clarity of Thought/Sentence Correction.* The word *affordable* and the phrase *that will fit within your budget* have the same meaning. Avoid repetition.

2. **(5)** *Sentence Structure/Clarity of Thought/Sentence Revision.* The phrases *on weekdays* and *from Monday through Friday* have the same meaning. Eliminate one to avoid repetition.

3. **(2)** *Usage/Subject-Verb Agreement/Sentence Revision.* The subject *playground* requires the singular verb *is.*

4. **(3)** *Sentence Structure/Parallel Structure/Sentence Revision.* All items in a series must use the same form in order to have parallel structure. Replace *to play* with *playing* to match the first two items in the series.

5. **(1)** *Sentence Structure/Clarity/Sentence Correction.* The words *routine* and *regular* have similar meanings. Use only one to avoid repetition.

6. **(3)** *Sentence Structure/Coordinators/Sentence Correction.* This sentence does not contain two complete ideas. Do not use a comma after one complete idea unless a second complete thought is joined to the first with a coordinate conjunction.

7. **(1)** *Sentence Structure/Subordinators/Sentence Revision.* The sentence is correct. Use a comma after a subordinate idea that begins a sentence.

8. **(5)** *Sentence Structure/Coordinators/Construction Shift.* The second idea gives an example of the women mentioned in the first idea. Use a semicolon with the coordinator *for example* followed by a comma.

9. **(4)** *Sentence Structure/Parallel Structure/Sentence Correction.* All items in a series must use the same form in order to have parallel structure. Replace *to cut* with *cutting* to match the first two items in the series.

10. **(1)** *Sentence Structure/Coordinators/Sentence Revision.* The sentence is correct. Use a comma after the first idea when two complete ideas are joined by a coordinate conjunction.

11. **(3)** *Sentence Structure/Coordinators/Sentence Revision.* The second idea is contrasted with the first, and the coordinator *however* shows contrast.

12. **(4)** *Sentence Structure/Placement of Modifiers/Construction Shift. Because they know the same technology, the counterfeiters can copy the card within a short period of time.* The modifying phrase *Knowing the same technology* is not by a word that it could logically modify. From the information in the passage, you can determine that the counterfeiters are the people who know the same technology.

Test-Taking Strategies 2

Strategy 2 Exercises

1. **(3)** *Sentence Structure/Subordinators/Construction Shift.* The word <u>if</u> shows that the material that will follow is a condition upon which the first part of the sentence is based.

2. **(2)** *Sentence Structure/Subordinators/Sentence Correction.* The subordinator *where* shows placement. The word *although* is correct because it shows that the two ideas are contrasting.

3. **(5)** *Sentence Structure/Parallel Structure/Sentence Revision.* All items in a series must use the same form in order to have parallel structure. In this sentence, each item should be in the noun form.

4. **(3)** *Sentence Structure/Run-on Sentences/Sentence Revision.* One way to correct a run-on sentence is by using a semicolon.

5. **(4)** *Sentence Structure/Clarity/Sentence Revision.* The construction is awkward and unclear.

Unit 2 Review

1. **(4)** *Sentence Structure/Improper Modification/Sentence Revision.* In the original construction, the phrase *which has 36 characters made up of one to six raised dots* appears to describe *Louis Braille.* The correction is one way in which the sentence can be written so that all modifiers are near the words they modify.

2. **(2)** *Sentence Structure/Comma Splice/Sentence Revision.* Two complete ideas cannot be joined with only a comma. Of the choices, only the second alternative shows the correct relationship between the two ideas.

3. **(5)** *Sentence Structure/Improper Modification/Construction Shift. Because he wanted to simplify the system, Louis Braille used only six dots.* Put words that modify as close as possible to the word they modify. The words *Because he wanted to simplify the system* refer to Louis Braille.

4. **(3)** *Sentence Structure/Combining Sentences/Sentence Revision.* Do not combine unrelated ideas.

5. **(4)** *Sentence Structure/Parallel Structure/Sentence Correction.* Change *for keeping* to *to keep* to be consistent with the first two items in the series *to prevent* and *to enhance.*

6. **(5)** *Sentence Structure/Clarity/Sentence Revision.* The phrase *that we eat and drink* has the same meaning as *consumption.* Eliminate one to avoid repetition of ideas.

7. **(1)** *Usage/Subject-Verb Agreement /Sentence Correction.* The plural subject of the sentence *dyes* requires a plural verb.

8. **(3)** *Usage/Vague Pronoun Reference /Sentence Revision.* It is unclear to whom or what the pronoun *they* refers. The third alternative eliminates the value pronoun reference since the word *they* in this revision clearly refers to *dyes.*

9. **(3)** *Sentence Structure/Subordinators /Construction Shift.* The two events described in these sentences occurred at basically the same time. The word *while* shows the correct relationship between the ideas.

10. **(5)** *Sentence Structure/Coordinators /Sentence Revision.* The second idea is in contrast to the first idea. The coordinator *nonetheless* shows contrast.

11. **(1)** *Sentence Structure/Coordinators /Sentence Correction.* When the word *and* is used to join two complete ideas, use a comma after the first complete idea.

12. **(2)** *Sentence Structure/Sentence Fragments/Sentence* Correction. Remove the relative pronoun to form a complete thought with both a subject and a verb.

ANSWER KEY
UNIT 3

Unit 3 Mechanics

Preview Unit 3

1. *There are 26 letters in the* **English** *alphabet.* Capitalize a nationality.

2. *Dorothy's aunt in The Wizard of Oz was named* **Aunt** *Em.* Capitalize a title when it is part of a person's name.

3. Correct. Proper nouns that name clubs and organizations are capitalized.

4. *During the* **American Revolution,** *the Battle of Bunker Hill was really fought on Breed's Hill.* Capitalize proper nouns.

5. *Fred and Wilma Flintstone lived at 39* **Stone Canyon Way.** Capitalize street addresses.

Lesson 1 Exercise

1. *The Mediterranean Sea is part of the* **Atlantic Ocean.** Capitalize the names of bodies of water.

2. Correct. Names of people, proper adjectives, and title of books are capitalized.

3. *The* **Presidential Medal of Freedom** *was established in 1963.* Capitalize awards that are proper nouns.

4. *In 1865 a* **steamboat** *explosion on the Mississippi River killed 1,653 people.* Do not capitalize common nouns.

5. *Using his research ship* **Calypso,** *Jacques Cousteau explored the oceans.* Capitalize proper names of boats and ships.

Lesson 2 Exercise

1. *The first woman to be appointed to the Supreme Court was* **Justice** *Sandra Day O'Conner.* Capitalize titles when used as part of a person's name.

2. *Carnegie Hall is located at* **Seventh Avenue and Fifty-Seventh Street** *in New York City.* Capitalize the words in a street name.

3. Correct. A title that is not used as part of a person's name is not capitalized.

4. *While he was* **President of the United States,** *Herbert Hoover gave all of his paychecks to charity.* Capitalize the title of the highest official in a country regardless of the way in which it is used.

5. *Our new officers are located at* **5310 South Gardner Road.** Capitalize the words in an address.

Lesson 3 Exercise

1. *The word* **"Monday,"** *referring to the second day of the week, was taken from an Old English word that meant "moon's day."* Capitalize the days of the week.

2. *The first day of* **winter** *is usually on December 21.* Do not capitalize the seasons of the year.

3. *Socrates, the famous Greek philosopher, died in 399 B.C., but his ideas had a major influence on the philosophers of the* **Christian Era.** Capitalize the names of historical periods.

4. *Babe Ruth Day was held on* **April** *27, 1947, at Yankee Stadium.* Capitalize the months of the year.

5. Correct. A numerical designation of a century is not capitalized.

Chapter 1 Review

1. *Cary Grant never won an* **Academy Award.** Capitalize the names of prizes and awards.

2. *Cleopatra was an* **Egyptian** *queen born in 69 B.C.* Capitalize adjectives made from proper nouns.

3. *Peter O'Toole starred in the 1962 movie* **Lawrence of Arabia.** Do not capitalize the word *of* in a title, unless it is the first word.

4. *Old Kent Road and Park Lane are two of the squares in the* **British** *version of Monopoly.* Capitalize proper adjectives.

5. Correct. The names of holidays and titles used as part of a person's name are capitalized.

6. *I asked my brother where he was going this* **summer** *for his vacation.* Do not capitalize the seasons of the year.

7. *The Tokyo World Lanes Bowling Center in* **Japan** *has 252 lanes.* Capitalize the names of countries.

8. *Sherlock Holmes's landlady was* **Mrs. Hudson.** Capitalize a title when it is part of a person's name.

9. *The Apollo II landed on the moon at 4:17 P.M. on July 20, 1969.* Capitalize this indication of a specific time.

10. *Lucas Santomee was the first known black* **doctor** *in the United States.* Do not capitalize color distinction of a race of people.

11. *The sneak preview of Kevin Costner's new movie will be shown on* **Friday.** Capitalize the days of the week.

12. *Janice Williams, our union representative, will be here on* **May** *17 to discuss the new retirement plan.* Capitalize the months of the year.

13. *Drive south six blocks until you come to Westlake* **Road.** Capitalize the words in a street name. Do not capitalize south when it refers to a direction.

14. *Marc Golov, one of the supervisors of the sales staff, invited* **Professor** *Scott Pierpont to present a workshop on customer service.* Capitalize a title when it is part of a person's name

15. *Desmond Tutu of* **South** *Africa won the Nobel Peace Prize in the year 1984.* Capitalize direction words when they are part of the name of a country, state, or region.

GED Review 6

1. **(4)** *Mechanics/Capitalization/Proper Nouns/Sentence Correction.* Capitalize the names of countries and geographic areas.

2. **(5)** *Mechanics/Capitalization/Titles of Persons and Addresses/Sentence Correction.* Do not capitalize direction words when they are not part of a place name or address.

3. **(3)** *Mechanics/Capitalization/Titles of Persons and Addresses/Sentence Revision.* Capitalize a direction word when it is part of the name of a specific region of a country.

4. **(2)** *Mechanics/Capitalization/Common Nouns/Sentence Correction.* Do not capitalize common nouns.

5. **(3)** *Mechanics/Capitalization/Seasons /Sentence Correction.* Do not capitalize the names of seasons.

6. **(4)** *Mechanics/Capitalization/Times /Sentence Correction.* Use small capital letters for abbreviations which show the time of day.

7. **(2)** *Mechanics/Capitalization/Common Nouns/Sentence Revision.* Do not capitalize common nouns. The word *hotel* in this sentence is not the specific name of the hotel.

8. **(4)** *Sentence Structure/Coordinators /Sentence Correction.* The second idea is a result of the first. Choose a coordinator that shows the correct relationship between the two ideas.

9. **(5)** *Mechanics/Capitalization/Sentence Correction.* This is a complex sentence, and it is punctuated correctly. All proper nouns are correctly capitalized.

10. **(3)** *Mechanics/Capitalization/Proper Nouns/Sentence Correction.* Capitalize the names of clubs, organizations, and associations.

11. **(3)** *Mechanics/Capitalization/Proper Nouns/Sentence Correction.* Capitalize the names of specific buildings.

12. **(2)** *Mechanics/Capitalization/Proper Nouns/Sentence Revision.* Capitalize the names of cities.

Chapter 2 Preview

1. *The first passengers to ride in a hot-air balloon* **were** *a duck, a sheep, and a rooster.* Do not use a comma before the first item in a series.

2. *The Statue of Liberty has special meaning to the United States,* **for** *it was a gift from France.* Use a comma before a coordinate conjunction in a compound sentence.

3. *Did you know that Memphis was also the name of an ancient city in* **Egypt?** A question ends with a question mark.

4. Correct. Use a comma after a subordinate idea at the beginning of a sentence.

5. *The honest,* **reliable candidate** *got the job.* Do not use a comma between an adjective or descriptive word and the noun that follows it.

Lesson 1 Exercise

1. *An evergreen tree keeps its leaves during the* **winter.** Use a period at the end of a statement.

2. *That woman needs a doctor* **immediately!** Use an exclamation point at the end of a statement if it shows strong emotion.

3. Correct. Use a question mark at the end of a question.

4. *Is Karl looking for a new **job?*** Use a question mark at the end of a question.

5. *Do not send the letter until Ms. Martin reads **it.*** Use a period at the end of a command.

Lesson 2 Exercise

1. *Sputnik 5 orbited the earth with **two dogs and six mice** aboard.* Do not use a comma when there are only two items in a series.

2. *The **tired, hungry** travelers could not find a motel room.* Use a comma between adjectives in a row before a noun.

3. Correct. When all the items in the series are separated by coordinate conjunctions, commas are not needed.

4. *George Washington, Abraham Lincoln, and James **Monroe** were descendants of England's King Edward I.* Do not put a comma after the last item in a series.

5. *The five basic swimming strokes **are** the crawl, the backstroke, the breaststroke, the butterfly, and the sidestroke.* Do not put a comma before the first item in a series.

Lesson 3 Exercise

1. *Charles Dodgson wrote Alice's Adventures in Wonderland, **but** he used the pen name Lewis Carroll.* Use a comma before the coordinator *but* in a compound sentence.

2. Correct. Use a comma before the coordinator *for* in a compound sentence.

3. *June is known as the month of romance and marriage; **however,** it also has one of the highest crime rates.* Use a semicolon before the coordinator *however* in a compound sentence.

4. *Our universe contains billions of galaxies; the nearest is two billion light-years away.* Do not use a comma alone to connect two complete ideas in a compound sentence. A semicolon can be used without a coordinator.

5. *Approximately fifty spacecraft have flown near the moon **or** visited it since 1958.* Do not use a comma because the words after the coordinate conjunction *or* are not a complete idea.

Lesson 4 Exercise

1. ***When it began in 1860,*** *the Pony Express mail service took ten days to deliver a letter from Missouri to California.* When a subordinate idea begins a sentence, it is followed by a comma.

2. ***Linda,*** *the meeting is about to begin.* Follow a term of direct address with a comma.

3. ***No,*** *she did not realize that the package arrived this morning.* Follow an introductory element with a comma.

4. ***To explain our new billing procedures,*** *we will send letters to our regular customers.* It is always correct to put a comma after an introductory element.

5. Correct. An introductory phrase of two words does not have to be set off by a comma unless the sentence would be misread without the comma.

Lesson 5 Exercise

1. *Major earthquakes can cause dangerous side effects such as a **tsunami, a gigantic sea wave.*** Set off a sentence interrupter that ends a sentence.

2. *Landslides, **of course,** are also associated with earthquakes.* Use a pair of commas to set off a sentence interrupter that is not essential to the main idea of the sentence.

3. ***I believe*** *that most earthquakes occur along fractures in the earth's crust.* Do not use a comma to set off words that are essential to the main idea of the sentence.

4. Correct. The sentence interrupter is not essential to the meaning of the sentence and is appropriately set off by commas.

5. *The Richter scale, **a system for measuring an earthquake's magnitude,** was developed during the 1930s.* Use a pair of commas to set off an interrupter that falls in the middle of a sentence.

Lesson 6 Exercise

There may be more than one correct way to edit these sentences.

1. *In 1920 Emer Smith of the Cleveland **Indians hit** the first grand-slam home run in a World Series game.* Do not use a comma to separate the subject and verb of a sentence.

2. *Dave DeBusschere played basketball for the New York Knicks **and** pitched for the Chicago White Sox.* Do not use a comma between two compound verbs joined by a coordinator.

3. *While playing water polo, one team wears white caps, **and** the opposing team wears blue caps.* Do not use a comma between two complete ideas without using a coordinator.

4. Correct. Commas correctly separate the items in the series.

5. *Bruce Jenner, Bill Toomey,* **and Rafer Johnson** *were all Olympic decathlon winners.* Do not use a comma after the last item in a series.

Chapter 2 Review

1. *Both the Bering* **Sea and** *the Coral Sea are in the Pacific Ocean.* Do not use a comma between only two items in a series.

2. *An owl can turn its head 270* **degrees, but** *it cannot move its eyes.* Use a comma before the coordinate conjunction in a compound sentence.

3. Correct. An introductory phrase of two words does not have to be set off by commas.

4. *The* **first automobile** *license plates were required by the state of New York.* A comma is not needed because the sentence does not sound "right" when either the order of the adjectives is changed or the word *and* is inserted between them.

5. *More dinosaur bones have been found in* **Canada, by the way,** *than in any other place in the world.* A sentence interrupter is set off by commas from the rest of the sentence.

6. **John,** *please order six cartons of paper for the copier.* Use a comma after a word used in direct address.

7. *Some birds that live in high places* **are condors,** *eagles, and hawks.* Do not use a comma before the first item in a series.

8. *Is it true that more than 60,000 bees can live in a single* **hive?** Use a question mark at the end of a question.

9. *The first space shuttle flight took place in 1981,* **and John** *Young was the commander.* Use a comma before a coordinate conjunction in a compound sentence.

10. Correct. Use a comma after an introductory element.

11. *A scientist* **who studies weather** *is called a meteorologist.* Do not use commas to set off an interrupting phrase that is essential to the meaning of the sentence.

12. **One hot dog or one ounce of cheese or one chicken drumstick** *provides seven grams of protein.* Do not use commas when the items in a series are all separated by coordinate conjunctions.

13. *Water is more dangerous than wind during a* **hurricane;** *ninety percent of all hurricane-related deaths are caused by storm surges and floods.* Do not use only a comma to join two complete thoughts in a compound sentence. Use either a comma and a coordinate conjunction or a semicolon. If a coordinating word is used with the semicolon, it should be followed by a comma.

14. *Deserts are found on every* **continent; in fact,** *deserts cover about one-third of the land area of the earth.* Do not use only a comma to join two complete thoughts in a compound sentence. Use either a comma and a coordinate conjunction or a semicolon. If a coordinating word is used with the semicolon, it should be followed by a comma.

15. *Pike's Peak,* **a famous tourist attraction in Colorado,** *stands 14,110 feet high.* Use a pair of commas to set off an interrupter that falls in the middle of a sentence.

GED Review 7

1. **(3)** *Mechanics/Punctuation/Commas Between Items in a Series/Sentence Correction.* Do not put a comma before the first item in a series.

2. **(2)** *Mechanics/Punctuation/Commas After Introductory Elements/Sentence Correction.* Use a comma after a subordinate idea that begins a sentence.

3. **(5)** *Mechanics/Punctuation/Commas with Sentence Interrupters/Sentence Revision.* Do not set off words or phrases that are essential to the meaning of the sentence.

4. **(3)** *Mechanics/Punctuation/Commas with Sentence Interrupters/Sentence Correction.* Use commas to set off common expressions that are used as sentence interrupters.

5. **(3)** *Mechanics/Capitalization/Titles of People/Sentence Revision.* Do not capitalize a title if it is not used as part of a person's name.

6. **(4)** *Sentence Structure/Coordinators /Construction Shift.* The second idea contrasts with the first. The coordinator *instead* shows contrast.

7. **(1)** *Mechanics/Punctuation/Commas with Sentence Interrupters/Sentence Correction.* Set off a descriptive phrase with commas if it is not essential to the meaning of the sentence.

8. **(4)** *Mechanics/Punctuation/Commas in Compound Sentences/Sentence Revision.* When a coordinator is used with a semi-colon to join the complete ideas in a compound sentence, put a comma after the coordinator.

9. **(5)** *Sentence Structure/Coordinators /Construction Shift.* The second idea emphasizes the first. Of the choices, only the coordinator *in fact* gives emphasis.

10. **(1)** *Usage/Pronoun Reference/Subject Pronouns/Sentence Correction.* Use the pronoun *he* as a subject.

11. **(4)** *Mechanics/Punctuation/Commas Between Items in a Series/Sentence Correction.* Do not separate the items in a series when there are fewer than three items.

12. **(4)** *Mechanics/Capitalization/Proper Nouns/Sentence Revision.* Do not capitalize the short word *and* unless it is the first word of the proper noun.

Chapter 3 Preview

1. *Most of* **Earth's** *physical changes are so gradual that we do not notice them.* Add apostrophe to show possession.

2. *Only two city council members thought it was* **all right** *to raise parking fees.* All right is two words.

3. **Besides** *teaching, Larry enjoys coaching basketball.* Add an *s* to *beside,* to give the meaning "in addition to."

4. *There were several* **misspelled** *words in the letter.* Misspelled has two *s*'s.

5. Correct. The contraction *you'd* means "you would."

Lesson 1 Exercise

1. *Recent* **discoveries** *in medicine have changed the way people live.* The noun *discovery* ends in *y* preceded by a consonant. The plural is formed by replacing *y* with *i* and adding *es.*

2. *In many* **cities,** *trolleys once ran along main streets.* The noun *city* ends in *y* preceded by a consonant. Its plural is formed by replacing *y* with *i* and adding *es.* The noun *trolley* ends in *y* preceded by a vowel. Its plural is formed by adding *s.*

3. Correct. To form the *-ing* form of arrive, drop the final *e* before adding *-ing.*

4. *The candidates* **running** *for office appeared to have similar views.* To form the *-ing* form of *run,* double the final *n* before adding *-ing.*

5. *Many families are* **preparing** *their children for school by helping them learn to read.* To form the *-ing* form of *prepare,* drop the final *e* before adding *-ing.*

Lesson 2 Exercise

1. *A person* **can't** *jump higher than a horse.* Position the apostrophe to show exactly where letters have been omitted in the contraction of *cannot.*

2. *Kangaroos carry* **their** *young in a pouch.* Do not confuse the contraction *they're* (they are) with the possessive pronoun *their.*

3. *Although it drinks huge amounts of water, a camel* **doesn't** *sweat.* Position the apostrophe to show exactly where letters have been omitted in the contraction of *does not.*

4. **It's** *a fact that light travels about 186,000 miles per second.* Use the apostrophe to form the contraction of *it is.*

5. Correct. *Isn't* is the contraction for *Is not.*

Lesson 3 Exercise

1. *The only flag on the moon is* **ours.** Do not use an apostrophe with a possessive pronoun.

2. **Americans** *spend over $1 billion on gum each year.* An apostrophe is not needed because the noun does not show possession.

3. Correct. The word *girls'* is the possessive of the plural noun *girls.*

4. *The anaconda, the world's largest snake, squeezes* **its** *prey to death and swallows it whole.* Do not use an apostrophe with a possessive pronoun. The word "it's" is a contraction.

5. **Beethoven's** *music teacher criticized him for not having musical talent.* The possessive form of a singular noun is formed by adding an apostrophe and the letter *s* to the noun.

Lesson 4 Exercise

1. *It is* **all right** *to smile when you receive a* **compliment.** Change *alright* to *all right* and *complement* to *compliment.*

2. *In the* **past,** *I have always eaten dessert because I enjoy sweets a lot.* Change *passed* to *past.*

3. Correct. *Whose* is a pronoun that shows ownership.

4. Next **week** the **council** will decide what **course** of action to take. Change *weak* to *week*, *counsel* to *council*, and *coarse* to *course*.

5. Don't **waste** stationery because it is **too** expensive. Change *waist* to *waste* and *to* to *too*. *Stationery* is spelled correctly.

6. The policy board will meet **all together** next Thursday. Change *altogether* to *all together*.

7. **It's** my opinion that our principal goal should be to improve employee morale. Changes *Its* to the contraction *It's*.

8. Your **role** at the meeting will be to make sure everyone has a chance to speak. Change *roll* to *role*.

9. I want to make it plain that we cannot afford to **waste** any time at the meeting. Change *waist* to *waste*.

10. Ms. Conover **heard** that the new site for our office had **already** been decided. Change *herd* to *heard* and *all ready* to *already*.

Lesson 5 Exercise

1. change *abundence* to *abundance*
   change *adress* to *address*
2. change *auxilary* to *auxiliary*
   change *benefitted* to *benefited*
3. change *calender* to *calendar*
   change *cheif* to *chief*
   change *committment* to *commitment*
4. change *coroborate* to *corroborate*
   change *critisism* to *criticism*
   change *dependant* to *dependent*
5. change *dissappoint* to *disappoint*
   change *entrence* to *entrance*
   change *exersice* to *exercise*
   change *exhileration* to *exhilaration*
6. change *Febuary* to *February*
   change *freind* to *friend*
7. change *grammer* to *grammar*
   change *hankerchief* to *handkerchief*
   change *manuever* to *maneuver*
8. change *newstand* to *newsstand*
   change *occassion* to *occasion*
   change *ommission* to *omission*
9. change *perserverance* to *perseverance*
   change *shephard* to *shepherd*
10. change *unecessary* to *unnecessary*
    change *vacuumm* to *vacuum*
    change *wierd* to *weird*

Chapter 3 Review

1. The flea can jump a distance that is 130 times the height of **its** body. The possessive pronoun *its* is spelled without an apostrophe.

2. Many lives were lost in the war for **independence** from England. This is a frequently misspelled word.

3. The children have **swimming** lessons on Monday and tennis lessons on Tuesday. Double the final consonant of a one-syllable word that ends in a single consonant when adding *-ing*.

4. The Caterpillar Club is an organization **whose** members have used parachutes to save their lives. The relative pronoun *whose* is spelled without an apostrophe. Do not confuse it with the contraction *who's*.

5. Correct. The frequently misspelled word *accommodate* and the word *principal*, meaning the head of a school, are spelled correctly as written.

6. The candidate doubted the voters would approve a raise in **taxes.** To form a plural, add *-es* to nouns that end in *s, x, ch,* or *sh*.

7. Many **weather** satellites take pictures of cloud formations that surround the earth. *Whether* and *weather* are homonyms; *weather* refers to climate.

8. Solar energy is an **efficient** way to use the sun's energy. This is a frequently misspelled word.

9. The committee's decision was the same as **yours.** Never use an apostrophe in a possessive pronoun.

10. The council proposed **putting** parking meters in the alleys from Fourth Street to Broadway Avenue. Double the final consonant of a one-syllable word that ends in a single consonant when adding *-ing*.

11. Correct. The frequently misspelled word *convenience* is correct as written.

12. On a **library's** shelves, rare books can be found under the number 090. The possessive form of the singular noun *library* is formed by adding an apostrophe and the letter *s*.

13. The **development** of the Popsicle is credited to an 11-year-old boy. This is a frequently misspelled word.

14. I am surprised that you **didn't** know about the recent job opening. Position the apostrophe to show where the letter has been dropped to form the contraction for *did not.*

15. *There is the* **stationery** *you ordered last month.* The words *stationary* and *stationery* are homonyms. The word *stationery* refers to writing paper.

GED Review 8

1. **(5)** *Mechanics/Spelling/Frequently Misspelled Words/Sentence Revision.* The word *receive* is often misspelled.

2. **(1)** *Mechanics/Spelling/Possessives /Sentence Correction.* Add 's to make a singular noun possessive.

3. **(3)** *Mechanics/Spelling/Contractions /Sentence Correction.* Use the contraction *they're* to mean *they are.*

4. **(5)** *Mechanics/Spelling/Basic Spelling Rules/Sentence Correction.* When a one-syllable verb ends in a single consonant, double the final consonant before adding *-ing.*

5. **(3)** *Usage/Subject-Verb Agreement /Sentence Revision.* The singular subject *body* requires the singular verb *produces.*

6. **(2)** *Mechanics/Spelling/Basic Spelling Rules/Sentence Correction.* Singular nouns that end in **y** preceded by a consonant are pluralized by replacing the *y* with *i* and adding *es.*

7. **(2)** *Mechanics/Spelling/Homonyms /Sentence Correction.* Use the possessive pronoun *Their* instead of *There.*

8. **(3)** *Mechanics/Capitalization/Proper Nouns/Sentence Correction.* Capitalize the name of a country or region of the world.

9. **(1)** *Mechanics/Spelling/Possessives /Sentence Correction.* Use the possessive pronoun *Your* instead of the contraction *You're* meaning *you are.*

10. **(5)** *Mechanics/Spelling/Frequently Misspelled Words/Sentence Correction.* The frequently misspelled words *emergency, procedures,* and *necessary* are all spelled correctly.

11. **(1)** *Mechanics/Spelling/Homonyms /Sentence Correction.* The word *miner* means *a worker in a mine;* the word *minor* means *of little importance.*

12. **(2)** *Mechanics/Spelling/Possessives /Sentence Revision.* Use the possessive pronoun *Its* instead of the contraction *It's* meaning *it is.*

Answers for Test-Taking Strategies 3

1. **(4)** *Mechanics/Spelling/Possessives /Sentence Correction.* Use the possessive pronoun form *their* to modify *shows* rather than the contraction for *they are.*

2. **(1)** *Mechanics/Capitalization/Proper Nouns/Sentence Correction.* All the important words in a proper noun should be capitalized.

3. **(4)** *Mechanics/Spelling/Frequently Misspelled Words/Sentence Correction.* This word is often misspelled.

4. **(4)** *Mechanics/Punctuation/Sentence Interrupters/Sentence Revision.* Use paired commas to set off sentence interrupters.

5. **(5)** *Mechanics/Spelling/Possessives /Sentence Revision.* Use an apostrophe to show possession.

Unit 3 Review

1. **(3)** *Mechanics/Spelling/Sentence Correction.* This word is often misspelled.

2. **(2)** *Usage/Verb Forms/Sentence Correction.* Use the correct verb form with a helping verb.

3. **(4)** *Mechanics/ Punctuation/Sentence Revision.* Set off a sentence interrupter with a comma.

4. **(5)** *Mechanics/Spelling-Homonyms /Sentence Correction.* Use the relative pronoun form *whose* rather than the contraction for *who is.*

5. **(1)** *Mechanics/Punctuation/Sentence Revision.* The sentence is correct as written.

6. **(1)** *Mechanics/Capitalization/Sentence Correction.* Do not capitalize the word *and* as part of a title unless it is the first word in the title.

7. **(3)** *Mechanics/Capitalization/Sentence Correction.* Capitalize names of people or words that are derived from other words that are capitalized. The word *American* is derived from the word *America.*

8. **(1)** *Mechanics/Punctuation/Sentence Revision.* The sentence is correct as written. The words *who study buying trends* is needed for the meaning of the sentence to remain the same.

9. **(2)** *Mechanics/Punctuation/Sentence Revision.* Put a comma before the conjunction that connects a series.

10. **(1)** *Mechanics/Punctuation/Sentence Correction.* Put pairs of commas around an unnecessary sentence interrupter, such as *for example.*

11. **(2)** *Sentence Structure/Subordinators /Construction Shift. In 1966 McDonald's billboards boasted, "2 billion sold" while in 1991 they claimed, "Over 80 billion served."* The subordinator *while* shows the correct relationship between the two ideas.

12. **(2)** *Mechanics/Capitalization/Sentence Correction.* Do not capitalize the names of the seasons.

13. **(1)** *Mechanics/Punctuation/Sentence Revision.* The sentence is correct as written. Put a comma after an introductory group of words.

14. **(4)** *Mechanics/Punctuation/Sentence Revision.* Do not use commas to set off an interrupter that is necessary to the meaning of the sentence.

15. **(5)** *Mechanics/Spelling/Sentence Correction.* This word is frequently misspelled.

16. **(3)** *Mechanics/Spelling/Sentence Correction.* The plural of a word does not need an apostrophe.

Part I Practice Test

1. **(3)** *Usage/Subject-Verb Agreement /Sentence Correction.* The compound subject, *home computers and television,* requires a plural verb.

2. **(4)** *Sentence Structure/Subordination /Sentence Revision.* Use only one subordinator at a time. The subordinator *while* makes the most sense in this sentence.

3. **(1)** *Mechanics/Punctuation/Construction Shift. Use commas to set off a sentence interrupter. A 1985 survey, conducted by the President's Council on Physical Fitness and Sports, showed the results of a lack of enough active participation in exercise.*

4. **(5)** *Mechanics/Spelling/Sentence Correction.* Do not confuse the troublesome words *though* and *through.*

5. **(4)** *Mechanics/Punctuation—Overuse of Commas/Sentence Revision.* Do not use a comma before a coordinator that connects a compound subject.

6. **(2)** *Mechanics/Capitalization/Sentence Correction.* Do not capitalize a word that is not used as a common noun unless it is the first word of the sentence.

7. **(4)** *Usage/Verb Tense/Sentence Correction.* Verb tenses in a sentence should be consistent. Change *increased* to the present tense, *increases,* to agree with the tense of the other verb, *illustrate.*

8. **(4)** *Usage/Pronoun Reference—Agreement with Antecedent/Sentence Revision.* The pronoun *their* agrees with the plural antecedent *children's.*

9. **(2)** *Sentence Structure/Sentence Fragment/Sentence Correction.* Removing the relative pronoun, *who,* changes this sentence fragment into a complete sentence.

10. **(4)** *Usage/Verb Tense/Sentence Revision.* Change *became* to the present tense, *become,* to agree with the tense of the paragraph.

11. **(5)** *Sentence Structure/Coordination /Sentence Correction.* The coordinators *neither* and *nor* are used correctly to connect the two verbs, *meets* and *uses.*

12. **(3)** *Usage/Subject-Verb Agreement /Sentence Revision.* Change the verb, *provide,* to *provides* to agree with its singular subject, *book.*

13. **(4)** *Sentence Structure/Subordination /Construction Shift. As you gather information about a particular job, you should think about these ideas.* A coordinator is not needed when ideas of unequal rank are joined by a subordinator.

14. **(2)** *Sentence Structure/Comma Splice /Sentence Revision.* Do not use a comma between two complete ideas that are not joined by a coordinator. Replace the comma with a semicolon, or create two separate sentences by changing the comma to a period and capitalizing the first word of the second complete idea.

15. **(3)** *Mechanics/Punctuation/Overuse of Commas/Sentence Correction.* Do not use a comma before a coordinator that connects two items in a listing.

16. **(1)** *Sentence Structure/Complex Sentences /Construction Shift. Fifth, (E) entry skills that include specific education and training requirements must be known.* The second idea has been put into a group of words that begins with the relative pronoun *that.*

17. **(4)** *Mechanics/Spelling/Homonyms /Sentence Correction.* Change the contraction *you're* to the possessive pronoun *your.*

18. **(5)** *Usage/Subject-Verb Agreement and Pronoun Reference/Sentence Correction.* The verb, *are,* agrees with its subject, *languages,* and the pronoun, *themselves,* agrees with its antecedent, *computers.*

19. **(2)** *Usage/Subject-Verb Agreement /Sentence Revision.* Change *are* to *is* to agree with the singular subject, *each.*

20. **(4)** *Mechanics/Punctuation/Construction Shift.* *LOGO, a specialized language that uses both graphics and words, is used to teach programming to children.* The idea in sentence 5 is changed into an interrupting phrase that describes the noun *LOGO* in the new sentence. Sentence interrupters are set off by commas.

21. **(3)** *Mechanics/Capitalization/Sentence Correction.* Do not capitalize *mathematician* because it is a common noun and not a title that is part of a person's name.

22. **(5)** *Usage/Pronoun Reference/Sentence Correction.* No correction is necessary. The relative pronoun *which* is used correctly because it refers to things.

23. **(2)** *Mechanics/Punctuation/Sentence Correction.* An introductory phrase should be followed by a comma.

24. **(2)** *Sentence Structure/Misplaced Modifiers/Construction Shift.* *FORTRAN, an acronym for Formula Translator, is used for mathematical and scientific applications.* A modifier should be placed as close as possible to the word being described. The modifying phrase *an acronym for Formula Translator* describes *FORTRAN,* not *applications.*

25. **(4)** *Usage/Verb Tense/Sentence Correction.* Keep verb tenses consistent. Change *evolved* to the present tense *evolve* to agree with the verb *arise.*

26. **(5)** *Mechanics/Punctuation/Sentence Correction.* This sentence is correct as written.

27. **(3)** *Sentence Structure/Run-On Sentence/Sentence Revision.* Sentence 8 is a run-on sentence. A period should follow *person* and the first word of the second complete idea should be capitalized.

28. **(2)** *Usage/Subject-Verb Agreement /Sentence Revision.* The subject. *processors,* is plural. It needs the plural form of the verb *have* for correct subject-verb agreement.

Part II Essay Writing - Part II Test

Introduction to Holistic Scoring

The following GED Essay Scoring Guide provides a general description of the characteristics found in GED essays that are scored by the Holistic Method.

GED ESSAY SCORING GUIDE

Papers will show *some* or *all* of the following characteristics.

Upper-half papers make clear a definite purpose, pursued with varying degrees of effectiveness. They also have a structure that shows evidence of some deliberate planning. The writer's control of English usage ranges from fairly reliable at 4 to confident and accomplished at 6.

6 Papers scored as a 6 tend to offer sophisticated ideas within an organizational framework that is clear and appropriate for the topic. The supporting statements are particularly effective because of their substance, specificity, or illustrative quality. The writing is vivid and precise, though it may contain an occasional flaw.

5 Papers scored as a 5 are clearly organized with effective support for each of the writer's major points. The writing offers substantive ideas, though the paper may lack the flair or grace of a 6 paper. The surface features are consistently under control, despite an occasional lapse in usage.

4 Papers scored as a 4 show evidence of the writer's organizational plan. Support, though sufficient, tends to be less extensive or convincing than that found in papers scored as a 5 or 6. The writer generally observes the conventions of accepted English usage. Some errors are usually present, but they are not severe enough to interfere significantly with the writer's main purpose.

Lower-half papers either fail to convey a purpose sufficiently or lack one entirely. Consequently, their structure ranges from rudimentary at 3, to random at 2, to absent at 1. Control of the conventions of English usage tends to follow this same gradient.

3 Papers scored as a 3 usually show some evidence of planning or development. However, the organization is often limited to a simple listing or haphazard recitation of ideas about the topic, leaving an impression of insufficiency. The 3 papers often demonstrate repeated weaknesses in accepted English usage and are generally ineffective in accomplishing the writer's purpose.

2 Papers scored as a 2 are characterized by a marked lack of development or inadequate support for ideas. The level of thought apparent in the writing is frequently unsophisticated or superficial, often marked by a listing of unsupported generalizations. Instead of suggesting a clear purpose, these papers often present conflicting purposes. Errors in accepted English usage may seriously interfere with the overall effectiveness of these papers.

1 Papers scored as a 1 leave the impression that the writer has not only *not* accomplished a purpose, but has not made any purpose apparent. The dominant feature of these papers is the lack of control. The writer stumbles both in conveying a clear plan for the paper and in expressing ideas according to the conventions of accepted English usage.

0 The zero score is reserved for papers which are blank, illegible, or written on a topic other than the one assigned.

Source: The 1988 Tests of General Educational Development: A Preview, American Council on Education, 1985. Used with permission.

To score your essay, compare it with the following model essays. These model essays represent scores of 3 and 5 respectively.

Compare your essay with the model essay scored 3. If it is as good as that essay, assign your essay a score of 3. If it is not as good as the 3 essay, refer to the answers for the Writing Skills Predictor Test (pages 12-18). Use the descriptions of the 1 and 2 essays there to evaluate your essay.

If your essay is better than the 3 essay, compare it to the model essay scored 5. If yours is better than the 3, but not as good as the 5, score your essay a 4. If your essay is better than the 5 model essay, score it a 6.

In addition, look at the notes and character trait analyses that accompany the model essays. These comments explain the strengths and weaknesses of these essays.

Model Essay—Holistic Score 3

Too many key points—lack of focus. Disorganized, illogical flow of ideas.

No paragraphs in the middle to explain the points made in the introduction.

Undeveloped ideas that don't lead to a point.

Concluding statement weak—needs support.

Voting is a right everyone should have. It is important to vote because thats how people get elected. Voting was not always given to everyone. There were times when not every person could vote. Without everyone voting we cannot have a complete democracy. Voting is everyones right and everyone should exercise this right.

Secondly, voting is important for our government to act right. The people need to let the senators and presidents and congressman know what they think about things. What better way to do that than to vote in all the elections and let them know what you feel about different issues that are important in an election. In summary, it is important for everyone to vote rich people and poor people too. If everyone voted it would be a better world to live in today.

Character Trait Analysis

1. The essay is organized into two paragraphs, an introduction and a conclusion.

2. Within those two paragraphs, many different points are made, but none are supported with examples or details. The total effect is one of disorganization and illogical flow of ideas. Points made do not lead logically to a conclusion.

3. The conclusion that is made is not explained or supported.

4. The essay is shorter than the required 200 words.

5. Errors in spelling, punctuation, sentence structure, and grammar detract from the essay's effectiveness.

Model Essay—Holistic Score 5

Essay begins with an interesting fact. Introduction states points of view.

Explains one key idea introduced in first paragraph. Uses facts to support argument.

More facts supporting argument. Uses appropriate transition words to move from point to point.

Summarizes ideas; concludes with important statement about the topic that is in keeping with point of view.

Before a major election is held in the United States, efforts are sometimes made to register more voters. However, the number of people who do vote in an election is often small. I believe that all eligible citizens should vote in every election.

The right to vote is a freedom that we should not take for granted. In some parts of the world, people do not have this right. Even in this country, everyone could not always vote. For example, black men could not vote until after the Civil War. Women could not vote until early in this century. Thus, the right to vote is a freedom we all should cherish.

Although people may argue that their votes do not matter, a few votes can sometimes make a real difference. History tells of several presidential elections that were determined by no more than 100,000 votes. That may sound like a lot, but out of millions of voters, it is really a very small percentage.

Even when an election is not close, it gives us a chance to state our views about government. Every vote is private, and every vote counts equally. Therefore, an important way to be involved in our government and to preserve democracy is to vote.

Character Trait Analysis

1. The essay is well organized. Ideas flow logically and lead to a conclusion.

2. Point of view is supported by details and facts.

3. All details and facts are consistent with the point of view and make the writer's opinion clear.

4. The essay reads well, although there are a few structural weaknesses and minor mechanical errors.

Answer Key Practice Items Part I

Practice Items, Part 1

1. **(4)** *Usage/Subject-Verb Agreement—Interrupting Phrase/Construction Shift.* *The history of sports is often fascinating.* The singular subject, *history*, requires a singular verb, *is*.

2. **(3)** *Usage/Verb Tense—Clues Within Sentence/Sentence Revision.* The phrase *in 1895* indicates that the verb should be in the past tense.

3. **(1)** *Usage/Verb Form/Sentence Correction.* Be careful when expressing the forms of irregular verbs, such as *to see*.

4. **(5)** *Mechanics/Sentence Correction.* The sentence is correct as written.

5. **(4)** *Mechanics/Punctuation—Introductory Elements/Sentence Revision.* Always put a comma after a group of words that introduces the sentence but is not part of the main idea.

6. **(4)** *Sentence Structure/Comma Splice/Sentence Correction.* In the original sentence, two complete ideas are incorrectly joined with a comma. Since the sentence is also wordy, the error is best corrected by removing ideas that are repeated.

7. **(4)** *Sentence Structure/Run-On Sentence/Sentence Correction.* The original sentence contains two complete ideas that are run together without punctuation. The error is eliminated by forming two separate sentences.

8. **(2)** *Mechanics/Capitalization—Proper Nouns/Sentence Correction.* Capitalize the names of countries.

9. **(4)** *Mechanics/Punctuation/Sentence Revision.* Use a comma to separate two complete ideas joined by connecting words such as *but, and, or, for*.

10. **(5)** *Mechanics/Spelling—Homonyms/Sentence Correction.* *Role* and *roll* sound alike but have different meanings.

11. **(4)** *Usage/Verb Tense/Sentence Correction.* The present tense is used throughout the paragraph.

12. **(1)** *Sentence Structure/Subordination/Construction Shift.* *As November of any election year approaches, we see the faces of candidates frequently on TV.* Use a comma to set off the subordinate idea when it comes first in the sentence.

13. **(5)** *Sentence Structure/Parallelism/Sentence Correction.* Use parallel structures to express similar ideas.

14. **(3)** *Usage/Relative Pronoun/Sentence Revision.* Use *who* to refer to people and *which* to refer to things.

15. **(4)** *Usage/Subject-Verb Agreement—Interrupting Phrase/Sentence Correction.* The plural subject, *Those*, requires a plural verb, *tend*. Do not be confused by the description following the subject.

16. **(5)** *Usage/Subject-Verb Agreement—Interrupting Phrase/Sentence Revision.* The plural subject, *people*, requires a plural verb, *are*.

17. **(4)** *Sentence Structure/Coordination/Construction Shift.* *There were some past American presidents who probably would have seemed awkward and plain on television, yet they made excellent leaders.* The original sentences are choppy; the combination makes the relationship between ideas more clear.

18. **(2)** *Sentence Structure/Sentence Fragment/Sentence Correction.* The fragment is corrected by providing a verb phrase, *do make*, for the subject, *people*.

19. **(3)** *Sentence Structure/Dangling Modifier/Sentence Revision.* *It* does not watch television; *we* do. Use a word that can logically be modified by *Watching television*.

20. **(5)** *Sentence Structure/Parallelism/Sentence Correction.* When you join two verbs with *and*, they should be in the same form: *take* and *inject*.

21. **(2)** *Sentence Structure/Subordination/Sentence Revision.* Use only one subordinator to introduce a subordinate idea.

22. **(4)** *Sentence Structure/Clarity—Wordiness/Construction Shift.* *In the late 1800s a doctor discovered that patients given shots of cowpox virus were protected from smallpox.* The new construction eliminates the vague word *something*.

23. **(4)** *Usage/Pronouns—Agreement with Antecedent/Sentence Revision.* The pronoun, *them*, must agree with the antecedent, patients.

24. **(5)** *Usage/Subject-Verb Agreement— Expletive/Sentence Correction.* This sentence has inverted structure. The verb, *have been*, agrees with the subject, *deaths*, even though the subject follows the verb.

25. **(1)** *Mechanics/Spelling/Sentence Correction. Believe* is a commonly misspelled word.

26. **(4)** *Usage/Subject-Verb Agreement— Interrupting Phrases/Sentence Revision.* The singular subject, *vaccination*, requires a singular verb, *is given*.

27. **(1)** *Mechanics/Capitalization/Sentence Correction.* Titles are capitalized only when they are used with a person's name.

28. **(2)** *Mechanics/Punctuation—Overuse of Commas/Sentence Revision.* Do not separate the subject, *vaccines*, from the verb, *are being developed*, with a comma.

29. **(1)** *Mechanics/Spelling—Homonyms /Sentence Correction.* Do not use the contraction *you're* meaning *you are* as a possessive pronoun.

30. **(3)** *Mechanics/Punctuation—Introductory Elements/Sentence Revision.* Always put a comma after a group of words that introduces the sentence but is not part of the main idea.

31. **(4)** *Mechanics/Punctuation—Items in a Series/Sentence Correction.* Use commas to separate three or more items in a series.

32. **(3)** *Sentence Structure/Parallelism /Sentence Revision.* When you connect two verbs with *and*, they should be in the same form: *stop* and *talk*.

33. **(1)** *Sentence Structure/Subordination /Construction Shift. Many children who do not like to read on their own are often willing to read for quite a while if you offer to take turns reading some of the paragraphs.* Remember to use *who* when referring to people and *which* when referring to things.

34. **(4)** *Sentence Structure/Sentence Fragment/Sentence Revision.* When a semicolon is used, it should separate two complete ideas. The second idea in this sentence is a fragment. Both the subject, *he*, and the verb, *begins*, must be supplied to make the second idea complete.

35. **(5)** *Usage/Subject-Verb Agreement /Sentence Revision.* When the connecting words, *either...or*, join singular and plural nouns, the verb agrees with the closer noun. The plural verb, *are*, agrees with the closer noun, *bookstores*.

36. **(2)** *Usage/Subject-Verb Agreement— Inverted Structure/Sentence Correction.* Although the usual order is reversed, the singular subject, *half*, requires a singular verb, *is*.

37. **(5)** *Mechanics/Capitalization/Sentence Correction.* Names of holidays, months, and days of the week are capitalized.

38. **(4)** *Usage/Verb Tense—Irregular Verbs/Sentence Revision.* With the helping verb, *has*, use the past participle. The past participle of *grow* is *grown*.

39. **(5)** *Usage/Verb Tense—Clues Within Paragraph/Sentence Correction.* The verb tense used, the present, is correct because it is consistent with that used throughout the paragraph.

40. **(5)** *Mechanics/Punctuation—Sentence Interrupters/Sentence Revision.* Descriptions that are not essential to the meaning of a sentence are set off by commas. Here, *especially in the middle of the year* explains *Having to change schools* but is not essential to the sentence's meaning.

41. **(2)** *Mechanics/Capitalization/Sentence Correction.* Do not capitalize family titles that are not used in place of a specific name.

42. **(4)** *Sentence Structure/Comma Splice/Sentence Correction.* Use a connecting word, such as *and*, or a semicolon to join two complete ideas. A comma alone is not enough.

43. **(4)** *Mechanics/Capitalization—Proper Adjectives/Sentence Correction.* Capitalize adjectives that are formed from proper nouns.

44. **(4)** *Usage/Vague Pronoun Reference /Sentence Correction.* In the original, it is not clear whether *they* refers to the parents, the parents and the child, or many such families.

45. **(3)** *Mechanics/Spelling/Sentence Correction. Absense* is a frequently misspelled word.

46. **(3)** *Sentence Structure/Comma Splice/Sentence Revision.* A semicolon can be used to separate two complete ideas; a comma may not used in this way.

47. **(4)** *Sentence Structure/Clarity /Construction Shift. Each branch of the military has set up family service centers to assist with a variety of problems.* Of all the choices, this one is the most concise way of eliminating confusion over to what *It* refers.

48. **(4)** *Usage/Verb Tense/Sentence Revision.* Look within a sentence for clues to verb tense. *When computers were invented* should be followed by *people were frightened.*

49. **(5)** *Usage/Verb Form—Irregular Verbs/Sentence Revision. To take* is an irregular verb. With the helping verbs, *would be,* use the past participle, *taken.*

50. **(3)** *Mechanics/Punctuation—Overuse of Commas/Sentence Correction.* Do not separate the subject, *thought,* from its verb, *made,* with a comma.

51. **(5)** *Sentence Structure/Coordination /Sentence Correction.* Two complete ideas are correctly separated by a semicolon. The second idea provides evidence supporting the first.

52. **(2)** *Mechanics/Capitalization—Proper Nouns/Sentence Correction.* Capitalize the names of cities, counties, states, countries, continents, and planets.

53. **(1)** *Usage/Relative Pronoun/Sentence Correction.* Use *that* or *which* when referring to things and *who* when referring to people.

54. **(1)** *Sentence Structure/Clarity /Construction Shift. Fortunately, the workplace has been made safer by robots.* The new construction is clearer and more precise than the original.

55. **(3)** *Mechanics/Spelling—Homonyms /Sentence Revision.* The word *passed* is the past tense of the verb *pass.* The word *past* refers to a time that has gone by.

Answer Key Practice Items Part II

Introduction to Holistic Scoring

The following GED Essay Scoring Guide provides a general description of the characteristics found in GED essays that are scored by the Holistic Method.

GED ESSAY SCORING GUIDE

Papers will show *some* or *all* of the following characteristics.

Upper-half papers make clear a definite purpose, pursued with varying degrees of effectiveness. They also have a structure that shows evidence of some deliberate planning. The writer's control of English usage ranges from fairly reliable at 4 to confident and accomplished at 6.

6 Papers scored as a 6 tend to offer sophisticated ideas within an organizational framework that is clear and appropriate for the topic. The supporting statements are particularly effective because of their substance, specificity, or illustrative quality. The writing is vivid and precise, though it may contain an occasional flaw.

5 Papers scored as a 5 are clearly organized with effective support for each of the writer's major points. The writing offers substantive ideas, though the paper may lack the flair or grace of a 6 paper. The surface features are consistently under control, despite an occasional lapse in usage.

4 Papers scored as a 4 show evidence of the writer's organizational plan. Support, though sufficient, tends to be less extensive or convincing than that found in papers scored as a 5 or 6. The writer generally observes the conventions of accepted English usage. Some errors are usually present, but they are not severe enough to interfere significantly with the writer's main purpose.

Lower-half papers either fail to convey a purpose sufficiently or lack one entirely. Consequently, their structure ranges from rudimentary at 3, to random at 2, to absent at 1. Control of the conventions of English usage tends to follow this same gradient.

3 Papers scored as a 3 usually show some evidence of planning or development. However, the organization is often limited to a simple listing or haphazard recitation of ideas about the topic, leaving an impression of insufficiency. The 3 papers often demonstrate repeated weaknesses in accepted English usage and are generally ineffective in accomplishing the writer's purpose.

2 Papers scored as a 2 are characterized by a marked lack of development or inadequate support for ideas. The level of thought apparent in the writing is frequently unsophisticated or superficial, often marked by a listing of unsupported generalizations. Instead of suggesting a clear purpose, these papers often present conflicting purposes. Errors in accepted English usage may seriously interfere with the overall effectiveness of these papers.

1 Papers scored as a 1 leave the impression that the writer has not only *not* accomplished a purpose, but has not made any purpose apparent. The dominant feature of these papers is the lack of control. The writer stumbles both in conveying a clear plan for the paper and in expressing ideas according to the conventions of accepted English usage.

0 The zero score is reserved for papers which are blank, illegible, or written on a topic other than the one assigned.

Source: The 1988 Tests of General Educational Development: A Preview, American Council on Education, 1985. Used with permission.

To score your essay, compare it with the following model essays. These model essays represent scores of 3 and 5, respectively.

Compare your essay with the model essay scored 3. If it is as good as that essay, assign your essay a score of 3. If it is not as good as the 3 essay, refer to the answers for the Writing Skills Predictor Test (pages 12-18). Use the descriptions of the 1 and 2 essays there to evaluate your essay.

If your essay is better than the 3 essay, compare it to the model essay scored 5. If yours is better than the 3, but not as good as the 5, score your essay a 4. If your essay is better than the 5 model essay, score it a 6.

In addition, look at the notes and character trait analyses that accompany the model essays. These comments explain the strengths and weaknesses of these essays.

Model Essay—Holistic Score 3

Weak statement of point of view, vague generalizations.

I think having a hobby is a very important way of doing that for several reasons. Many people like to do things that don't have anything to do with their work. They like to get away from their work for a change and find something different to think about.

First, if you have a hobby like jewelry making it can help you see some talent you never knew you had. This might be a good way of making a living that you never thought of before.

Undeveloped ideas that don't support the writer's point of view.

Second, a hobby is a grate way to forget about all the worries of the day. It can give you something to think about other than work. Thinking about the bracelets or rings you made is a lot better way to fall asleep than thinking about a fight you had with your boss. Hobbies breaks up your routine. It gives you something different to talk about at the dinner table.

Weak conclusion.

In the end people think they don't have time for a hobby but it is important for everybody to have a hobby. When you make the time, you will find out that it is worth it. Weather you try jewelry making or something else, you will find out that it relaxes you and it helps you to face going to work a lot easier.

Character Trait Analysis

1. The essay is organized in three parts: an introduction, the body, and a conclusion.

2. An attempt is made at supporting points with examples and reasons, though they are not clearly stated. Other points are made without supporting detail. The overall effect is one of disorganization and an uneven flow of ideas.

3. Inconcise language makes the purpose of the essay unclear and the conclusion less effective.

4. Errors in spelling, punctuation, sentence structure, and grammar detract from the essay's effectiveness.

Model Essay—Holistic Score 5

States point of view.

Finding time for activities outside of work and home is difficult in this face paced world we live in. It seems as though there is always more work to be done. Making time for yourself is more important than ever, and having a hobby lets you do just that.

Develops key ideas and uses specific, personal examples to support the writer's point of view.

Uses appropriate transitional words.

Your hobby might be gardening, hang gliding, fishing, or collecting stamps. You might work much harder at any of these than you do at your regular job. But time spent doing something you find pleasurable is rewarding. It will make those jobs at work and home much easier.

For example I spend every Saturday working in my yard. I get up early to pull weeds, mow the lawn, and water the flowers. I work out in the sun all day, but I am never tired in the same way that I am after a regular day's work. In fact, I sometimes continue working after dark. My Saturdays make my Monday mornings much easier. I don't mind getting up to go to work because I've spent time doing something that was important to me.

Summarizes ideas and restates point of view.

Having some activity took forward to is extremely important for adults today. One day or even a few hours spent enjoyably working at a hobby can make every other day of the week much richer. When you find a hobby you also find a part of yourself you never knew you had before.

Character Trait Analysis

1. This essay is well organized. Ideas flow logically and support the conclusion.
2. The point view is supported by specific details.
3. Sentences are smooth and controlled.
4. Though there are a few structural weaknesses and minor mechanical errors, the essay reads well.

ANSWER KEY PRACTICE TEST

Practice Test, Part I

1. **(4)** *Usage/Subject-Verb Agreement /Sentence Correction.* The subject of the sentence *Thinking* requires the singular verb *is*.

2. **(1)** *Mechanics/Spelling-Homonyms /Sentence Correction.* The words *presents* and *presence* sound alike but mean different things.

3. **(2)** *Usage/Subject-Verb Agreement /Sentence Correction.* The subject of this sentence is a plural noun — *members*. The verb must be changed to the plural form to agree with the subject.

4. **(4)** *Sentence Structure/Clarity /Construction Shift. With a calculator, they can easily figure out the tip.* In the original sentence, *Using a calculator* is a dangling modifier.

5. **(3)** *Usage/Verb Tense/Sentence Revision.* The phrase *Before they decide* provides a clue that the past tense of *use* is inappropriate.

6. **(4)** *Sentence Structure/Clarity /Construction Shift. Determining how much paint to buy is no problem with a calculator.* The new organization eliminates repetition of the pronoun *they*, and the overall wordiness of the sentence.

7. **(4)** *Mechanics/Capitalization—Proper Nouns/Sentence Correction.* Capitalize the names of specific places.

8. **(5)** *Mechanics/Punctuation—Items in a Series/Sentence Revision.* Separate three or more items in a series with commas.

9. **(4)** *Sentence Structure/Coordination /Sentence Revision.* Only one connecting word—*but* or *however*—should be used to show how the two parts of this sentence are related. When *however* is used as a connecting word, it is preceded by a semicolon.

10. **(2)** *Sentence Structure/Comma Splice/Sentence Revision.* A comma is used incorrectly to join two complete sentences. A question mark must be added at the end of the first sentence.

11. **(4)** *Usage/Pronoun Reference—Agreement With Antecedent/Sentence Revision.* Make sure that a pronoun agrees with the word it replaces. The pronoun in sentence 3, *they*, does not agree in number with its antecedent, *Occupational Outlook Handbook*, in the previous sentence.

12. **(1)** *Sentence Structure/Subordination /Sentence Correction.* Only one subordinator should be used to connect the subordinate idea with the main idea. In the original sentence, two subordinators, *if* and *in case*, are used.

13. **(2)** *Usage/Subject-Verb Agreement— Inverted Structure/Sentence Correction.* The plural subject, *cards*, requires a plural verb, *are*, even though the verb comes before the subject.

14. **(2)** *Mechanics/Spelling/Sentence Correction. Journels* is spelled incorrectly. The endings *al, el, le, il*, and *ile* often sound alike.

15. **(2)** *Usage/Verb Tense/Sentence Correction.* The present tense is appropriate; throughout the paragraph, the writer discusses sources of information that exist right now.

16. **(1)** *Usage/Pronoun Reference/Sentence Revision.* To be consistent with the implied subject (*You*), use *yourself. Who*, not *whom*, is required as the subject with the verb *wrote*.

17. **(3)** *Sentence/Structure/Clarity /Construction Shift. Sometimes, for example, employers pay writers to write pamphlets about a company.* The new construction improves the wordy original by using the word *for*.

18. **(5)** *Sentence Structure/Coordination /Construction Shift. The pamphlets may exaggerate job benefits and fail to mention problems with the job.* Two sentences are combined by joining the verbs in each sentence—*may exaggerate* and *may fail*—to form the phrase *may exaggerate and fail*.

19. **(1)** *Mechanics/Spelling—Contractions /Sentence Correction.* Use the contraction *It's* to mean *It is*. The pronoun *Its* is a possessive pronoun.

20. **(4)** *Sentence Structure/Clarity— Modification/Sentence Revision. To make sure that high school graduates have basic computer skills* is used as a modifier. In the original sentence, the word modified is unclear. *School officials,* not *computer literacy,* want *to make sure that...*

21. **(4)** *Mechanics/Spelling/Sentence Correction.* Remember the *d* in knowledge. The endings *age, ege, edge, idge* and *ige* all sound alike.

22. **(4)** *Usage/Verb Tense/Sentence Revision.* The word *future* provides the clue that the future tense, *will be,* is needed.

23. **(3)** *Mechanics/Punctuation—Commas With a Series/Sentence Correction.* A comma is never used after *and* before the last item in a series.

24. **(3)** *Sentence Structure/Coordination /Construction Shift. Students learn about computers in both special computer classes and regular classes.* The new construction avoids repetition by using a coordinator to join similar elements.

25. **(2)** *Mechanics/Punctuation—Commas After Introductory Elements/Sentence Correction.* When the subject comes in the middle of a sentence, use a comma to separate the introductory words from the subject.

26. **(1)** *Mechanics/Capitalization/Sentence Correction.* The names of languages are proper nouns and should therefore be capitalized.

27. **(2)** *Usage/Subject-Verb Agreement— Expletives/Sentence Revision.* The plural subject, *programs,* requires a plural verb, *are.* The word *there* is an expletive; an expletive is never the subject of a sentence.

28. **(5)** *Usage/Subject-Verb Agreement /Sentence Correction.* The singular subject in the second part of the sentence—*use*— requires a singular verb, despite the interrupting phrase, *in a variety of areas.*

29. **(4)** *Usage/Pronoun Reference—Pronoun Shift/Sentence Revision.* Use pronouns consistently within a sentence. The pronoun *you* is used in the second part of the sentence (in *you've won*), as well as throughout the paragraph.

30. **(5)** *Sentence Structure/Parallelism /Sentence Correction.* Express similar ideas in similar form. The news comes in three ways: *in a letter, on a post card,* or *on a computer form.*

31. **(2)** *Usage/Pronoun Reference—Agreement With Antecedent/Sentence Correction.* The plural pronoun *they* in the original sentence is incorrect because it does not agree in number with its antecedent, *someone.*

32. **(4)** *Sentence Structure/Comma Splice/Sentence Correction.* Two complete sentences are incorrectly joined by a comma. The run-on sentence is corrected by replacing it with two separate sentences.

33. **(2)** *Mechanics/Punctuation–Overuse of Commas/Sentence Correction.* Do not use a comma between the subject and verb of a sentence.

34. **(5)** *Sentence Structure/Sentence Fragment/Sentence Revision.* The fragment is corrected by adding the verb *is* and creating a subject, *description,* from *describing.*

35. **(5)** *Mechanics/Capitalization—Proper Nouns/Sentence Correction.* Words such as *County* and *Mountains* should be capitalized when they are part of specific place names.

36. **(3)** *Sentence Structure/Parallelism /Sentence Revision.* Express similar ideas in similar form. The sales pitch may be about *buying land* or *renting vacation property.*

37. **(2)** *Usage/Pronoun Reference/Construction Shift. Don't be one of those unfortunate people who waste their time and money on these scams.*

38. **(5)** *Sentence Structure/Sentence Fragment/Sentence Revision.* The fragment is corrected by providing a verb, *last,* for the subject, *jobs.*

39. **(2)** *Mechanics/Spelling/Sentence Correction.* The endings *int, ent,* and *ant* are frequently confused.

40. **(5)** *Sentence Structure/Coordination /Construction Shift. Agencies that handle temporary jobs are advertised in the telephone book and in the classified section of your newspaper.*

41. **(2)** *Mechanics/Capitalization/Sentence Correction.* Capitalize words such as *agency* or *company* only if they are part of a proper noun.

42. **(4)** *Usage/Verb Tense/Sentence Correction.* Keep the tense of verbs consistent throughout the paragraph. *An agency that handles...will probably test...*

43. **(5)** *Usage/Pronoun Reference—Pronoun Shift/Sentence Revision.* The pronoun *you* should be used to be consistent with the understood subject of the sentence and with the other sentences in the paragraph.

44. **(1)** *Usage/Verb Tenses/Sentence Correction.* The passage is written in the present tense. Change the past tense *was* to the present tense *is* to be consistent.

45. **(3)** *Sentence Structure/Clarity/Sentence Correction.* Eliminate unnecessary words. The word *because* is sufficient to express the relationship between the two ideas in the sentence.

46. **(3)** *Mechanics/Punctuation/Sentence Revision.* Use a comma after the coordinating word in a compound sentence.

47. **(4)** *Sentence Structure/Clarity—Dangling Modifier/Sentence Revision.* The first part of this sentence, *Having decided...the drawbacks*, does not clearly modify any of the words in the sentence.

48. **(4)** *Usage/Pronoun Shift/Sentence Correction.* The sentence shifts from the second person (*you*) to the third person (*we*). Since the rest of the paragraph is written in the second person, use the second person consistently in this sentence.

49. **(1)** *Sentence Structure/Subordination /Sentence Revision.* The comma correctly separates the subordinate idea from the main idea. The verb in the subordinate idea, *grows*, agrees with the subject, *chick*.

50. **(5)** *Usage/Relative Pronoun/Construction Shift.* You might think that your elderly aunt who lives alone needs a guard dog. The relative pronoun *who* refers to a person.

51. **(2)** *Mechanics/Capitalization/Sentence Correction.* Capitalize the names of holidays.

52. **(4)** *Sentence Structure/Misplaced Modifier/Sentence Revision.* The words *that crawled into your yard* modify, or describe, *turtle*, not *brother*. Place the description as close as possible to the word it modifies.

53. **(5)** *Usage/Verb Tense—Irregular Verbs/Sentence Revision.* With the helping verb *have*, use a past participle as the main verb. The past participle of *think* is *thought*.

54. **(2)** *Mechanics/Punctuation—Items in a Series/Sentence Correction.* Separate three or more items in a series with commas: *Food, vaccinations, and emergency trips...*

55. **(2)** *Mechanics/Punctuation—Introductory Elements/Sentence Correction.* Use a comma after an introductory group of words that is separate from the main idea.

Practice Test, Part II

Introduction to Holistic Scoring

The following GED Essay Scoring Guide provides a general description of the characteristics found in GED essays that are scored by the Holistic Method.

GED ESSAY SCORING GUIDE

Papers will show *some* or *all* of the following characteristics.

Upper-half papers make clear a definite purpose, pursued with varying degrees of effectiveness. They also have a structure that shows evidence of some deliberate planning. The writer's control of English usage ranges from fairly reliable at 4 to confident and accomplished at 6.

6 Papers scored as a 6 tend to offer sophisticated ideas within an organizational framework that is clear and appropriate for the topic. The supporting statements are particularly effective because of their substance, specificity, or illustrative quality. The writing is vivid and precise, though it may contain an occasional flaw.

5 Papers scored as a 5 are clearly organized with effective support for each of the writer's major points. The writing offers substantive ideas, though the paper may lack the flair or grace of a 6 paper. The surface features are consistently under control, despite an occasional lapse in usage.

4 Papers scored as a 4 show evidence of the writer's organizational plan. Support, though sufficient, tends to be less extensive or convincing than that found in papers scored as a 5 or 6. The writer generally observes the conventions of accepted English usage. Some errors are usually present, but they are not severe enough to interfere significantly with the writer's main purpose.

Lower-half papers either fail to convey a purpose sufficiently or lack one entirely. Consequently, their structure ranges from rudimentary at 3, to random at 2, to absent at 1. Control of the conventions of English usage tends to follow this same gradient.

3 Papers scored as a 3 usually show some evidence of planning or development. However, the organization is often limited to a simple listing or haphazard recitation of ideas about the topic, leaving an impression of insufficiency. The 3 papers often demonstrate repeated weaknesses in accepted English usage and are generally ineffective in accomplishing the writer's purpose.

2 Papers scored as a 2 are characterized by a marked lack of development or inadequate support for ideas. The level of thought apparent in the writing is frequently unsophisticated or superficial, often marked by a listing of unsupported generalizations. Instead of suggesting a clear purpose, these papers often present conflicting purposes. Errors in accepted English usage may seriously interfere with the overall effectiveness of these papers.

1 Papers scored as a 1 leave the impression that the writer has not only *not* accomplished a purpose, but has not made any purpose apparent. The dominant feature of these papers is the lack of control. The writer stumbles both in conveying a clear plan for the paper and in expressing ideas according to the conventions of accepted English usage.

0 The zero score is reserved for papers which are blank, illegible, or written on a topic other than the one assigned.

Copyright 1985, GED Testing Service, September, 1985

Source: The 1988 Tests of General Educational Development: A Preview, American Council on Education, 1985. Used with permission.

To score your essay, compare it with the following model essays. These model essays represent scores of 3 and 5 respectively.

Compare your essay with the model essay scored 3. If it is as good as that essay, assign your essay a score of 3. If it is not as good as the 3 essay, refer to the answers for the Writing Skills Predictor Test (pages 12-18). Use the descriptions of the 1 and 2 essays there to evaluate your essay.

If your essay is better than the 3 essay, compare it to the model essay scored 5. If yours is better than the 3, but not as good as the 5, score your essay a 4. If your essay is better than the 5 model essay, score it a 6.

In addition, look at the notes and character trait analyses that accompany the model essays. These comments explain the strengths and weaknesses of these essays.

Model Essay—Holistic Score 3

Point of view is unclear. Sometimes consumers buy products because they are influenced by the way they are advertised. In this essay I will tell why that is so.

When people go to the grocery store they usually have a pretty good idea of what they want to buy there. Sometimes something may catch their eye that they have not planned on buying, for example, they could see a new kind of spagetti sauce in a fancy jar. They remember the picture on the jar from the TV commercial they saw last night. Even if they weren't planning on having spagetti they will put it into their shopping cart anyway.

Haphazard listing of details rather than clear examples that support a point of view. As they go threw the store they may forget their shopping list all together. They may buy canned goods, because they thought the song about them on the radio was clever. They can buy one brand of vitamins because they think those vitamins are new and improved. They can buy a certain bar of soap. That costs to much money because they think it will help them get a date.

Weak unsupported conclusion. Shoppers should be careful because sometimes they will buy things they don't really want to buy. They will only get them because they liked the commercials for the things.

Character Trait Analysis

1. The essay is organized into three parts: an introduction, the body, and a conclusion.

2. The writer does not clearly state his or her point of view on the topic.

3. Specific examples and details are used to support the writer's points, but the haphazard listing of examples doesn't lead to a logical conclusion.

4. Errors in spelling, punctuation, sentence structure, and grammar detract from the essay's effectiveness.

Model Essay—Holistic Score 5

Strong introduction, clear point of view.

Consumers want to buy quality products, but they can be influenced to buy an inferior or more expensive product because of the way it is marketed. Manufacturers know they can make their products attractive to the public my associating attractive images with their products.

Uses a specific example to support writer's point of view.

As a consumer, when I buy a pair of jeans, I am concerned about how well they are made, how long they will last, and how much they cost. But I also want to buy a brand that the people around me will think are in style. Commercials and advertisements fool the public into thinking that some brands will make you more popular than others.

Explains idea introduced earlier.

Many consumers think that a manufacturer cares about the quality of the product if the advertisements are slick and exciting. Often this is true. But it takes using the product at least once to tell whether or not the advertising claims are true. Too often, consumers think that the attractiveness of the packaging will rub off on them. For instance, if all the anti-wrinkle creams really worked, no one would have wrinkles. Consumers have to try products out for themselves and judge how well they do what they're supposed to do.

More supporting details.

You cannot always tell a book by it's cover. The same is true with advertising claims. It is difficult for consumers today not to be drawn in by fancy advertising. But products that have proven their quality are the ones that will survive in the marketplace.

Summarizes ideas, concludes with important statement about the topic that is in keeping with point of view.

Character Trait Analysis

1. The essay is well organized. Ideas flow logically and lead to a strong conclusion.
2. The point of view is supported by examples and reasons.
3. The examples and reasons are consistent with the writer's point of view.
4. The essay reads well, although there are a few errors in sentence structure and mechanics.

Answer Key—Simulated Test

Simulated Test Part I

1. **(5)** *Usage/Pronoun Reference—Agreement with Antecedent/Sentence Correction.* The pronoun *them* does not agree with the word it replaces, *a lunch.*

2. **(2)** *Mechanics/Punctuation—Overuse of Commas/Sentence Revision.* Commas should be used to separate items in a series, with the final comma appearing before the *and, or,* or *nor* preceding the last word in the series.

3. **(2)** *Sentence Structure/Comma Splice/Sentence Correction.* Use a semi-colon, not a comma, to separate complete ideas that are connected by *nevertheless, however, thus,* or *therefore.*

4. **(1)** *Usage/Subject-Verb Agreement /Construction Shift.* *Meat, fish, chicken, nuts, and beans contain protein.* The plural subject requires a plural verb.

5. **(4)** *Mechanics/Capitalization/Proper Nouns/Sentence Correction.* Capitalize the names of regions of the world.

6. **(2)** *Sentence Structure/Comma Splice/Sentence Revision.* Do not use a comma to separate two complete ideas. The error is corrected here by forming two sentences.

7. **(3)** *Usage/Subject-Verb Agreement /Sentence Revision.* When both subject words connected by *either...or* are singular, use a singular verb.

8. **(2)** *Mechanics/Spelling—Frequently Misspelled Words/Sentence Correction.* The *-ing* form of *proceed* is *proceeding;* the *-ing* form of *precede* is *preceding.*

9. **(5)** *Mechanics/Spelling—Contractions /Sentence Correction.* Use the contraction *it's* to mean *it is.*

10. **(3)** *Sentence Structure/Coordinators /Sentence Correction.* Some coordinators are used in pairs such as *either...or* and *neither...nor.* When the coordinator *not only* is used, it should be paired with *but also.*

11. **(5)** *Usage/Pronoun-Antecedent Agreement/Sentence Revision.* The antecedent *presidents* requires the plural pronoun *their.*

12. **(1)** *Mechanics/Punctuation—Commas with Sentence Interrupters/Construction Shift. Economic issues, those financial matters concerning goods and services, have gotten less attention.* Use commas to set off an interrupting phrase from the rest of the sentence.

13. **(4)** *Sentence Structure/Sentence Fragment /Sentence Correction.* The sentence fragment is corrected by providing a verb, *receive,* that agrees with the subject, *issues.*

14. **(4)** *Usage/Verb Tense Error—Clues to Tense in Paragraph/Sentence Revision.* The present tense is used consistently throughout the paragraph.

15. **(5)** *Sentence Structure/Dangling Modifier/Sentence Revision.* A sentence should be worded so that a modifier clearly and logically modifies a word in the sentence. *The U.S.,* not *drugs, works with Mexico...*

16. **(3)** *Mechanics/Spelling—Homonyms /Sentence Correction.* Use the possessive *their* when referring to ownership.

17. **(4)** *Usage/Relative Pronouns/Sentence Correction.* Use the pronoun *that* or *which* to refer to nonliving things.

18. **(1)** *Sentence Structure/Subordination /Construction Shift. For example, they feel that keeping peace in the Middle East should take priority over the question of whether or not to raise our minimum wage a few cents.*

19. **(5)** *Usage/Vague Pronoun Reference /Sentence Correction.* Make sure the antecedent of a pronoun is clear. It is not clear whether *they* refers to *many people* or *Presidents.*

20. **(5)** *Sentence Structure/Run-On Sentence/Sentence Correction.* The run-on sentence is corrected here by rewriting it as two sentences.

21. **(3)** *Mechanics/Punctuation—Comma After Introductory Elements/Sentence Correction.* When a subordinate idea appears at the beginning of the sentence, it is followed by a comma.

22. **(4)** *Mechanics/Spelling—Contractions /Sentence Correction.* In a contraction, put the apostrophe (') where the missing letter should be.

23. **(1)** *Sentence Structure/Subordination /Construction Shift. Studies show that the more television children watch, the worse they are likely to do on reading tests.*

24. **(4)** *Usage/Subject-Verb Agreement— Interrupting Phrase/Sentence Correction.* The singular subject, *Television*, requires the singular verb, *is*, despite the phrase that separates the two.

25. **(2)** *Mechanics/Capitalization/Sentence Correction.* Capitalize the names of the days of the week.

26. **(2)** *Sentence Structure/Fragment /Sentence Revision.* The subject *children* requires a verb. Changing *developing* to *can develop* makes the sentence complete.

27. **(2)** *Usage/Pronoun Reference/Sentence Revision.* Do not shift pronouns within a sentence or paragraph. Continue with *you* to be consistent.

28. **(3)** *Sentence Structure/Sentence Fragment/Sentence Revision.* The sentence fragment is corrected by supplying the verb, *should control*, required by the subject, *Parents*.

29. **(3)** *Mechanics/Punctuation—Commas in Compound Sentences/Sentence Correction.* Use a comma before the coordinator that connects two complete ideas in a compound sentence.

30. **(3)** *Sentence Structure/Complex Sentences/Construction Shift. Before you do anything for someone who is choking, wait a moment to see if he coughs it up himself.* Make sure you put a comma after a subordinate idea that introduces a sentence.

31. **(2)** *Mechanics/Spelling—Frequently Misspelled Words/Sentence Correction.* Don't confuse the spellings of *breathe* and *breath*. When you breathe, you take a breath.

32. **(5)** *Mechanics/Spelling and Capitalization/Sentence Correction.* The sentence is correct as written.

33. **(4)** *Usage/Subject-Verb Agreement /Sentence Revision.* The singular subject, *One*, requires a singular verb, *is*, despite the interrupting phrase, *of the most common ways to start.*

34. **(4)** *Sentence Structure/Subordination /Sentence Revision.* Don't forget to include both words of the subordinator in such combinations *as so/that, such/that, as/as, more/than.*

35. **(4)** *Usage/Subject-Verb Agreement— Inverted Structure/Sentence Correction.* The subject determines the form of the verb, even when it follows the verb. Here, the singular subject, *thumb*, requires a singular verb, *is*.

36. **(3)** *Sentence Structure/Comma Splice/Sentence Revision.* Do not use a comma to separate two complete ideas. Here, the error is corrected by making the first idea, *With your other hand cupped over the fist*, subordinate to the second, *give a hard upward pull.*

37. **(4)** *Sentence Structure/Run-On Sentence/Sentence Revision.* If the two ideas in a run-on sentence are closely related, a semicolon may be used at the end of the first complete sentence.

38. **(1)** *Usage/Verb Tense—Word Clue to Tense in Sentence/Sentence Revision.* The words *have* and *usually* indicate that a present-tense verb, *has*, is required.

39. **(2)** *Usage/Verb Tense—Word Clue to Tense in Paragraph/Sentence Correction.* Use the present tense to be consistent with that used throughout the paragraph.

40. **(2)** *Usage/Subject-Verb Agreement /Sentence Revision.* The verb form that agrees with the singular subject, *arguing*, is *takes*.

41. **(3)** *Sentence Structure/Subordination /Construction Shift. Anger that has been suppressed for months or even years may erupt when family members see each other again.* The new construction makes the relationship between ideas clearer.

42. **(2)** *Usage/Subject-Verb Agreement— Compound Subjects/Sentence Correction.* The compound subject, *Fatigue and irritability*, requires a plural verb, *go*.

43. **(4)** *Mechanics/Spelling—Homonyms /Sentence Correction.* The words *brake* and *break* sound the same but have different meanings.

44. **(3)** *Mechanics/Capitalization/Sentence Correction.* Capitalize words such as *Island* and *City* when they are part of the name of a place.

45. **(2)** *Usage/Subject-Verb Agreement /Construction Shift. Neither waiting in line to buy six pumpkin pies nor baking six of them leads to feeling very relaxed.* Since *neither* and *nor* join singular nouns (*waiting* and *baking*), a singular verb, *leads*, is required.

46. **(3)** *Mechanics/Punctuation—Contractions /Sentence Revision. You're* is a contraction that means *you are.*

47. **(5)** *Sentence Structure/Complex Sentences/Sentence Correction.* The sentence is correct as written. Do not put a comma before *because.*

48. **(3)** *Sentence Structure/Subordination /Construction Shift. Although dentists' offices have changed in appearance over the years, the dentist's role is basically unchanged.*

49. **(3)** *Usage/Verb Tense—Clue within Sentence/Sentence Correction.* The words *goes around...while* provide the clue that the present tense, *are taken,* should follow.

50. **(5)** *Usage/Verb Tense/Clues within Sentence/Sentence Revision.* The word *now* provides the clue that the present tense, *uses,* should follow.

51. **(3)** *Usage/Ambiguous Pronoun Reference/Sentence Revision.* It is not clear whether *her teeth* refers to the child's teeth or the dentist's. The ambiguity is cleared up by eliminating the pronoun.

52. **(3)** *Mechanics/Spelling/Sentence Correction. Procedure* is a frequently misspelled word.

53. **(3)** *Sentence Structure/Parallelism /Sentence Revision.* A verb that is parallel to *brush* is needed in the second part of the sentence. *Use* is parallel to *brush.*

54. **(1)** *Sentence Structure/Subordination /Sentence Correction.* Use only one subordinator to introduce a subordinate idea.

55. **(1)** *Mechanics/Capitalization—Proper Nouns/Sentence Correction.* Capitalize words such as *Association* or *Company* if they are part of the name of a group.

Simulated Test, Part II

Introduction to Holistic Scoring

The following GED Essay Scoring Guide provides a general description of the characteristics found in GED essays that are scored by the Holistic Method.

GED ESSAY SCORING GUIDE

Papers will show *some* or *all* of the following characteristics.

Upper-half papers make clear a definite purpose, pursued with varying degrees of effectiveness. They also have a structure that shows evidence of some deliberate planning. The writer's control of English usage ranges from fairly reliable at 4 to confident and accomplished at 6.

6 Papers scored as a 6 tend to offer sophisticated ideas within an organizational framework that is clear and appropriate for the topic. The supporting statements are particularly effective because of their substance, specificity, or illustrative quality. The writing is vivid and precise, though it may contain an occasional flaw.

5 Papers scored as a 5 are clearly organized with effective support for each of the writer's major points. The writing offers substantive ideas, though the paper may lack the flair or grace of a 6 paper. The surface features are consistently under control, despite an occasional lapse in usage.

4 Papers scored as a 4 show evidence of the writer's organizational plan. Support, though sufficient, tends to be less extensive or convincing than that found in papers scored as a 5 or 6. The writer generally observes the conventions of accepted English usage. Some errors are usually present, but they are not severe enough to interfere significantly with the writer's main purpose.

Lower-half papers either fail to convey a purpose sufficiently or lack one entirely. Consequently, their structure ranges from rudimentary at 3, to random at 2, to absent at 1. Control of the conventions of English usage tends to follow this same gradient.

3 Papers scored as a 3 usually show some evidence of planning or development. However, the organization is often limited to a simple listing or haphazard recitation of ideas about the topic, leaving an impression of insufficiency. The 3 papers often demonstrate repeated weaknesses in accepted English usage and are generally ineffective in accomplishing the writer's purpose.

2 Papers scored as a 2 are characterized by a marked lack of development or inadequate support for ideas. The level of thought apparent in the writing is frequently unsophisticated or superficial, often marked by a listing of unsupported generalizations. Instead of suggesting a clear purpose, these papers often present conflicting purposes. Errors in accepted English usage may seriously interfere with the overall effectiveness of these papers.

1 Papers scored as a 1 leave the impression that the writer has not only *not* accomplished a purpose, but has not made any purpose apparent. The dominant feature of these papers is the lack of control. The writer stumbles both in conveying a clear plan for the paper and in expressing ideas according to the conventions of accepted English usage.

0 The zero score is reserved for papers which are blank, illegible, or written on a topic other than the one assigned.

Source: The 1988 Tests of General Educational Development: A Preview, American Council on Education, 1985. Used with permission.

To score your essay, compare it with the following model essays. These model essays represent scores of 3 and 5 respectively.

Compare your essay with the model essay scored 3. If it is as good as that essay, assign your essay a score of 3. If it is not as good as the 3 essay, refer to the answers for the Writing Skills Predictor Test (pages 12-18). Use the descriptions of the 1 and 2 essays there to evaluate your essay.

If your essay is better than the 3 essay, compare it to the model essay scored 5. If yours is better than the 3, but not as good as the 5, score your essay a 4. If your essay is better than the 5 model essay, score it a 6.

In addition, look at the notes and character trait analyses that accompany the model essays. These comments explain the strengths and weaknesses of these essays.

Model Essay—Holistic Score 3

Weak, impersonal point of view. The essay topic asks for the writer's opinion, not vague generalizations about life today. List of undeveloped, unconnected ideas that don't support a personal point of view; needs specific examples.

Weak conclusion—unsupported by examples in essay.

Having a role-model is especialy important for young people today. Each year the world seems to get more and more confusing and it is important for young people to know that there are individual people out there who can achieve success.

These role-models may be parents, grandparents, a relative, someone you know, or someone you read about in the paper. These role-models show young people that they can make a contrabution to the world. They show that it is possible to make your dreams come true. They show that not all rock stars are bad.

Young people today get so much information thrown at them mainly from the media that it can be confusing. A role-model can be someone who shows them how they handle living in a complacated world, and still manage to be successful.

It is important that young people today have role-models all people should have them for that matter. If everybody had a role-model then they would find comfort knowing that success in the modern world is really possible, not just some dream.

Character Trait Analysis

1. The essay has been organized into three parts: an introduction, the body, and a conclusion.

2. The point of view is weak and impersonal throughout the essay.

3. Several different points are made, though none are backed up with specific supporting examples and reasons. Total effect is one of disorganization and illogical flow of ideas.

4. The conclusion could have been made stronger with supporting details.

5. Errors in spelling, punctuation, sentence structure, and grammar detract from the essay's effectiveness.

Model Essay—Holistic Score 5

Point of view is clearly stated.

I believe that is is still very important that young people have role-models. Without strong individuals to look up to, the next generation may be defeated before it has even given the future a chance.

Key idea is explained using general examples.

Role-models help define the choices young people have. By being an excelent biochemist, gym instructor, or astronaut, they are showing young possible roads their own careers could take. These could be careers a young person never would have thought of if they hadn't been introduced to the role-model.

Another key idea is explained; uses a specific example to support the idea.

Young people also need to know that success is possible. They need to know that someone has come along before them and achieved goals that might seem impossible to the rest of the population. Helen Keller was a role-model for many young people. Though she was heavily handicapped when she was born, she learned to read and write. She became a famous writer.

Another key idea is explained; a specific example is used to support the idea.

Role-models also help show young people how to get where they want to go. Their own careers can be like charts or maps for young people to follow. Knowing how Gary Carter worked hard to become the excellent baseball player he is shows young people how they can accomplish this, too.

Uses appropriate transition words to move to final point.
Summarizes ideas.
Concludes with important statement that is in keeping with the point of view.

But most importantly, role-models show young people that they are not alone in their dreams. Someone else has dreamed something similar to their dream before them. Our young people need to get to know the courage, strength, and other good qualities role-models have had. Unless they discover how individuals have striven to succeed, they may never achieve their dreams. And there may be no role-model candidates for future generations.

Character Trait Analysis

1. The essay is well organized. Ideas flow logically and lead to a conclusion.

2. Point of view is supported by substantive ideas.

3. Specific examples have been used to support these ideas in the essay.

4. Though there are a few structural weaknesses and minor mechanical errors, the essay reads well.